Your Cubase® Studio

Steve Pacey

Course Technology PTR
A part of Cengage Learning

COURSE TECHNOLOGY
CENGAGE Learning

Australia • Brazil • Japan • Korea • Mexico • Singapore • Spain • United Kingdom • United States

COURSE TECHNOLOGY
CENGAGE Learning™

Your Cubase® Studio
Steve Pacey

Publisher and General Manager, Course Technology PTR: Stacy L. Hiquet

Associate Director of Marketing: Sarah Panella

Manager of Editorial Services: Heather Talbot

Marketing Manager: Mark Hughes

Executive Editor: Mark Garvey

Project Editor: Dan Foster, Scribe Tribe

Technical Reviewer: Greg Ondo

PTR Editorial Services Coordinator: Erin Johnson

Copy Editor: Brad Crawford

Interior Layout Tech: Macmillan Publishing Solutions

Cover Designer: Mike Tanamachi

Indexer: Katherine Stimson

Proofreader: Kate Shoup

For product information and technology assistance, contact us at
Cengage Learning Customer & Sales Support, 1-800-354-9706

For permission to use material from this text or product, submit all requests online at **cengage.com/permissions**
Further permissions questions can be emailed to
permissionrequest@cengage.com

Cubase and Cubase Studio are trademarks of Steinberg Media Technologies GmbH.

Library of Congress Control Number: 2007936029

ISBN-13: 978-1-59863-452-5

ISBN-10: 1-59863-452-6

Course Technology
25 Thomson Place
Boston, MA 02210
USA

Cengage Learning is a leading provider of customized learning solutions with office locations around the globe, including Singapore, the United Kingdom, Australia, Mexico, Brazil, and Japan. Locate your local office at:
international.cengage.com/region

Cengage Learning products are represented in Canada by Nelson Education, Ltd.

For your lifelong learning solutions, visit **courseptr.com**

Visit our corporate website at **cengage.com**

Printed in the United States of America
1 2 3 4 5 6 7 11 10 09 08

This book is dedicated to my lifelong friend Matt Piper for always sharing the desire to learn more and more about music and technology and for keeping me in check on some of the latest developments in this industry.

Acknowledgments

Thanks to Course Technology for giving me the opportunity of writing this book. Thanks to everyone there who has worked hard in making this book a reality. Special thanks to Mark Garvey for his support and for believing in me. Thanks to Dan Foster for taking care of the details, for his expertise, and for having patience with a guy who didn't major in English. Thanks to Cubase master Greg Ondo for taking the time to check and recheck my wording and instructions to assure that everything I've written makes sense. Also, thanks to Brad Crawford and all the editors for adding their valuable perspectives. Thanks to the people at Steinberg for continuing to take Cubase to levels I never dreamed possible when I first started using the program. Thanks to Tom Meyers at Mackie for help in configuring the Mackie console to work for my example. Special thanks to all my friends and family for their continuous love and support. Last, but not least, thank you (the reader) for having the desire to learn and explore MIDI. Your desire will continue to fuel the future of music for generations to come.

About the Author

Steve Pacey has held an interest in music since he was just a child. His desire to learn more about music took him from piano lessons to playing trombone in the grade school band, to writing songs, to rapping and learning how to beat box, to playing keyboards and singing in a rock band, to attending a specialized music school, to owning and working in recording studios, to writing music for theater, TV, video, and film, to producing bands, to editing technical music books, and to writing this book. His first computer was an Apple IIe. He later moved on to an Atari 1040Ste and now he uses a Dell desktop with Windows XP. Steve has been a devoted Cubase user since attending the Grove School of Music where he studied songwriting and recording engineering in Los Angeles in 1990. He is currently writing and producing music for several TV shows, including the television series "The Ultimate Blackjack Tour" on CBS. Steve is a member of ASCAP and NSAI. He owns his own music publishing company (Spot On Music) and recording studio and lives in "Music City" Nashville, TN, where he continues to write music for fun and for a living.

Contents

Chapter 2
Accessorizing Your Cubase Studio   55

Chapter 3
Before You Record...   89

Chapter 4
Recording MIDI   111

Chapter 5
Recording Vocals   153

Chapter 6
Recording Guitar and Bass   183

Chapter 7
Recording a Whole Band or Multiple Tracks at Once   209

Chapter 8
Basic Editing   251

Chapter 9
Mixing It Down   295

Epilogue: After the Mix   325

Index   329

Introduction: Making Cubase Work for You

Congratulations! Picking up this book will help you take the steps you need to get serious about setting up your Cubase studio so you can start making music. This book works as a companion to the Cubase manual. Its purpose is not to lead you in a direction specific to any version of Cubase, but instead to help you understand how Cubase works as a DAW (digital audio workstation) and how to get the most out of Cubase in your home studio. If Cubase is the first DAW you've used, this book will help you understand not only Cubase but also how most DAWs function should you want to work with another brand later.

The Cubase users who will most benefit from reading this book are those who have limited computer and recording experience. This book is sort of an "all-in-one" Cubase studio handbook and mostly covers the basics in every possible area of working with Cubase and interfacing the rest of your studio with Cubase.

A Cubase User's Option Anxiety

You may already be familiar with the several versions of Cubase. This book will work with any of them. Even though versions will change and advance over the years, the basics of interfacing Cubase with your home studio should be similar enough so that you won't have to buy a new book each time a software update appears. To get you started, let's go over the differences among the current versions of Cubase to make sure that you have the version that suits your needs best.

Cubase versus Nuendo

The biggest question is, "What's the real difference between Steinberg's Nuendo and Cubase?" Even though both programs record with exactly the same sound quality, there are several differences. Both can be used to create music recordings, but Nuendo has also been geared to compete with some high-end audio post-production software.

Note: Audio post-production is a term used to describe the process of replacing the audio in media such as TV, film, and video. It is usually the last step in the process of creating a film or video and could involve adding sound effects, premixed music tracks, Foley (sound effects tied to on-screen action, such as footsteps), and voice-overs or dialog replacement from actors.

Even though Cubase can be used similarly to Nuendo to handle post-production, Nuendo offers a lot more control when working with video and mixing for the silver screen. Cubase does offer a lot of control for screen composers, but not as much for the audio engineer primarily interested in handling audio associated with pictures in the post-production world. Nuendo's price tag could lead users to believe that there is no better software for music production. However, Nuendo's higher price merely reflects its broader offering of post-production tools. That said, Nuendo is priced very competitively for what it has to offer the post-production market.

The bottom line is this: If you're primarily recording music in your studio, Cubase is all you need. The only reason to purchase Nuendo would be compatibility with professional studios (because most pro studios have either a Pro Tools or Nuendo setup). Still, you should be able to open a Cubase project on a Nuendo system. Keep in mind that you can always have compatibility issues because there are so many different software versions. Plus, if the studio you go to doesn't have the same plug-in effects or VST instruments, you could end up with a project that isn't going to function properly in that studio.

This book is focused primarily on music production, which is where my strengths lie. Even though there are several programs on the market that offer similar working environments, Cubase is the only program you will need to create and mix music that could be heard on any medium, whether it's TV, radio, or the Web. There are several versions of Cubase on the market: the *full* version of Cubase, the *lite* version of Cubase, and a few different *intro* versions of Cubase. There are also a lot of users with older versions no longer sold by Steinberg.

Steinberg has changed the name of its versions so many times that it can be difficult to keep track of which version is the latest and greatest. This book was written with the full version of Cubase, currently Cubase 4, in mind. The current lite version of Cubase 4 is called Cubase Studio 4. The current intro versions of Cubase are called Cubase SE3, LE, and AI.

Note: Cubase LE and AI usually come with the purchase of a pro soundcard or Yamaha product. These are the most basic versions of Cubase you can possibly own. The main purpose of these "free" versions is to give you a taste of what Cubase has to offer. As these are the most limited versions of the program, I will refer to them collectively as "Cubase SE," the most similar stand-alone version that Cubase sells.

Realize that these versions will change. Sometimes the changes will dramatically affect the way you work. Sometimes the changes simply reflect a higher-quality recording. If you are truly serious about growing with the music technology, understand that no matter how comfortable you feel with your current system, you will need to change your software and your computer within the next couple of years. Change is inevitable. Therefore, I will focus less on the "how to" details discussed in your current Cubase manual and more on helping you understand why the software works the way it does and adapt to new software in the manner that every working professional must as the versions are updated. My goal is to prevent you from having to buy a similar book in two years when the details have changed.

Note: Yamaha purchased Steinberg in 2005 from another company, Pinnacle Systems. When a major corporation buys a smaller company, there are *major* changes in the way things are done. My personal feeling is that things will continue to work out with Yamaha in control and continue to develop beyond what Steinberg was capable of doing as a small company, but who's to say what the future will be? Sometimes keeping an eye on the business side can give you a heads up on the direction the technical side is going.

I have to level with you. I've been creating music for TV and film for years. In fact, I started creating music for TV before you could even record audio on a computer. Ten years ago, I would have killed for today's "intro" version of Cubase. So, if you own the intro version of Cubase, don't feel inferior to those guys with the full version because you're still superior to guys who have fallen off the technological wagon and are using their ADATs and drum machines to record music. And don't pay attention to price tags. There are plenty of systems on the market that cost a lot more than the intro version of Cubase, but they perform the same functions.

Cubase, Cubase Studio, and Cubase SE: The Big Differences

There are big cost differences among the various Cubase versions, but there are also very good reasons for that. Cubase Studio 4 is half the retail price of Cubase 4, and Cubase SE is less than half the price of Cubase Studio 4. The interesting thing is, you can create music that is suitable for radio, TV, and film using any of the three software versions. So you may ask, "If quality isn't an issue, why would I pay five times more for the full version of Cubase?" The simple answer: You get a lot more bells and whistles.

Let's start by comparing Cubase 4 with Cubase Studio 4. Both programs record unlimited audio tracks, allow unlimited use of virtual instruments, include SoundFrame, have the exact same Audio Warp and Time Warp features, and allow you to print and edit scores in the same way. This makes Cubase Studio 4 appear very attractive. But Cubase 4 also has a valuable Control Room feature, allows you to mix in surround sound, includes almost 20 additional plug-ins (programs that work within Cubase), includes four additional VST instruments (software-based synths), and contains a full print manual (as opposed to the newly standardized PDF document manual that comes with most programs these days), as well as boasting several other major improvements.

Cubase SE is a slightly older technology than Cubase 4 and Cubase Studio 4 (more similar to Cubase SX and SL), but nonetheless it delivers a powerful bang at a fraction of the cost of its bigger brothers. Its biggest limitations aren't very limiting at all. For instance, instead of being able to record an unlimited number of audio tracks, you can have only 48 tracks. Did you know that some of the most popular recordings the Beatles made were done with only four tracks and that other recordings still popular today were recorded on two tracks? The truth of the matter is, most of the time, if you're using more than 24 tracks at a time, you're using too many! I won't mention any names, but I've been to some of the best studios in the world with the best equipment and heard some really horrible-sounding tracks, and I've also heard some amazing recordings that were done on a four-track cassette recorder. It all comes down to recognizing that your gear isn't worth anything if you don't know how to get the most from it.

Cubase SE comes with 24 plug-in audio effects and three VST instruments. The only real drawback I can see is that if you really need to produce a score (printed sheet music), you can't do it with Cubase SE. The other thing that comes to mind is that since the technology is slightly older than Cubase 4, you'll probably need to completely relearn the way the program works the next time there's an update. I have a sneaking suspicion that the next update to Cubase SE will be similar to Cubase Studio. If you're working with an older version of Cubase, such as Cubase LE, Cubase SL, or Cubase SX, you'll find that they're very comparable to Cubase SE. A lot of times, if you can't afford to have the latest/fastest computer on the market, the older software actually works better than newer software. But I always recommend keeping up with the technology, because you'll find that support for older hardware and software eventually fades away.

If price is an issue for you, consider how much money you make from music. If you make less than $1,000 a year from music, don't sweat it—Cubase SE is an incredible bargain. If you make more than $5,000 a year, both Cubase 4 and Cubase Studio 4 have a lot more to offer. The best reason to purchase Cubase 4 over Cubase Studio 4 is the additional plug-ins and VST instruments, and if you record live musicians on a regular basis, the Control Room feature is nice to have. I guarantee that every available version of Cubase is well worth the retail price. Please don't use "crack" versions of the program. I understand that most musicians are counting their pennies, but using "cracks" will not only limit your product support but also hurt the entire music industry by taking away the funding it needs to further develop the software.

Note: A "crack" is a program that has been developed to override the piracy control security that prevents software from being illegally copied and distributed. "Crack" versions are illegal.

As the technology continues to develop, you'll see that each of these versions of Cubase will add more and more extras, but you can't sit around and wait for that to happen. You just have to jump on that fast-moving train and try to keep from falling off.

A Multitude of Ways to Record Using Cubase

Just opening Cubase for the first time can be a little intimidating. It's a massive program. It puts most everyday-type programs to shame with its complexity. The funny thing is that most people who jump into this software come from a background in music, not computers. Half the time, beginning Cubase users barely understand their computer's operating system, let alone this massive program. The truth of the matter is that when you open a project in Cubase, you can do one of only three things: record, edit, or mix. And when you are starting with a clean slate, your only option is to record.

The idea behind recording sounds fairly simple, but it can get complicated. The first question you need to ask yourself is, "Where do I start?" Do you want to simply record a keyboard part? If so, do you want to record the MIDI data from the keyboard, or do you want to record the actual audio you hear from your keyboard? Maybe you'd like to record some guitar. Acoustic or electric? Maybe you just want to record a vocal. What if you want to record an entire band at the same time?

If these are the questions that are holding you back from taking Cubase to the next level, then you will get a lot out of this book. It covers everything step by step, from how to make the most basic recording to how to stay in control of a very advanced recording scenario. I not only go over Cubase and how it functions as the center of your studio environment, but I also go over other types of programs and equipment that you will need to use along with Cubase to get the recording you want and get the most out of Cubase.

By the time you've read this book, you should have the answers you need to record with Cubase, or at least know where to look for them. Working with Cubase requires not only a deep understanding of the program itself, but also a deep understanding of music and all the outboard equipment you will need to record music. It also requires a deep understanding of the computer you're using and the operating system itself. There are no real secrets to creating music using Cubase. The answers are all out there. The trick is knowing the questions, and where to find the answers for the questions you may already have. Your ultimate goal after reading this book should be to feel confident enough about the technical side that you can relax and enjoy making music.

What This Book Will and Will Not Cover

Your Cubase Studio was written for someone who already owns Cubase and is getting serious about recording with it. It covers everything from choosing your computer platform and setting up your computer system to work most efficiently with Cubase to using the automated mixing functions and achieving a detailed mix of your project.

There are some things that this book will barely touch on or not cover at all. One is score creation/editing in Cubase. Creating and editing a score lies beyond what the average Cubase user needs to know. The Media Bay (found in Cubase and Cubase Studio) is a fairly new feature to Cubase and a nice addition to the program, but it isn't really necessary for creating music—so I've skipped over it here. That also goes for several other features: the Play Order Track, SoundFrame, Tempo Track, and Time Warp.

Even though this book does cover MIDI editing, the subject goes much deeper than the average Cubase user might require. I will be touching on several MIDI editors, including the Key Editor, the In-Place Editor, and the Drum Editor; however I will *not* cover the Score Editor, List Editor, Sys Ex Editor, or Logical Editor. I will not go into detail on MIDI effects and modifiers or other MIDI functions. I will, however, explain in detail the steps you need to take to set up and record both MIDI and audio with a MIDI keyboard. For more information on MIDI editing, please check out my book *MIDI Editing in Cubase: Skill Pack*.

Although this book goes over what I consider to be the fundamentals of audio editing, audio editing in itself is another very deep subject. The basics that I go over here will open doors to more advanced audio editing for you down the road.

Everyone's home studio setup is going to be different. Because not everyone has a $250,000 mixing console sitting in their living room, I will focus on interfacing your Cubase studio with some of the best and most affordable options on the market today. I will also reference more expensive models and explain why you may want to shell out a few extra dollars in certain areas depending on the type of music you are recording. A high-pressure sales guy at the music store could probably point you in a lot of directions, but I'm interested only in your building a system that does what you want it to do without wasting your money.

Using This Book as a Companion to Your Cubase Manual

As I mentioned earlier, I'm not going to get too caught up in details specific to particular versions of Cubase. As a result, you will definitely need to use the Cubase manual as a resource along with this book. I will also refer to Web sites and other resources that will help you gather all the information you will need in order to achieve the results you want in your Cubase studio. It will be very helpful for you to have an Internet connection (but not necessarily from your Cubase computer setup).

The Cubase manual isn't always the best reference. The manual is written by several people, then edited and translated into other languages and released with last-minute changes very quickly. Sometimes it's incomplete. It's amazing that this is accomplished at all, as a 500-page book can take months to write—I know first-hand! Anyway, this is the nature of the racing technological beast, and unfortunately, we just have to accept it.

But it gets worse (and some of you may have already witnessed this). Because of rising operating costs in today's fast-paced market, many manufacturers of audio/music products have decided to cut off or outsource their customer support. (I remember the good ol' days when I could contact Steinberg and speak to a human being fairly easily about a technical issue I was having.) Even though Steinberg tech support has improved, sometimes you still have to wait a while on the line in order to speak to someone, and when you do, you still occasionally get the standby stock answer: "I'm sorry. We don't support that…" followed by the name of a particular model of sound card or computer. After waiting for an hour on the phone, that's the last thing you want to hear, especially in the middle of a recording session! The good news is there are ways to work around some of these issues, and I will go over some of them in this book. I will not refer to specific page numbers or chapters in the Cubase manual. Instead, I will give you keywords to use in your search for more information. Again, this approach is designed to help you understand the workings of your Cubase studio so that you know where to look when you need more information, regardless of the version of Cubase you have.

1 Setting Up Cubase on Your Computer

After the Cubase software itself, the most important part of your setup is your computer. When you bought your computer, were you thinking about using it to make music, or did you want to use it to do *everything*? Do you think most major studios are running Microsoft Office on the same system with the latest and greatest DAW setup? Just how serious are you about recording music?

When I finally traded in my Atari computer for a Windows system in the mid-'90s, I thought, *Wow! A computer that can do everything!* I bought the latest video games. I had this digital answering machine software going on. I had the coolest screensavers. I was surfing the Internet like a madman. Of course, Cubase was still my priority, and I was using it to record audio for the first time on a computer! I was pretty new to using Windows, and after about one month, I started seeing error messages. Then one day I came home to check my cool digital voice mail and found out about the infamous "Blue Screen of Death" (BSOD). My computer was fried. I lost everything I recorded and some cool programs. I had to spend a lot of money rebuilding my computer. That was my *first* lesson. You Mac guys are laughing right now, but maybe you haven't seen all the little "bombs" that pop up on Macs when something goes wrong.

It's funny, because even though I don't see the BSOD so often anymore, it still occasionally comes up—and it's *still* just as ugly as it was in 1996!

The goal of this chapter is to prevent you from seeing bombs or BSODs when you're working in Cubase.

Mac or Windows?

All right, by now you've probably come to the conclusion that I use Windows on my system, and you are correct.

Even though most people I know went down the Mac road, I dared to be different. To be honest, the only reason I really chose the Windows system was because there was a greater selection of software available. After having a lot of PC problems, I tried Mac because so many people I know said, "These things never crash." I crashed the Mac. In fact, that Mac kept saying, "It's not my fault" in a robotic voice, which only made me want to hurl the computer out of a window even more. The point is that whether you choose a Mac or a Windows computer to run Cubase, there are going to be issues that you will have to deal with. There is no such thing as a perfect system. Use the computer that you feel most comfortable with.

I have a theory that Macs tend to hide the workings of the computer from the user to create the illusion that everything just works like magic and that Windows is set up so you can more easily "peek behind the curtain" to see the workings. But, my theory goes, because Windows is easier to manipulate in this way, it's also more vulnerable to dummies erasing important system files. If you jump under the sink when the garbage disposal makes a funny sound, you may be more of a Windows person. If you call a plumber when you hear the same sound, you're probably a Mac person. If you try to fix the garbage disposal and end up with a broken sink and garbage disposal, and a bump on your head, maybe you're a Windows person who should be using a Mac. Most people that I know who use Macs and have problems spend more time on the phone with Mac support. On one hand, Macs are built with some pretty high-quality hardware that is the state of the art (at least for a month); on the other hand, the majority of the world uses Windows, and parts for PCs can come cheaper because of the wild, ever-fluctuating computer-component market. That being said though, Windows computers are more susceptible to computer viruses if they are connected to the Web because everyone uses them.

Pick your poison—Mac or Windows. Just remember not to get too attached to your computer because you'll probably need a new one in two to three years. I've been using Dell computers for years just because they are so easy to configure and build from the company's Web site. These days, it's more affordable to update an entire computer system every couple of years than to upgrade a system piece by piece. When it comes to upgrading your operating system, I recommend that you avoid doing it unless you are buying a new computer. Most new operating systems are designed to run on the latest hardware technology. If your computer is not up to speed, chances are it will perform more poorly after the new operating system is installed.

Note: In case you're already getting confused, your computer and every physical component in it is considered *hardware*. Cubase and all the other programs on your computer are considered *software*.

Regardless of which operating system you choose, consider yourself lucky that, with Cubase, at least you have a choice. Steinberg has made it a point from the beginning (or at least since the great fall of Atari) to make Cubase available for Windows *and* Mac. There are a few other very popular DAWs out there intended only for Mac (mostly due to the fact that Mac *owns* them). Other, lesser-known software (at least on a pro level) is available only on Windows-based computers. I guess if you have a split personality, you can run Windows on a Mac, or you can just own two different computers.

Speaking of owning two computers, it's not a bad idea. Remember how I said I was trying to run screensavers, video games, and an answering machine on my first computer along with Cubase? Well, if you really want to keep it simple and you can afford this option, it's great to have a dedicated DAW computer and another computer to do everything else (if you're a geek like me who lives in a computer world). And when I say everything else, I mean that you wouldn't even have your DAW computer connected to the Internet or a network of any sorts. The more software and hardware that you have running on your DAW computer, the greater the chances are that you will see system errors and Cubase program error messages. Running Cubase alone is enough to tax most computer systems, not to mention that if you're running Cubase, you will most likely be running plug-ins and other music-creation programs.

Optimizing Your Computer for Music Production

The thing that a lot of people don't seem to understand when they first buy a computer is that there are a lot of variables in the hardware alone that can make or break the way the software runs. This is because when you go to the store and see them all sitting side by side, they tend to look very similar. There are people who simply buy computers because they look "cool" or the monitor display looks impressive. In fact, a computer's appearance and its monitor have very little to do with how well the computer is going to run your software. It's the "guts" of the computer that really make the difference. I call Macs the pretty computers, because Apple usually takes the time (and money) to make a computer look a little snazzier on the outside. But what's inside a Mac and what's inside a Windows computer are not very different, and they're becoming more similar all the time. Figure 1.1 shows my

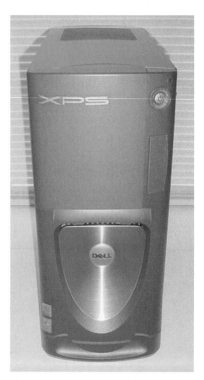

Figure 1.1 An external shot of my Dell XPS Gen 3 computer.

current computer. At the time I purchased this (2005), it was the top of the line for Dell's home computers.

When you open up a computer and expose the "guts" of the machine, things look a little different (see Figure 1.2).

Figure 1.2   The "guts" of my Dell XPS Gen 3.

Note: Laptop or desktop? Unless you're constantly on the road, traveling, or you require a laptop to perform live, stick with a desktop computer. Desktop computers will always be better computers for music production because it takes time just to develop the technology to make hardware small enough to fit into a laptop. Sure, it's nice to be able to stick a studio in your pocket, but let's get serious here!

Obviously, most store owners aren't going to allow you to take apart their display computers to see their guts, so it's important to know what to look for before you go shopping.

The CPU/Processor

The CPU/processor is the single most important part of the computer and often the most expensive part. Usually, when you talk about how fast a computer is, you're referring to the CPU (much like the engine of a car). There are many different types of CPUs on the market. You may have heard of companies such as Intel or AMD (two of the most popular), which specialize in making CPUs. These companies are always competing to make a processor that is faster than the "other guys'." Because there are several different companies making these and they're always changing, you're going to run into a lot of choices.

The latest and supposedly fastest processor is not always the best choice. Because of the speed of technological development, developers (such as Intel and Steinberg) have a hard time making sure everything is working the way it should. Dual processors are two processors that are linked together to perform as one faster processor. This type of processing has been available for quite some time but is just now becoming standard because it didn't work as well with Cubase systems from the start. To get an idea of the processing speed, refer to the GHz (gigahertz) number usually associated with a computer. At the time of this book's publication, a fast Intel Core 2 Quad core processor (four processors working together) was 2.66 GHz.

There is another field to be concerned with called the FSB (Front Side Bus) setting. This can get pretty technical, but the higher the FSB setting, the better off you are. A higher FSB helps in any multi-tasking you do on your computer system. Most manufacturers put a sticker of the processor type on the outside of a computer (such as Intel Pentium 4 or AMD Athlon). The best way to make sure you're getting the best processor for your Cubase studio is to visit Steinberg's Web site and browse the user's forum (specific to your version of Cubase) for information on bugs or errors associated with particular processors. You should also check with the manufacturer of the sound card you wish to use for compatibility issues. Personally, I don't enjoy browsing the forums, but I have learned quite a bit from them, and I'm glad they're out there. Another reason I buy my computers from Dell is because they currently offer a 30-day 100 percent satisfaction guarantee on their computers. This gives me plenty of time to load Cubase into the system and do some major tests with my setup to make sure that everything is working correctly before I commit. If you can find a company that will let you test drive its computers so that you can make sure everything works properly, that's often worth spending a few extra dollars.

As of 2007, Steinberg recommends dual or quad-core processors, and they seem to be working best with Cubase, but they're still in testing. The single-core processors, such as mine, are on their way out. Even though my computer is 3.6 GHz, because it's a *single* processor, a 2.66 GHz *dual* core is about twice the speed. Time for me to upgrade! If you go to the Support tab at Steinberg's Web site (http://www.steinberg.net), you should be able to find more information on currently supported DAW components.

Note: If you're super nerdy, you may try something called "over-clocking" your processor so that it works even faster, but I don't rec-ommend it. When you "overclock" your processor you start voiding warranties, you could create more system problems, and (even worse) you could cook your computer!

Note: Another thing you may see a lot when comparing processors is the word "cache." The more cache your processor has, the better off you are. Cache acts like a buffer that helps direct traffic to and from your processor to save valuable processor resources.

The CPU Fans

The fans in your computer do a lot more than just make noise. The main purpose of the fan is to cool the CPU and prevent your computer from actually melting down (which is not something you want to experience). I was a little disappointed after I bought my Dell computer because when I turned it on for the first time, it sounded like a race car. The race car sound is usually not the sound you want to hear when your computer is in the same room as your vocal mic. After opening the computer, I realized why it was so noisy. There are four large fans in the computer. I've had computers where I saw one or two fans, but four? The reason it has four fans was because the CPU works hard and gets super hot. In fact, using my computer is very similar to using an electric space heater (no exaggeration!). Again, my computer has a 3.6 GHz (single) Intel Pentium 4 processor, and at the time I bought it, I thought that because it was so fast, I would just have to live with the fan issue. If I had it to do over, I probably would've asked a few more questions about the fans. If you look hard enough within the manufacturer's specs, you should be able to find a dB (decibel) measurement for fan noise.

There are companies such as Sound Construction & Supply (http://www.custom-consoles.com) that create cabinets where you can put your computer to reduce fan noise, but I don't see this as a clever alternative. Even though these cabinets have internal fans, the computer still needs to "breathe," and putting it in a cabinet is not going to help it breathe any better and puts it at greater risk for meltdown. The only alternative to a noisy fan is replacing it with a quieter fan. This can be tricky because you definitely want to make sure you get a fan suited to your computer and processor. Most computers also have heat sinks that work along with the fans to cool the CPU. Every few months you should spray out your fans and your computer with a can of compressed air. Cleaning your fans will prevent worse noise down the road and will also keep your computer from overheating. Don't be so squeamish about opening a computer to clean it out. Unlike a TV or a synthesizer, computer towers are designed to open easily for cleaning or installing other hardware. Check your computer's manual for more on this. The biggest thing to worry about is static electricity, but if you follow your computer manufacturer's instructions, you should have no problems.

Note: When you're buying a computer, if it includes "quiet" in its product description, it's usually a good sign. If it doesn't use the word "quiet," it could have loud fans!

The Hard Drive

The hard drive is where everything happens. All your programs, including the operating system, are stored on your hard drive. When you save an audio file or a project, it is saved to your hard drive. There are a few things that are important when you're looking at hard drives: size, speed, and reliability are the main ingredients.

First let's look at size. Hard drive size is measured in bytes (1 byte equals 8 bits). One kilobyte (kB) is 1,024 bytes. One megabyte (MB), or "meg," is 1,048,576 bytes (or 1,024 kB). One gigabyte (GB), or "gig," is 1,073,741,824 bytes or 1,024 MB. One terabyte (TB) is 1,099,511,627,776 bytes, or 1024 GB. One minute of CD-quality audio requires about 15 MB of hard drive space. I have learned that it's not possible to buy a hard drive that is too big. My current hard drive is 1.2 TB, and it is almost completely full. The only problem with owning large hard drives is that for every large hard drive you own, you need another to have around just as a safety backup. Losing 1.2 TB of work and software is going to cost me a lot more money in time than the dollar value of a hard drive. I have had three hard drive crashes within the last 10 years. Hard drives crash for different reasons: mechanical failure, electrical surge, or maybe even a virus (which attacks the operating system, not the physical hard drive). Each time my hard drive crashed, I lost everything on the hard drive. Those files (recordings) were lost forever. Fortunately, I learned my lesson from this, and I now back up my hard drive regularly. Having multiple hard drives is better than having one hard drive. By using multiple hard drives, you can store your operating system on one drive and your files (such as Cubase projects or recordings) on the other. The files that you've worked on so hard are the ones that are the most important to back up. This means having at least two hard drives is more than a luxury—it's a necessity.

There are two types of hard drives you can get: internal or external. Every computer needs at least one internal hard drive. That internal hard drive needs to run the operating system for the computer (Windows/Mac). Most of the time, the same hard drive is used to also hold all the programs that run on that computer (Cubase, Reason, etc.).

Where you store your files is up to you. Some people prefer the same (system) hard drive or another internal hard drive because it keeps everything in one place. Others like the external hard drive because they can take that hard drive to use with other computers and it prevents the files from all being in the same place. It's also been said that using external hard drives creates less of a load on the power supply of your computer (because external hard drives have their own power supply), which in turn helps your computer run better. External hard drives are more expensive, but if you can afford them, they seem to be a very safe, efficient alternative to internal hard drives.

As I mentioned before, size isn't all that matters. Speed is very important. A hard drive is actually a magnetic disk (so don't put it around any magnets!) that spins and stores information the way a record on a record player stores tracks. When audio is being recorded, a lot of information is being stored, so that disc needs to spin pretty fast, at least 7,200 RPM (revolutions per minute). You can record on slower drives, but you're looking for trouble if you do, especially if you get into recording or playing back multiple tracks at once (which is what Cubase is all about!). I believe 7,200 RPM is becoming more and more of a standard in hard drives, but I'm also seeing hard drives at 10,000 RPM, which is even better. Other than disk speed, the transfer rate is the other factor that determines the speed of the hard drive. The faster the transfer rate, the better off your Cubase studio will be. The transfer rate is especially important when you are working with a lot of edits in Cubase or you are using a virtual sampler (such as HALion or Kontact) from within Cubase. The transfer rate determines how much info can come and go to the hard drive at once. Currently the rate of 3 GB/second is pretty darn fast. If you can find a drive that fast, or even above 1 GB/second, you should be in good shape for a while.

Note: Once again, the word "cache" can come up when referring to hard drives. The bigger the cache a hard drive has, the better the chances are that the hard drive will perform well when handling large amounts of data (or, in Cubase, a lot of audio tracks).

When it comes to reliability (particularly for audio recordings) it's really difficult to single out a particular manufacturer's hard drives or specific model. I'm sure that a pro music retail store such as Guitar Center (GC) will point you in one or two directions, but you may be able to find more words of wisdom in the Cubase Web site's forum. I've had drives that never let me down, only to suffer a crash when I bought another one of the same type. The most important thing you can do is back up, back up, and back up some more.

The Motherboard, Casing, and Power Supply

The casing of the computer is what you see on the outside of the computer. When you open up the computer, you'll find a large circuit board (called the *motherboard*) attached to the casing. The motherboard holds the CPU and connects it to just about everything in the computer. The power supply is also connected to the casing and converts the current from your wall socket into something that your computer can use. Steinberg claims that the motherboard (also known as the *chipset*) is the most crucial ingredient to a DAW's success, but in order to resolve any issues, you need to refer to your sound-card manufacturer's Web site for any information it has regarding compatibility issues. The truth of the matter is that unless you're building your own computer, you won't get much choice when it comes to these three important parts, but I have a few notes about each of them.

A computer whose ad uses the word "integrated" in its pitch has whatever feature is referenced built into the motherboard. It's becoming very popular to see computers with integrated sound, video, and modem. Having integrated features can be handy, but my theory is that when you try to cram more into something, you usually have to alter it so that it fits—and that process usually doesn't involve a change for the better. The worst part is that if you don't like the integrated feature, you're stuck with it because it's a part of the motherboard. I'm starting to see a lot more of this in computers, and it's getting hard to avoid, but my advice is to stay away from integration as much as possible. You especially want a separate video card and a separate audio card when you're running Cubase. Integrated video or audio is just one more thing to create problems for you down the road. If you are building your own computer and are looking for advice on mother-boards to avoid, check your sound-card manufacturer's Web site for a list of compatible mother boards.

The "skinny" on skinny computers is this—stay away from them. If you think that the narrow-profile casing on a skinny computer looks cool, let me tell you what they had to sacrifice in order to make it look that way: *quality*. The worst part is that the sound and video cards that interface into your computer's motherboard are a standard size and won't even fit in most skinny computers. Skinny computers are usually chock-full of integrated features. Apple tends to make some funky casing designs. Because of this, sometimes you don't really have a choice and you will be more limited with your sound-card choices. The more vents on your casing, the better the ventilation may be for your CPU, but the more often you'll need to clean out the inside of your computer with compressed air (because dust can slow down and even kill a computer).

A bad power supply can be the death of a computer system. I have twice fried a hard drive and replaced every component in my computer only to discover it was the power supply that was bad all along. Since most casings come with a built-in power supply, I can only offer one very valuable bit of advice: buy a surge protector. The best type of protection you can get is a battery backup system. A battery backup system will not only prevent you from frying your computer during a storm; it will also keep your computer on when the power goes out and allow you to save whatever it is you're working on. APC makes a backup surge protector that you can find at just about any office supply store for around $50. That $50 investment has been the best investment I have made and the best insurance you can have besides a backup hard drive for your system.

The Video/Graphics Card and Monitors

Without a video card in your computer, you wouldn't be able to see anything on your computer. I don't think most computers will even work without some sort of video card installed. A video card offers several features. The most basic and important benefit is that you can plug an external monitor into it to see what you're doing. Because working with Cubase requires working with many windows open at once, I highly recommend a video card that will support at least two monitors.

Note: Single- or dual-monitor setup? If time is valuable to you, spend a little extra and get a dual-monitor setup. If I could have a four-monitor setup, I would. The extra monitor helps save so more time when you're in the studio.

Besides monitor outputs and hookups, the most important thing a video card does is help the processor display video on the screen. Did you know that every time anything changes in the display, the computer has to redraw the entire screen? You can probably guess, then, why video games require some serious graphics buffering. Cubase may not be quite up to par in looks with games such as *Halo*, but because Cubase is so audio-intensive, sometimes it has to steal resources from the video end of your computer. When this happens, you'll see flickering on your screen, or it will freeze altogether. Once screens freeze, the rest of the system starts to freeze and you can lock up your whole system, forcing you to reboot and lose whatever it was you were working on. Even though advances in technology have made video cards much less of an audio concern, the balance between video and audio is still very important. If you don't have a sufficient video card and the graphics are complex (maybe you're monitoring video as you play back in Cubase), you may run into problems with your audio as well as your video. I remember the days when a video card that had 4 MB of VRAM was pretty cool. Now I see video cards with 768 MB of VRAM.

Note: VRAM is video random access memory. It's a special type of memory chip developed strictly for video-card usage. This has nothing to do with your RAM (discussed later in this chapter).

With graphics becoming more and more important on computer systems, I predict that it won't be long before video cards are graded by how many gigabytes of VRAM they offer. The more VRAM on your video card, the less of a load video will be on your CPU. There are several models of video cards on the market. Video cards and pro audio cards require a certain "chemistry" in order to work together. Unless you have the option of trying out the video card and running some tests on your system before you buy, I highly recommend that you visit your sound-card manufacturer's Web site to see if there are any compatibility issues between your sound card and your video card. Assuming that your priorities for this computer revolve around your Cubase usage, your sound card is the more important choice. If you have to live with a slightly less desirable video card, so be it.

Another thing that's becoming more of a consideration when buying computer systems is their ability to edit video. The system required for video editing is very similar to the system required for audio editing. The biggest difference is that video requires even more hard-drive space and a stronger video card than for audio editing. I don't recommend putting consumer-grade video capture cards in your Cubase computer. If you must have video editing on your Cubase system, I highly recommend looking into some pro capture cards (those by such manufacturers as Blackmagic or Matrox) and checking with the manufacturers of both your sound card and your video card for compatibility issues. Once you have both cards together in a system, you should do some major testing before you jump into any serious Cubase projects. If you decide later on you want to add something like this to your system or change your video card, realize that this is not something you want to do when you're in the middle of an important project. It takes finding a good *balance,* and upsetting that balance could lead to system failure.

When it comes to monitors and a Cubase system, there's not a lot to discuss. Just find one that will be easy for you to look at for hours at a time. If you haven't moved into the new millennium and upgraded to LCD flat-panel monitors, I highly recommend them. The flat panels not only take up less space in your studio, they also use less electricity and are easier to read for long hours. They're also much less susceptible to video "burn in," which happens when an image remains on the screen for long hours at a time. The bigger the monitor is, the better it is for working with Cubase. But if you're debating whether you want to get one really big monitor or two smaller monitors, get the two smaller monitors. Cubase works best with multiple monitors, hands down.

The Sound Card (or Audio Interface)

Finally we get to the part that is going to make the biggest difference in the way your Cubase projects come out sounding: the sound card. When you buy a computer that's been pre-assembled, it's going to come with a sound card installed. Unless you bought a system that was built specifically for Cubase, the sound card in your computer is most likely a consumer-grade sound card. No matter how much an ad insists that the sound card is "top of the line," it's not going to be best suited for working in Cubase. Most of the time, these consumer models will work in Cubase, but they aren't capable of producing broadcast-quality audio recordings. If your computer doesn't have a sound card installed, it probably has integrated sound (which is a cheaper sound card that is built directly into the motherboard).

My personal feeling is that I'd rather pay to have a cheap sound card (one I can remove from my computer) installed in my system than have integrated sound (permanently fused to the motherboard) that I'll be stuck with in my system. After you install your pro sound card, you don't want some cheap integrated sound card still on your system and conflicting with your pro sound card. Technically, you should be able to function normally with multiple sound cards in your setup, but I tend to follow the "keep it simple" rule of thumb when it comes to these things. But if you have a Sound Blaster sound card installed and you just want to use it for playing back other applications, such as CDs, iTunes, your PC sounds, etc., that's fine. Your pro sound card will probably conflict less with other sound cards than a video card that isn't a good match.

There are several directions you can go when choosing a new pro sound card for your Cubase studio. If you're like me, you'll want the sound card that has the highest quality and the best price. If price is not an issue, you'll probably just aim for the best quality. There are also other things to consider, such as: What will you be recording, and how do you need to interface your audio to the sound card? What type of computer do you have, and how do you need to interface the sound card to the computer? What sort of driver does the sound card require?

First, let's start off as simple as possible. Let's say you're a keyboard player who simply wants to be able to record MIDI and you'll be using VST instruments (either included with Cubase or plug-ins) without using external synths in your setup. All you'll really need is something to play back the audio through your speakers so you can mix your tracks and something that's designed to record MIDI. Even though you can find this in plenty of all-in-one sound cards on the market, you can also easily find it in some small individual parts. Now, you already have choices at this point, and only *you* can decide what is right for you.

On the flip side, a complex situation would be that you're a keyboard player with multiple external synths and MIDI controllers, and you want to be able to record 96 audio tracks simultaneously from multiple sources, including a drum kit, vocalists, guitar and bass, and an eight-piece string section. The good news is that you *can* do this in Cubase Studio or Cubase 4 (but not in Cubase SE). The bad news is it's going to cost you more in regards to your sound card.

Following is a bulleted list of third-party sound-card manufacturers that currently offer Cubase-compatible sound cards. After the name of each manufacturer, I've included a Web site link so that you can find more information on its current line of sound cards. Also next to each manufacturer, I have rated the price range from low to high with $–$$$$, quality with *–****, and have given a rating of #–#### for the number of audio interfaces available to give you a better idea of where to look.

- Alesis ($–$$) (*–**) (#) http://www.alesis.com
- Apogee ($$$$) (****) (##) http://www.apogeedigital.com
- ART ($–$$) (*–***) (#) http://www.artproaudio.com
- AUDIOTRAK ($$) (**) (##) http://www.audiotrak.net

- Behringer ($$) (**) (###) http://www.behringer.com

- Echo Digital Audio ($–$$) (**) (##) http://www.echoaudio.com

- EDIROL (Roland) ($) (**) (###) http://www.edirol.com

- E-MU ($) (*) (#) http://www.emu.com

- Focusrite ($$$) (**) (##) http://www.focusrite.com

- Lexicon ($) (**) (#) http://www.lexiconpro.com

- Line 6 ($) (**) (#) http://www.line6.com

- M-Audio ($–$$) (***) (####) http://www.m-audio.com

- Mackie ($$–$$$) (**–***) http://www.mackie.com

- Mixvibes ($) (*) (#) http://www.mixvibes.com

- MXL ($) (*) (#) http://www.mxlmics.com

- Native Instruments ($$) (**) (#) http://www.native-instruments.com

- PreSonus ($$$) (***) (##) http://www.presonus.com

- RME ($$$–$$$$) (***–****) (###) http://www.rme-audio.com

- SONIC CORE ($$$) (***) (##) http://www.sonic-core.net

- Steinberg ($$) (***) (##) http://www.steinberg.net

- Tascam ($$–$$$) (***) (###) http://www.tascam.com

- TC Electronic ($$$) (***) (##) http://www.tcelectronic.com

- Universal Audio ($$$$) (***) (#) http://www.uaudio.com

- XPSound ($) (*) (#) http://www.xpsound.com

- Yamaha ($–$$$) (***) (###) http://www.yamaha.com

If you find this list a little overwhelming, I would suggest looking to M-Audio for high-quality, low-cost sound cards, Steinberg or Yamaha for middle-of-the-road sound cards, and Apogee or RME for higher-cost/higher-quality sound cards. I've been using Steinberg's VSL 2020 sound card for two years. It cost me $200, and I've been impressed with the sound quality. Since I don't record live bands very often, I find that the interface suits my needs fine.

The sound card can be interfaced to your computer in multiple ways.

- USB 1.1
- USB 2.0
- FireWire 400 (IEEE 1394)
- FireWire 800 (IEEE 1394b)
- PCI
- PCMCIA

USB 1.1 (usually referred to simply as USB), USB 2.0, FireWire 400 (or just FireWire), and FireWire 800 audio interfaces all provide a simple connection thru a USB or FireWire cable to a USB or FireWire port on your computer. This makes it incredibly convenient to interface your audio to a computer system.

PCMCIA sound cards usually work with laptop computers.

PCI sound cards, such as my Steinberg VSL 2020, fit into PCI slots inside a desktop computer (see Figure 1.3).

My personal experiences with sound cards make me lean a little more toward PCI-based sound cards. These sound cards usually come with a

Figure 1.3 Steinberg's VSL 2020 sound card.

special breakout box, and even though the tech specs seem to match up the same with most FireWire/USB sound cards, I have had higher sound quality and better overall performance with PCI cards. In some computers, you don't always have the luxury of using PCI cards because PCI slots (located on the motherboard) are limited (usually to two or three), sometimes not available, and are usually occupied by other devices (other sound cards, a modem, etc.). So make sure you have an available PCI slot before you buy something you can't use.

Getting back to recording 96 audio tracks simultaneously: The only way you're going to be able to do it is by using Cubase Studio 4 or Cubase 4 (or later). With Cubase Studio 4, you can record up to 128 tracks at once, and with Cubase 4 you can record up to 256 tracks at once. With Cubase SE, you can record only eight tracks at once. Most of the sound cards you'll find on the market have only eight analog inputs, so if you are serious about recording 96 tracks of audio at one time, you're going to have to shell out some bucks for hardware. Most people aren't going to need to record 96 tracks at once from home, but it's nice to know that the option is available. I think the biggest question at this point is: Do you have a computer that can even handle recording 96 tracks of audio at once?! Probably not!

I will cover more on sound card configurations throughout the book. My goal is to help you better understand what it is that you're going to need so that you'll know what to look for and where to look when you need it.

RAM

RAM stands for random access memory. If you want a very good technical definition for it (or for anything else, for that matter), I suggest turning to Wikipedia online.

Note: If you're not familiar with Wikipedia (http://www.wikipedia .org) and you want to feed your brain, please look up anything you have a question about or don't understand. Wikipedia's filled with all sorts of great technical information on computers.

There are lots of different types of RAM. When you buy a new computer, RAM doesn't come cheap. It's important that you understand how RAM is going to help your recording experience. RAM is like your desktop (not the desktop on your computer, but the desktop that your computer sits on). The larger your desktop, the more things you can put on your desk and the more tasks you can have going on at once. Putting more RAM in your computer is sort of like adding some more length or width to your desktop. When you're working with Cubase, it's very likely that your "desktop" is going to get pretty full, so the larger your "desktop," the better—meaning the more RAM, the better.

RAM runs at different speeds, and every computer has a limit on how much RAM you can install. Operating systems also limit the amount of RAM they can use. For instance, Windows XP Home limits you to using 2 GB of RAM. This means that if you have 4 GB of RAM installed, you'll only get the benefit of using 2 gigs of RAM. It's important to do some research before you rush out and buy RAM that isn't going to work for your computer system.

Currently there are no versions of Cubase that can run on under 512 MB of RAM. This means that if you don't have at least 1 GB of RAM, you're in trouble. RAM specs seem to change even faster than processor specs, so it's a race you can't win. My suggestion is to buy enough RAM to work with Cubase (check the Cubase site for system requirements), but *don't* buy too much RAM when you buy your computer. RAM is the one smart upgrade on a computer system (and then only if you really need it). This is because you'll save money (the price of RAM will drop over time) and it's easy to install without really changing the functionality of your system.

Certain types of RAM can cause conflicts with Cubase, but most likely Steinberg will work these bugs out of the program if they come up. This sort of conflict would affect many Cubase users.

There may be people who will tell you that a certain type of RAM is faster or better (and it may be), but don't worry about that. Just buy enough RAM, don't use up all your computer's RAM slots right away, and you'll be fine. One important tip: RAM is sometimes sold in pairs or in single chips (parity and non-parity). This doesn't make much difference, but you should know that if the RAM is supposed to work in a pair and you have only one of the chips installed, it will not work properly.

The actual DRAM chip is called a DIMM. This means that if you have 4 GB of DRAM and you have 2 DIMMs, you have two 2GB DRAM chips. If you have 4 GB of DRAM and you have 1 DIMM, you have 1 4GB DRAM chip. When you're buying your computer, it's important to make sure that you have enough slots available for future upgrades. You have a limited number of RAM slots in your motherboard, and each motherboard can only hold so many DIMMs, thus limiting your RAM.

USB/FireWire

A lot of sound cards now operate using USB or FireWire. FireWire was originally a Mac thing, and USB was originally a PC thing, but nowadays you can get either type installed in either computer. Every computer has a limited number of USB or FireWire inputs, but this has nothing to do with the load on the computer itself. Pro sound cards pull a lot of juice from a computer's hub. This means that if you're trying to run several USB/FireWire devices at once, all from the same computer, you may be asking for trouble.

I simply don't recommend running more than one or two of these devices at once, but if it is absolutely necessary, it's better to have an additional USB/FireWire hub installed through a PCI slot on your motherboard. This will free up some of your resources. USB/FireWire cards are not expensive. You should always opt for getting the latest technology (such as USB 2.0 or FireWire 800 at this time), because the newer technology is usually *backwards compatible*.

Note: *Backwards compatible* means that you can interface the newer technology with the older technology, but when combining the two, you will be forced to work within the older technology's restrictions. You can use a USB 1.1 drive with a USB 2.0 hub and get the same performance you could with a USB 1.1 hub, but if you try to use a USB 2.0 drive with a USB 1.1 hub, it will perform like a USB 1.1 drive.

Since USB and FireWire have both been around for several years now, I wouldn't be surprised if very soon we didn't see a new type of interface that was even better than these. All I can say is that if you're still using SCSI, get with the program!

Network Card, Modem, Bluetooth, Thumb Drives, and Dongles
Network cards and modems have very little to do with Cubase unless you need to connect your computer to the Internet or another local network. If you are using Windows and you can avoid connecting your PC to the Internet, I recommend it. It's not safe to surf the Internet or download e-mail on a Windows computer without antivirus/anti-spyware software. And running antivirus software while running Cubase is almost worse than contracting a computer virus! It's another no-win situation. If I had to choose, I'd take my chances with the viruses! I have two computers: one dedicated to working with music/audio (and Cubase) and one for everything else. Maybe this sounds excessive, but how many TVs do you own? How many musical instruments? It makes sense if you can afford it. Even though you'll need to download program updates from the Web, you can download them on your "everything" computer and then transfer the files to a USB thumb drive (flash drive) so that you can easily transfer the files to your DAW computer (see Figure 1.4).

Figure 1.4 A cheap alternative to viruses ($20).

Bluetooth wireless is exciting to me because it's pretty new. Similar to other wireless technology (such as wireless network cards), you can use Bluetooth to transfer data from a Bluetooth-compatible wireless device to your computer with the help of a Bluetooth *dongle* (see Figure 1.5).

Figure 1.5   A Bluetooth wireless dongle.

Note: A *dongle* is very similar to a thumb drive. It's usually small and plugs into a USB port. Cubase comes with a dongle that you need to have installed on your computer to run the program (see Figure 1.6). This dongle prevents piracy of the program. Whatever you do, don't lose that dongle! Steinberg will not replace it if it gets lost. They will make you buy a whole new program. Ouch!

Dongles require very little effort from a USB and can come in very handy because they're small and easy to take from computer to computer.

Bluetooth is something you may eventually want to get for your computer, but you don't need to have it installed because the Bluetooth dongle is so easy to install. So far Cubase hasn't really found a way to use Bluetooth technology, but with cell phones and ringtones becoming more popular, I wouldn't be surprised if they were able to integrate it a little further down the road.

You could opt for a Bluetooth wireless mouse or computer keyboard to enhance your Cubase system. At this time, I'm unaware of any technical

Figure 1.6 The Cubase dongle.

side effects of using Bluetooth, but since Bluetooth sometimes uses sound devices such as microphones and speakers, if you can live without Bluetooth, your Cubase studio will most likely run better.

CD/DVD Readers/Writers

Don't forget to install a CD/DVD writer (also known as a burner) in your system. Even though you currently can't burn a CD directly from Cubase, you need a DVD-ROM in order to install the software. Instead of owning a DVD-ROM drive (which cannot write to disc) and a CD writer, I recommend just owning a DVD writer. With a DVD writer, you can read and write CDs *and* DVDs.

Another important thing about owning a DVD writer, as opposed to a CD writer, is that you can store over 4 GB of data on one standard DVD-R (a write-once format). This means you can usually back up entire projects on one DVD-R. To do that, you will need other software besides Cubase. I'll tell you more about that in Chapter 2, "Accessorizing Your Cubase Studio."

DVD writers have a few different specifications. There are DVD+R, DVD-R, DVD+RW, DVD-RW, and DVD±RW. You definitely want a DVD±RW writer. This type of DVD writer ensures that you can read or write DVD+Rs, DVD-Rs, DVD+RW and DVD-RW (rewritable) discs, as well as CD-R and CD-RW discs, with no problems. For more information on DVD formats, search Wikipedia for "DVD format."

Note: DVD-RW and DVD+RW discs (DVD rewritable) are DVDs you can reuse over and over again. I don't recommend them. DVD-Rs are cheap. Maybe they aren't as environmentally friendly, but they burn better, faster, and they are recognized in more DVD-ROMS.

Another spec to look for is the *x* speed. You may have a DVD writer that's 16x. This means that if you're writing a 16-minute-long CD, in theory it should write the CD in one minute. This is not 100-percent accurate because it usually takes a minute before it actually starts writing, but this should give you an idea. This means a 52x writer should be able to write a 52-minute CD in one minute as well. Here's the catch: In order to write at the max speed, your media (whether it's DVD or CD) must also be rated at that speed. Not all media are created equal, so speeds vary. Most programs allow you to burn CDs at lower speeds than the max speed. This is nice because, when quality is important, you want to make sure there are no write errors, and writing at a slower speed lessens the chances of write errors. Currently Cubase does not offer a way to burn CDs internally.

The last spec to consider is dual (or double) layer. If you can find a DVD writer that is dual-layer capable, this means you can write more than 8 GB of data on a dual-layer disc. This can come in handy when you need to back up a project that's larger than the standard 4.7GB DVD-R.

Note: HD DVD burners and Blu-ray technologies are both fairly new to computers. These both offer even better disc-burning alternatives but are currently very high priced and work with media that isn't as compatible as a standard DVD or CD. I'm positive that there will be a dramatic price drop in this technology within the next five years, and it will not be necessary for most Cubase users to own either until that time.

Increasing Your Operating System's Performance

Whether you have chosen to go down the Mac road or the Windows road, there's something you have to understand: Neither Apple nor Microsoft designed its operating systems solely to work with Cubase. There are a lot of built-in compatibility issues for both Windows computers and Macs from the moment Cubase is installed on your system. Before you start to cry and run back to your banjo or harmonica for comfort, let me tell you that taking care of these little issues is no big deal. That's what we're going to work on in this section.

By the time this book is available, Mac will have released OS X Leopard and Microsoft will probably have a few updates available for Vista. Because operating systems are always changing, I'm going to give you some general advice.

Using Multiple User Accounts

The first tip regards trying to "do it all" on one computer. If you must surf the Web, edit video, or use Microsoft Word on the same computer as the one on which you run Cubase, you should look into setting up your machine for *multiple users*.

Setting up a user profile strictly for audio production (your Cubase studio) and another user profile for everything else has proved beneficial for Cubase users. For Mac, I recommend downloading free software called Diablotin to help you set up your preferences. To find Diablotin, try Googling "Diablotin" and look for downloads.

Note: *Googling* refers to using the search engine Google (http://www.google.com) to find information based on key words that you input. Try it sometime.

Keep in mind that if you can avoid multiple users on a computer, you'll be better off. There's also something in both Mac and Windows computers called *fast user switching* that enables you to quickly jump from your Cubase studio to the profile set up to do everything else. This can come in pretty handy for your all-in-one system, but it's a major resource hog that will always be running in the background. If you have a dedicated Cubase computer, disable *fast user switching* to help give Cubase a performance boost.

Clean Install

Reformatting your hard drive (erasing everything on your hard drive, including the programs that are installed) is something that only the brave should do. When you reformat your hard drive, you have the option of starting over from scratch and reinstalling Windows from the roots up (this is referred to as a *clean install*, and some people do this every so often just as a maintenance routine). This gives you more options. Windows Vista uses the NTFS file system. It is possible to configure your computer as a *dual-boot system* if you would like to run Windows XP as well. Sometimes users choose to run a dual-boot system so they can A/B the way Cubase functions on both operating systems. Again, I usually stick to the "keep it simple" principle and recommend choosing just one operating system. You'll probably end up using just the newest operating system down the road. For Macs with Intel processors, this means you can run Windows on your Mac.

Note: If you want to find more info on dual-boot systems, try Googling your operating system (Mac or Windows) along with the words "optimize" and "audio." Various publications and Cubase user groups are always putting new information on the Web. Whether it strictly pertains to Cubase or another DAW doesn't matter. They all require something similar from an operating system.

Windows Messenger and Instant Messaging

When you're working with Cubase, do you really need to be IMing your buddy on the other side of the world? Windows Messenger has a lot of great features, but it's a resource hog. If you want your Cubase studio to be at peak performance, you need to disable Windows Messenger, even if you aren't connected to the Internet. To do this, find Windows Messenger in the program list or task tray, open it, and select Tools > Options > Preferences. In the Preferences window, uncheck any box that says "Run this program when Windows starts" or "Allow this program to run in background." Click OK, and then close Windows Messenger.

Visuals and Audio

This is a big one. It seems like every time they come up with a new operating system, it has more little animated graphics and photos. Although these things are fun to play with, they are system hogs. In Windows, right-click anywhere on your desktop and click Display (from a Mac, locate the Dock submenu from the Apple menu). Then go through and disable automation, background photos, and screensavers. I know it takes a little bit of fun out of the user experience, but you'll be making your Cubase experience as good as it can be. For Macs, you can download a freeware program called Shadowkiller (Google it!) that will help you get rid of some of those frills and fluff. From the display setup, you'll also be able to access your video card's setup menu, from which you should be able to change the resolution of your display. With the rapid development of video cards, this is something you probably won't have to do, but if necessary you can change these settings to meet the minimum requirements of Cubase as a last resort.

Note: When it comes to built-in power-saver features, such as ones that make hard drives "sleep" or shut monitors off after a period of time, disable them all. Those features tend to lock up a system or are just plain annoying. When you're not using your computer, shut it down. Shutting down your computer not only saves power, it *could* save your computer!

As bad as these fun little visual effects are for performance (and both Mac and Windows are guilty), sound effects might be worse. Those little beeps and bonks or "it's not my fault" audio warnings can crash your audio setup. In Windows, find the Control Panel, locate the Sounds and Audio Devices section, and choose No Sounds. On a Mac, under System Preferences, choose Sound, and under Sound Effects, choose No Sound Effects.

In Windows, in the control panel's System settings, select the Advanced tab. Under the Visual Effects tab that appears, choose Adjust for Best Performance. Under the processor settings, choose Adjust for Best Performance of Background Services. This will aid the ASIO drivers that are used with most Windows sound cards.

Note: ASIO technology was actually developed by Steinberg in order to achieve higher-quality results in audio recording on a computer. This technology is used by many sound-card manufacturers and DAW software developers today. Go Steinberg!

Virtual Memory

I went over RAM earlier and the importance of having a lot of RAM in your system. Windows and Mac operating systems also employ something called *virtual memory*. Virtual memory uses a designated portion of your computer's hard drive to help ease the load on your processors and RAM. Again, under the Advanced tab in the System settings of your Windows computer, you will find the Virtual Memory settings. I personally recommend disabling virtual memory, but you should try adjusting it to see if you notice a difference in the way your system runs. A good rule of thumb is to set your virtual memory to twice the amount of RAM you have in your system (4 GB of RAM = 8 GB of virtual memory). This also holds true for Macs. On Macs, you can find the Virtual Memory setting in the Memory control panel.

Auto-Start/Startup and System Services

Whenever you first boot up your system, Windows and Macs automatically launch several programs. These are usually applications your computer thinks you're going to need right away. These *auto-start* programs and other *system services* tend to stay on in the background, taking away valuable system resources for your Cubase studio. Disabling all these is not an option because Cubase requires that some of them *are* running in the background (e.g., the Syncrosoft license control software for your Cubase dongle).

You have to careful what you disable, but if you think you're up to the challenge, here's how you can do it. In Windows, open Run from the Start menu and type in "msconfig." A window will open with various tabs. Select the Startup tab and uncheck any boxes for software you don't need. Again, be very careful! If there is something that you don't recognize, your best bet is to leave it alone. For Macs, check your Startup Items folder and move any programs that you don't need at startup to another location on your computer.

Write Behind Caching

Windows has a feature called *write behind caching,* which is used to buffer data before it's actually written to disk. With Cubase, it works best when you write directly to disk. In order to bypass this, right-click on My Computer from the Start menu and choose Properties. Select the Hardware tab and Disc Drives, and then select a hard drive on your system from the list (if you have multiple hard drives, you need to do this for each of them). Right-click on the hard drive and select Properties. In the Properties window, locate and select the Policies tab. Under Policies (if it is available for your hard drive), uncheck Enable Write Caching on the Disk. Click OK. If this isn't an option, don't sweat it: You'll probably be fine with your current setting.

Multiple Hard Drives

Cubase really knows how to make your hard drive sweat. If you are recording and playing back multiple large audio files (the computer sees this as large bits of data) from one hard drive, there is a lot of data being transferred to and from the hard drive at once. I'm continually amazed at how well this process actually works considering what's going on. I've been recording audio on computers since Cubase started recording audio on computers, and I know that this process has dramatically improved over the last five years and will continue to improve. You should easily be able to play back 24 tracks at one time on a 7,200 RPM hard drive. If you start running into problems, such as audio stuttering, distortion, or clicking, it may be because you've pushed your hard drive past its limits. When this happens, I recommend recording and playing back files from another hard drive in addition to your main hard drive. I personally prefer to have all my files in one location because it becomes messy when you have guitar tracks on one hard drive and your drums on another and you need to back up, but sometimes using multiple hard drives is a necessity.

If you want to use a virtual sampler VST instrument (such as HALion or GigaSampler), you're best off keeping your samples on a hard drive different from the one you use to record and play back your audio. This is because running each virtual sampler is like running a mini-Cubase within Cubase. Each note played on a sampler can trigger multiple recordings that are stored and played back simultaneously from your hard drive (just like the audio tracks in Cubase are triggered and played back in Cubase). If you have a lot of samples happening at once and a lot of audio tracks and edits, you're pushing Cubase into the danger zone.

Besides juggling multiple hard drives, there is another way to solve this problem that's been around for years–a solution that continues to simplify our lives today. It's a technique called *bouncing* audio tracks. When you bounce an edited audio track, for example, from four edits into one track, you prevent your computer from having to access the hard drive four times, thus saving a lot processing power on your whole system. Also, when you convert the audio from a VST instrument or sampler into an audio track (using a similar method), you also free up system resources. I will give you more input on how to bounce audio in Chapter 9, "Mixing It Down."

Where multiple drives really start to become an issue depends on how many tracks you need to record and play back at one time. If you plan to record 24 tracks while you're playing back 24 tracks, you may want to consider multiple hard drives. If you're not recording more than eight tracks at a time and monitoring 24 tracks at a time, you should be fine with one good hard drive, assuming you aren't running too many virtual samplers at once.

Antivirus/Anti-Spyware and Automatic Updates

Antivirus/anti-spyware software is by far the worst thing you can do to your Cubase setup besides install a computer virus. It continuously runs and acts as a filter for everything that goes to your hard drive. It's supposed to work in the background, but there's nothing quite as annoying as your recording session coming to a halt by a warning message from McAfee or Norton. If you're serious about your Cubase studio, do yourself a favor and stay away from this type of software. Use it only if you need to surf the Internet and download e-mail from your DAW computer. If you absolutely need to have it, disable it when you're not online and especially while you're running Cubase.

Automatic operating system updates are almost as bad as antivirus software. Turn off automatic updates on your computer and instead of letting Microsoft or Apple decide when it's time to update, *you* can decide when it's time to update your computer (preferably when you aren't recording or mixing your next masterpiece). It *is* important to stay up to date with your operating system. Before you install major updates, however, visit Steinberg's site (http://www.steinberg.net) for news regarding any conflicts that an update may have with your current version of Cubase. It's also good to check with your sound-card manufacturer for information on the operating-system updates, although these updates are not as likely to disrupt your audio hardware setup as they would any software you are running.

Deleting Programs and Defragging Your Hard Drive

I've learned a lot from my mistakes, and deleting programs was something I used to do the wrong way. When you're working in

Windows, whatever you do, don't drag a program (or some other file that you aren't sure what the purpose of it is) into your Recycle Bin and then empty the bin. You'll be deleting that file or files from your hard drive for good. Even though this may seem like the right thing to do when you don't want that program on your computer anymore, there is a proper way to delete programs, and that is not the way. To delete a program, locate the program's *uninstaller* (located in the program's menu under the Start menu in Windows), select it, and follow the on-screen instructions. If you cannot find the uninstaller for a program there, use the Add or Remove Programs feature in the control panel. I recommend you remove any programs that you don't use. Mac users can drag programs into the trash, but if they would like to remove some of the things that are left behind, they can purchase third-party software such as Yank. This isn't necessary, however.

A lot of times, there is dead space left on a heavily used hard drive because of file fragmentation. Defragging your hard drive compacts these file fragments and reorganizes the files so that they are easier for your computer to find. When you're working with large audio files, you should defrag routinely (once a month or bimonthly). Sometimes the fragments that Cubase creates can be extremely large, and defragging your hard drive frees up some much-needed hard-drive space as well as helps its performance.

To defrag your Windows hard drive, open My Computer, select the hard drive you wish to defrag, right–click, and select Properties. In the Properties window, select the Tools tab, and then select Defragment Now in the Defragmentation section. Once again, select the hard drive and click Defragment. Macs are set up to automatically defrag when they feel it's necessary, and there is no software included with a Mac to defrag a drive. You can download third-party software that will enable you to defrag your Mac's hard drive. An action that can be performed periodically on a Mac that could be helpful is repairing disk permissions. For more information on repairing disc permissions, try Googling the action along with your operating system.

Note: A Mac's automatic hard drive defrag utility is not necessarily always a good thing. When you're in the middle of a recording session, this utility can slow your system down. Unfortunately, there's no way to disable this. Currently the only way to avoid this is to use third-party defrag software on a regular basis when you aren't in a session.

Setting Up Your Pro Sound Card with Cubase

Once you've gone through the installation procedures for your sound card, you've installed Cubase using the DVD or CD-ROM that came with the software, and you've installed the Syncrosoft piracy-protection software and USB key (dongle), you're ready to open Cubase and set up your sound card.

Understanding Latency

The Wikipedia definition of latency is "a time delay between the moment something is initiated, and the moment one of its effects begins or becomes detectable." For anyone using a VST software–based DAW, this is similar to an audio delay. Trying to record through an audio delay would be really difficult and unnatural, so the sound card can be configured to compensate for latency by using a "buffer" that delays the input signal until the delayed audio plays back, thus creating a recording that is perfectly in sync.

The biggest issue with latency is monitoring a live performance, because you need to hear what you're doing while you're listening to what has already been recorded and is playing back. To compensate for this, Steinberg has what is called *direct monitoring*. Direct monitoring is the process of monitoring the signal going into the sound card's input as well as monitoring the output signal. This is still not an exact science because you end up getting the signal that is "now" and the signal that is milliseconds from "now," which in turn creates a slapback delay (a very short delay). The good news is that Steinberg has also created ASIO 2.0 drivers, which enable computers to play back audio with a latency as low as 32 samples.

Digital audio is created by sampling a continuous audio waveform. The process of sampling converts that waveform into samples at a rate determined by your sample rate setting. So with your audio sample rate (44.1 kHz, 48 kHz, 96 kHz, and so on) and latency set (32 samples), through calculated conversions you can determine that the delay time might be as little as .333 ms (at 96 kHz) and as much as 1 ms (32 kHz). That's a pretty darn quick delay!

To better understand delay, you have to be aware that there are delays happening all the time when you record audio. Delays are natural. The delay you hear when you clap your hands in any room is longer than 1 ms. There is a delay that occurs as your voice travels to the microphone. There is a delay that occurs between the microphone and the computer. Are you starting to get the picture? A 1 ms delay is not going to get in your way during the recording process.

The VST Audio System

Now that you understand what all this latency is about, let's work on setting it appropriately on your computer system. With Cubase up and running, locate the Devices menu on the menu bar across the top of the screen. Locate and select Device Setup from the Devices menu. The Device Setup window opens. It should look similar to what you see in Figure 1.7.

What you should look for is the VST Audio System control, as shown on the left side of Figure 1.8. The top right side of the Device Setup window contains an ASIO Driver drop-down menu. By opening this menu, you should be able to select the driver from your sound card (if you have installed your sound card properly). There may be other drivers listed here (e.g., one for your built-in PC sound card), but for the best sound, choose the software driver that came with your pro sound card. (Hopefully, your pro sound card's driver uses ASIO 2.0, or Core Audio drivers at the very least.) Keep in mind the software drivers are always being updated by manufacturers, so check your manufacturer's Web site for updates to existing drivers, and you'll be always stay up to speed with the world.

A new driver can make a huge difference in the performance of your pro sound card. The advanced options shown are for tweaking if you are having problems and are for advanced users only. You can play

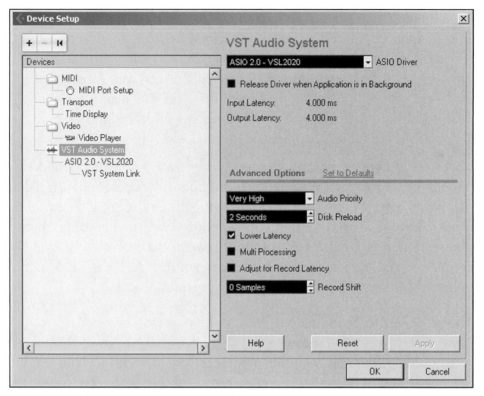

Figure 1.7 Cubase 4's Device Setup window.

around with these if you're having problems, but otherwise they are okay to leave in their default settings. If you are using Cubase along with other programs (such as WaveLab) and you need to switch back and forth between the two, you may experience audio issues because once Cubase is up and running, it is always "fighting" to be in control of the audio. Checking the Release Driver when Application is in Background checkbox should solve this issue, but it also depends on how your other software is set up. If you don't need to run Cubase and another program that shares audio capabilities at the same time, then you should just leave this box unchecked.

Once you've chosen these basic settings, on the left side of the screen, select the driver's name (as it also appears in the menu from which you just selected it) from under the VST Audio System control. The driver's display window may look similar to mine, shown in Figure 1.8.

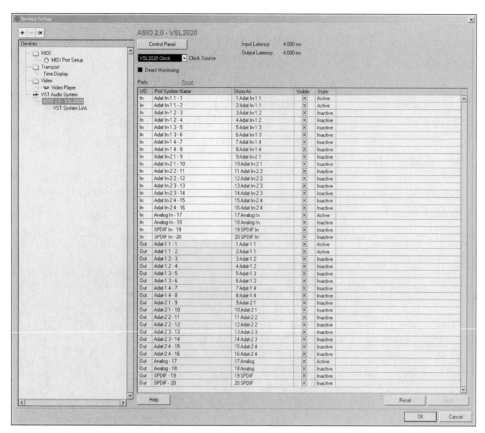

Figure 1.8 The sound card's driver panel in Cubase.

This new window displays all the ins and outs of your sound card. In the Show As window, you can select the input or output of your sound card and rename it whatever you want (e.g., VSL 1 In, or Guitar In, etc.). You can also uncheck the box to the right of the Show As field if you want to hide the input from your input and output setup menus. (This is a nice feature if you have a sound card with 20 ins and outs and you only use two.) This is the screen where you can enable direct monitoring (as I mentioned previously in the "Understanding Latency" section). Depending on the way you're recording, you may want to use direct monitoring. You can always toggle this switch while you're recording to determine which works best. The Clock Source selection menu displays what is currently in control of Cubase's sound and what makes Cubase function. What is displayed in this menu entirely depends on your sound card's driver and how it is set up. If your sound card is being controlled by another device's clock (such as when syncing to external video), Cubase will chase the external source (the *master*), and the word "external" may be displayed here since Cubase is acting as a *slave* to the external master clock source. The Cubase VSL 2020 driver that I'm using in this example has no options in this menu. The options are all available from driver's control panel, which is shown in see Figure 1.9.

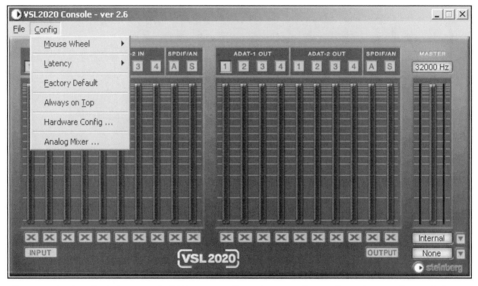

Figure 1.9 My Steinberg VSL 2020's sound card control panel, as shown from Cubase's Device Setup window.

Clicking on the Control Panel tab in your sound card's driver window will open the actual sound card's graphical control panel, which will allow you to manipulate the workings of your sound card. When it comes to adjusting quality, latency, and synchronization, you will most likely be making the changes you need from this panel. Since everyone's control panel is going to look a little different, I'll just tell you what to look for.

Setting the Right Latency

First off, latency should be adjustable from somewhere within your sound card's control panel. Now, you may be wondering, Why should

I have to adjust latency? Why can't I just leave it always set to the least amount of latency? The answer is that your system's limits are based on how you're using your system. For instance, if you are running a lot of tracks at once, your system has to work harder. This means that your system's resources are going to be more limited. You should be aware that working with Cubase (or any DAW) is a constant performance "balancing act." Your computer and sound card have to work pretty hard to achieve ultra-low latency. If you're running a lot of VST instruments, you're also pushing the limits of your processor. In order to compensate for that, you may need to make adjustments to your setup. Of course, you could run out and buy a new computer or some more RAM, but before you do that, try adjusting the latency. A little more latency may cause more of a delay when you go to record, but a little less latency may cause crackling or distortion if your system is maxed out. The capabilities of Cubase definitely exceed the capabilities of most computer systems, and as long as Steinberg and other DAWs keep pushing the envelope, it will continue to be that way. You have to *learn* your system's limits and adapt to them. I adjust my latency from 32 samples to 2,048 samples all the time. It all depends on the project you're working on and the capabilities of your computer system.

Recording Quality versus System Efficiency

Like latency adjustments, your recording quality setting should take into account not only how good you need your project to sound, but also your system's limitations. Two things come to mind: sampling frequency and bit depth. The higher either number is, the better the quality is. Figure 1.10 shows how bit depth and sampling frequency affect a sound wave.

To break this down in audio layman's terms, the greater the bit depth, the greater the headroom and bandwidth, the greater the sampling frequency, and the more accurate the replication of the sound wave. Think of a sample as a frame in a filmstrip and the number of frames that go by in one second as the frequency rate of those samples (30 frames per second is pretty standard). A sample rate of 16 bits at 44.1 kHz (the CD-quality standard) means 44,100 samples per second

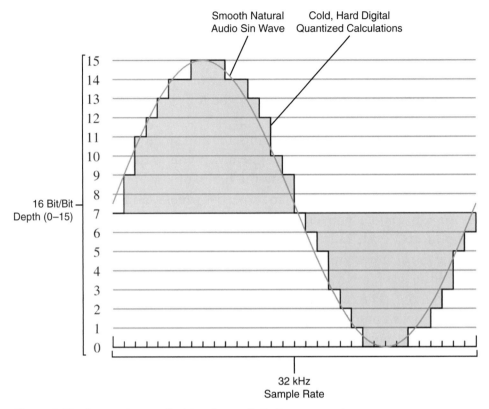

Figure 1.10 A sound wave that has been digitally processed.

at a maximum of 16-bit depth. As I mentioned before, one minute of stereo audio at this quality uses about 15 MB of space on a hard drive. Most pro sound cards can record at a bit depth of 24 bits, which is becoming more of a standard. Changing the bit depth alone will dramatically increase the size of an audio file (e.g., a stereo 24-bit file recorded at 44.1 kHz equals more than 26 MB). As you can probably guess, the file size of a stereo 24–bit, 96 kHz track is going to be high (around 35 MB). Twenty-four tracks of stereo files, each more than three minutes with these same settings, come to 2.46 GB of audio. Maybe that doesn't sound like a tremendous number, but when you start adding everything up, it can quickly eat up hard-drive space and create a greater burden on your CPU, and the transfer rate of your hard drive may become more of a concern.

In your sound card's control panel, you should be able to find the controls you'll need to adjust the sampling frequency. Another way to

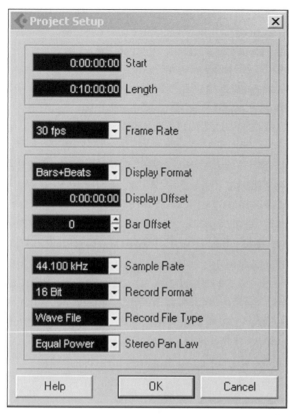

Figure 1.11   The Project Setup window as shown in Cubase 4.

adjust the sample rate and also the bit depth (record format) of the audio tracks you record is through the Project Setup window, which you access by selecting Project Setup from the Project menu (see Figure 1.11).

Note: Keep in mind that different versions of Cubase may vary when it comes to setting up a project's bit depth. The important thing to remember is that this is something you change within a Cubase project setup and not from your sound card's control panel.

The Project Setup window is the main place to make changes to the overall sound quality of your project. From here, you can toggle your bit depth to 16 bit, 24 bit, or 32-bit floating point.

Note: *32 bit floating point* is not 100-percent 32 bit, but it captures a bit depth of up to 25 bits flawlessly and can increase the sound quality even more than 24-bit recording. Even though your sound card may only support 24-bit recording, 32–bit floating point will add an even greater dimension to your internal audio processes.

You can change your bit depth (record format) while you're working on your project, but if you try to change your sampling frequency, it will ask if you would like to convert the sampling frequency of the other files you have created in the project. It prompts you to convert the sample rates of the previously recorded files because if you try playing back a file that was recorded at a higher sample rate on a lower sample rate setting, the file will sound as if it is playing back at a lower speed and pitch. You get the opposite effect when you play a track recorded with a lower sample rate with a higher sample rate setting. This is because even though the rate has changed, you still have the same number of samples; they just get moved closer together or spread farther apart.

Note: When changing bit depth and sample rate, it's usually a better idea to "downsize" (go from high to low) than to upgrade to a higher level when you're converting tracks within your project. When it's time for mixing and mastering, using a higher bit depth and sampling frequency is always better.

Recording File Formats

Along with bit depth and sample frequency, another setting that can greatly affect the sound and the size of your audio file (recording) is your choice of audio file format. Using different file formats can become messy because there are so many to choose from. Windows computers' default audio file format is the WAV file, and a Mac computer's default audio file format is the AIFF file. If you listen very closely on a good system, you may be able to hear the difference between the different file formats recorded at the same bit depth and sample frequency on the same system. Cubase offers four high-quality choices when it comes to file format: WAV, AIF, Broadcast WAV, and WAV 64. The four formats can be selected from the Project Setup window as well. You can also import other popular file formats (such as MP3s) using the Import Audio File function from the File menu. When you export a mixdown, you're also given more file formats to choose from. The important thing to remember is that WAV and AIFF files are the most common and universal pro file formats (for compatibility reasons), but I highly recommend experimenting with different file formats to change the sound of a recording within Cubase. Broadcast WAV is the highest quality format and is becoming more of a standard on both Mac and PC platforms. Format does make a significant difference to the sound.

2 Accessorizing Your Cubase Studio

As mentioned in Chapter 1, Setting Up Cubase on Your Computer, Cubase and your computer system (including the sound card) are the most important elements in a great Cubase studio. In that chapter, you also learned how quickly technological changes can affect the way your Cubase system runs. After writing the last chapter, I decided to upgrade to a new Dell computer with a 2.4 Quad-Core processor, 4 GB RAM, and Windows XP Pro, with two 1 TB external hard drives. This system update is going to require about a month of heavy testing to make sure Cubase and my sound card have no major compatibility issues.

But without the proper accessories, you will find that your system is very limited. The good news about Cubase accessories is that they don't become outdated nearly as quickly as the actual computer system. Most other hardware accessories that you'll be using with Cubase will last you years without costing you much in updates or maintenance.

The accessories you will require with Cubase depend on the type of music you wish to produce. In this chapter, I go over some basic accessories, and I explain where these accessories come into play and why they are useful in certain types of music production.

On another note, musicians can get a little carried away with accessories and it's important that you understand how some accessories are a waste when Cubase already has so much to offer. This chapter has been designed to give you a clear idea of what other equipment you might require to make the most of your Cubase studio.

MIDI Keyboards

Whether you are a keyboard player or not, one of the most valuable Cubase accessories you can own is a MIDI keyboard. I started out a keyboard player (piano) as a child, so my opinion may be a little biased, but what I've discovered over years of using Cubase is that I use my MIDI keyboard for a lot more than just programming MIDI keyboard/ instrument parts. For instance, a MIDI keyboard can be the perfect tool for non-drummers to program drum parts (the only reason I say "non-drummers" is because there are even better tools available for those who actually know how to play a drum kit or play with drum sticks). Also, because of the popularity of virtual synths and DAWs, most keyboards contain a wide variety of controllers that enable you to get the most out of performing tasks in Cubase, such as programming pitch bend, volumes changes, or synth parameter changes; mixing, changing, or automating EQ settings—the list goes on. Having all of these features in one place definitely makes the MIDI keyboard one of the most practical accessories a Cubase user can own.

If you've been doing your sound-card homework, you may have already realized that some manufacturers understand the importance of owning a MIDI keyboard so much that they have combined MIDI keyboards with sound cards. There are several of these types of MIDI controller/ sound cards on the market, and they may seem like the perfect solution for those using Cubase with a laptop on the road (see Figure 2.1).

Being a keyboard player and a fan of the "keep it simple" principle, I find the idea of owning a MIDI keyboard that can do it all pretty exciting. However, there is a good reason I don't own an M-Audio Ozonic, and it has to do with another principle I usually stick to: When someone tries to cram too much into one box, they usually have to take shortcuts, so be very cautious. Even though the idea is incredible, think about it: If something with so many features retails for $600 and there are other sound cards that have the simple purpose of capturing and playing back audio from a computer for the same list price, shouldn't the stand-alone sound card sound better than the all-in-one keyboard? The bottom line is that if sound quality is important to you, try to avoid any sort of all-in-one unit. All-in-one keyboards are designed to make things convenient for live performers and aren't meant to be used

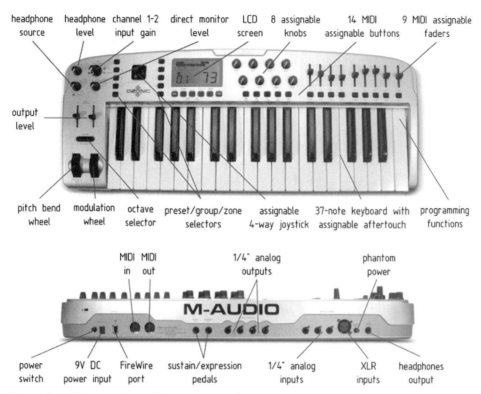

Figure 2.1   The amazing all-in-one M-Audio Ozonic audio interface keyboard.

in a studio. M-Audio makes some other fantastic MIDI keyboard controllers that aren't sound related, and I'll go over some of those shortly.

Note: Simple MIDI keyboard controllers *do not* contain any sort of internal sounds (such as an organ or drum kit). A MIDI keyboard controller is designed to be the trigger (or MIDI input) device into Cubase. Once the MIDI info has been programmed into Cubase, Cubase will output that MIDI information to external synths or internal VST synths (or controls). There is no need to own a MIDI keyboard that includes sounds unless you are a keyboard player who also plays live (without a computer) or you just happen to like the way a particular keyboard's internal sounds function, or the way the keyboard feels. For the most part, if you're not a keyboard player or synth programmer, a simple MIDI keyboard controller will suit your needs fine.

If you consider yourself to be a virtuoso pianist, do yourself a favor and buy a keyboard controller with 76 to 88 keys. Weighted keys are optional. As a keyboard/piano player, I don't find any similarity between the feel of weighted keyboard keys and piano keys, and I opt for the unweighted keys for a cheaper, lighter, and easier-to-play keyboard. Keep in mind that if the MIDI keyboard you buy has internal sounds that you would like to use, you will need to hook up the audio outputs to your sound card's audio inputs. This is explained in more detail in Chapter 4, "Recording MIDI." If you're not a keyboard player or you rarely play with both hands on the keyboard at once, save some valuable studio space by getting a keyboard with fewer than 49 keys. Just because a keyboard has only 49 keys doesn't mean that you can't cover the range of a keyboard with 88 keys. All keyboard controllers are capable of adjusting the octave range in which you wish to work.

Note: What if you have a MIDIfied piano? Can you use that as a MIDI controller? The simple answer is, *anything* that has a MIDI output can be used as a MIDI controller. The question you should ask yourself is: Does the MIDI controller actually perform the functions you require? A MIDIfied piano won't really help you *mix* a track in Cubase, but you would be able to lay down some killer MIDI piano parts. Sometimes it's necessary to use *multiple* MIDI controllers. It all depends on your personal studio needs.

If you consider yourself to be a tweaker who likes to manipulate sound in almost unimaginable ways, you may want a MIDI keyboard controller with a lot of knobs or sliders. That said, even though using the knobs and sliders is fun, you can perform the same tweaking as with a knob or slider on your MIDI keyboard using your mouse. The other thing to note is that if you want to make the most out of knobs and sliders on a MIDI keyboard, spend some time doing some setups with Cubase. If you like to do a lot of tweaking, you'll save precious studio time by using knobs and sliders instead of a mouse. Don't worry about cramming too many knobs or sliders on a MIDI keyboard. It will not degrade the sound quality in any way. The worst problem excess knobs or faders could cause would be a system crash or MIDI delay, and you'd have to be using a *lot* of knobs and sliders simultaneously to make that happen.

Other Types of MIDI Controllers

If for some reason you're completely against the idea of having a MIDI keyboard in your setup but you still want to be able to tweak your faders and knobs with Cubase remotely, there are several other directions you can go. I used to own a Tascam US-428 MIDI control surface that boasted a mini-mixer with faders and knobs and an external sound card. The new Mackie MCU Pro (see Figure 2.2) has everything you need to tweak a mix without having a built-in sound card.

Figure 2.2   The Mackie MCU Pro MIDI mixing control surface.

If you're a DJ, a guitar player, or a drummer and you want to take full advantage of Cubase, there are several MIDI control surfaces currently on the market just for you. For DJs who want to be able to record and perform edits to the scratching (such as timing corrections and pitch bend), check out control surfaces such as the Vestax VCI-100 (see Figure 2.3).

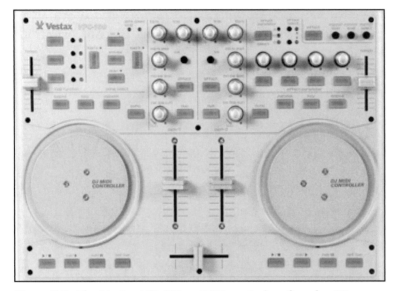

Figure 2.3 The Vestax VCI-100: a MIDI control surface for DJs.

For drummers who want to use their skills to the fullest in Cubase, one of the best (and pretty standard) options around is a set of Roland V-Drums. The important thing to realize is that you aren't limited to the sounds that come with MIDI drum kits. In fact, if you use the MIDI kit appropriately, you can bypass the MIDI drum kit's internal sounds completely. Even though most drummers I know are purists when it comes to playing on particular kits, there are several very valuable reasons to use a MIDI drum kit when recording. The biggest reason is, you don't need to spend hours getting drum sounds. Most of the time, in order to achieve a desired acoustic drum recording, a drummer must set up the drums in a properly tuned room, tune the drums perfectly, and then find proper microphones to use on each drum and enlist the services of a great engineer to get the perfect drum mix. With a set of MIDI drums, you can simply plug a MIDI cable into your computer and start recording in Cubase. If you don't like the sounds you used at the time you recorded, you can change them later! Another benefit is automatic *quantizing* of drum parts. For instance, let's say there was a part where the drummer played a kick drum a little off beat, but the rest of the track was perfect. Instead of retaking a section, you could simply quantize the kick drum to fall in the appropriate place. You'll learn more about quantizing within Cubase in Chapter 8, "Basic Editing." When shopping for a MIDI kit, the important thing to keep in mind is, what is the drummer going to feel most comfortable playing? The more comfortable a drummer feels during a recording, the better the performance you're going to get. You can actually trigger an acoustic kit with microphones, but you will not achieve the *dynamics* in the MIDI recording that you would with a MIDI kit such as the Roland V-Drums (see Figure 2.4).

Guitar players seem to like to accessorize more than any other type of musician. Because of this, there are a lot of different guitar interfaces

Figure 2.4 The widely popular Roland V-Drums.

available in today's market. Most of them appear as a guitar-plug-to-USB adaptor and convert the guitar's audio signal from analog to digital audio. If you have a pro sound card installed in your system, there is no need for a cheap guitar interface to plug your guitar into your computer. Using these convenient little devices could actually *decrease* your recording quality. I will go over this and much more in Chapter 6, "Recording Guitar and Bass." What I'd like to discuss here is the option of recording MIDI with a guitar. Recording MIDI with a guitar has been done for years. Due to the complex nature of the guitar itself, the MIDI guitar has never been perfected. Like recording MIDI drums, there are definite plusses to recording MIDI with a guitar. For instance, let's say you own a guitar, but you want to record a sitar or banjo part. Because a guitar is very similar to a banjo or sitar, using a sampler you can achieve some very realistic-sounding parts for instruments that fall into the guitar family. Also, if you're a great guitar player and a horrible keyboard player, it may be easier for you to program other types of MIDI parts via your guitar as opposed to using a MIDI keyboard.

Again, another great quality of MIDI guitar is having the ability to quantize your playing or play something at a slower tempo so that you can speed it up later and sound like Yngwie Malmsteen or Eddie Van Halen. Most guitar-to-MIDI interfaces require a device that translates the string vibrations and audio pitch from the guitar to an actual MIDI note with certain characteristics. The audio-to-MIDI "translation" is very complex, and the results are far from perfect and usually require that the guitar player change the way he/she plays in order to achieve the desired results (which takes a lot out of a performance!). The only strictly MIDI guitar that I'm aware of today is made by a small company called Starr Labs, and it's called the Z-tar (see Figure 2.5). It replaces each fret with a touch-sensitive button and comes highly recommend by guitar greats such as Stanley Jordan.

For those of you who do nothing but sit around, there is even a guy who designed a MIDI sofa controller (that's right, a MIDIfied *couch*). If you want to explore more about MIDI, you can do so at http://www.midi.org

Figure 2.5   The all-MIDI Z-tar!

Note: When purchasing a MIDI controller (particularly a keyboard, guitar, or drum controller), it's important to look for *velocity-sensitive* keys or pads. This enables you to record *dynamics* (soft or loud) in a performance. You should also look for a keyboard that has *after-touch*. Aftertouch allows you to alter the tonality of a pitch by applying physical pressure on a key once the key has been struck and held. This enables you to do slight pitch bends and other tricks (as you would do with a guitar string on the neck of a guitar).

Setting Up Your MIDI Controller with Cubase

Once you've determined which type(s) of MIDI controller(s) you're going to need with Cubase, the next step is interfacing the controller to work with your computer and Cubase.

MIDI controllers normally interface thru a MIDI cable, a USB cable, or a FireWire cable. I wouldn't be surprised to see wireless MIDI devices in the near future (wireless MIDI has been around for quite some time but hasn't really become popular for DAW systems).

For the most part, you'll need to follow the instructions that came with your MIDI device to ensure proper installation on your system. In the following example, I demonstrate how to use your MIDI controller in Cubase once it has been properly installed. I use a simple M-Audio Keystation 49e MIDI keyboard in this example. The Keystation 49e interfaces with a standard USB cable directly to a USB port on the computer.

Note: When you use a USB interface, most of the time the device will receive its power through the USB cable (meaning that you won't need to plug the device into an outlet; it receives its power through your computer's power supply). This can be very handy, although it does place a slightly greater load on your computer system.

MIDI Port Setup

Once the MIDI device has been installed, the first place you explore should be the Device Setup window, accessed by selecting Device Setup from the Devices menu on the menu bar. Once you've opened this window and selected MIDI Port Setup from the left side of the Device Setup window, it should appear similar to Figure 2.6.

The MIDI Port Setup screen displays every MIDI in and out in my Cubase studio. Close examination of the MIDI Port Setup screen should reveal that I have in fact three MIDI inputs on my system and seven MIDI outputs, which are way more than I need for this exercise. The reason I have so many inputs and outputs listed here is that not only does the Keystation 49e offer one MIDI in and one MIDI out, but the sound card that came with the computer (Sound Blaster) also comes with four MIDI outs (three of which operate internally and another

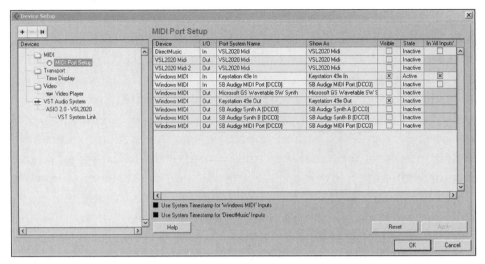

Figure 2.6 The MIDI Port Setup screen within the Device Setup window.

that works as a MIDI out port by using the FireWire output on Sound Blaster), and my pro Steinberg card offers one physical MIDI in and out, and one internal MIDI out port. To simplify matters, I have marked only the Visible checkbox next to the Keystation MIDI in and out. This will hide the other choices later when I need to make a selection. If the MIDI device you want to use is *not* listed in the MIDI Port Setup screen, it has not been installed correctly. (Try your installation again, or contact your MIDI device's customer support.)

Understanding MIDI Signal Flow

In order to help you understand what this MIDI in/out nonsense is all about, you really need to understand *signal flow*. When you truly understand signal flow, you will be able to make sense of all your ins and outs no matter how complicated things get. You determine signal flow by defining the path that a signal needs to travel to get from point A to point B. For example, let's analyze what happens as a key is struck on a piano. A finger strikes a piano key, and the key moves a hammer, which in turn strikes multiple strings, which creates a pitch. The pitch is then amplified by a soundboard in the piano and heard by some guy sitting across the room. Even though this may seem detailed to some, it's actually a fairly simple description of what really happens when a key is pressed on a piano.

Now let's create a simple signal-flow map starting with striking a key on a MIDI keyboard. Your finger strikes a key on the MIDI keyboard, then the signal travels out of the MIDI Out on the keyboard and in to the MIDI In on the computer through a USB or MIDI cable. Now, once the signal is in the computer, the signal must flow out to a synth or sampler's (MIDI sound source) MIDI In. Once the signal has reached the MIDI sound source, it is translated into an audio signal, and the audio signal then must go out of the MIDI sound source and through some sort of speaker so that you can hear the key your finger just struck. Whew! That was a lot of ins and outs (and that was a shortened version of what really happens to the signal)! If you can follow this example and always ask yourself where the signal needs to go in detail, you should be able to figure out *when* you'll need to use an in or out and *which* in or out you need.

Note: MIDI synths, samplers, digital pianos, or any other MIDI device that contains its own sounds can be referred to as a MIDI sound source whether it is software or hardware based.

Getting MIDI Signal from Your Controller to a MIDI Track

If you paid close attention to understanding MIDI signal flow as described in the previous section, you should be able to follow along with this example; and if things appear slightly different in the Cubase version you're working with, you should be able to find what you need to make your proper connections.

Now that my Keystation 49e is set up properly within the MIDI Port Setup, I need to create a MIDI track in Cubase so that I have a final destination to output my MIDI signal. To create a MIDI track in any project, select the Project menu, select Add Track, Add Track again from the resulting submenu, and choose MIDI as the type of track you would like to create. Cubase may prompt you to enter how many MIDI tracks you would like to create. One track is sufficient for this exercise.

Select your newly created MIDI track, and then, from the toolbar (see Figure 2.7), select the View Inspector button. The Inspector should appear on the left side of your MIDI track display. Use Figure 2.7 and the Inspector to determine your MIDI In and MIDI Out setting for the selected MIDI track. If the MIDI device you wish to use is not already listed in the track's MIDI In setting, click in the MIDI In setting to display a list of your available MIDI inputs (see Figure 2.8).

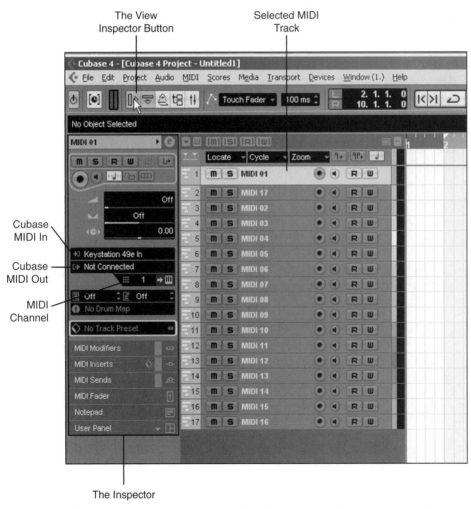

Figure 2.7 Using the Inspector to set the MIDI In and MIDI Out for the new MIDI track.

Figure 2.8 Finding the right MIDI In.

You may notice something called All MIDI In in Cubase. All MIDI In is the default selection of Cubase and simply means that all MIDI being received by Cubase will be received on that channel. This sort of opens up the MIDI floodgates so that any signal that's trying to get in can get in. If you are working with multiple MIDI devices at once, this could create a problem. Otherwise, you can use this as an alternative to selecting a specific MIDI In as we are doing with the Keystation 49e in Figure 2.8.

Note: The wording on ins and outs can become very confusing sometimes. Even though the Keystation 49e (used in this example) reads "Keystation 49e In," it is actually the MIDI *output* signal of the Keystation 49e's connection to the MIDI *input* of Cubase. The MIDI signal is going in to *Cubase, not* to the Keystation 49e. Unfortunately, every manufacturer calls its MIDI ins and outs whatever it wants, and not everyone thinks alike. The good news is that if your MIDI ports are set up correctly, then when you select the MIDI device from Cubase's MIDI Input drop-down list, only the MIDI outputs for your MIDI devices will appear.

Now that you have routed your MIDI device's MIDI output to Cubase's MIDI input for the selected track, you should get a reading

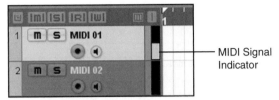

Figure 2.9 A MIDI signal from the Keystation 49e is detected by the track's MIDI Input Signal meter and the transport's MIDI Input meter when a key is struck.

on the selected track's MIDI Input Signal meter and on the transport's MIDI Input meter when you strike a key on the MIDI device, as shown in Figure 2.9.

Just because you can now see a MIDI signal in Cubase does not mean that you will be able to hear a sound. The reason you aren't hearing anything is you haven't directed the MIDI signal to a MIDI sound source. You can record MIDI at this point, if you'd like, but this may be hard to do without monitoring what you're playing, and even if you do record something, you will have to direct the sound to a MIDI sound source before you can hear what you've recorded.

I will go over recording MIDI and setting up VST instruments in much greater depth in Chapter 4.

Headphones and Reference Monitors

For most of us, it would be hard to imagine working in a studio without being able to *hear* anything. Besides the importance of having a good ear to achieve a mix, you're most likely going to need some sort of audio monitor setup for your Cubase studio. The cheapest alternative could be as simple as using the speakers built into your computer, some external PC speakers, or a pair of cheap headphones.

If you are planning on doing a final mix (making CDs) from your Cubase studio or recording live instruments, having a good set of reference monitors and/or headphones is a must. Most professional studios have not just one good set of reference monitors; they have multiple sets. Some professional engineers are so particular about their monitors they actually take them from studio to studio.

Note: The reference monitors that I'm referring to are speakers that are designed to truly represent audio. A lot of consumer speakers are built to "color" or enhance sound. This coloration effect makes it difficult to judge the *true* sound of a recording or mix. The word "flat" is often used to describe a good true pair of reference monitor speakers. *Flat* means that there is very little tonal coloration from the speaker itself.

There are a lot of choices out there when it comes to selecting good reference monitors. A monitoring setup consists of an amplifier and a speaker. Both of these elements can dramatically affect the sound of a mix or recording. Twenty years ago, the idea of using a speaker cabinet with a built-in amplifier was unheard of for studio-monitoring purposes. Today, most people are using these all-in-one monitor setups mostly because they sound great and are very easy to use.

Truth be told, your *ears* are the only real judge for what monitors you need. If you're new to mixing and you don't really understand how to listen for certain characteristics in a recording, you can spend $400 or $10,000 on a pair of monitors, and it may not make much of a difference in the sound when it's all said and done. Most of the best engineers in the world would rather die than mix on a pair of all-in-one monitors. But if you're mixing in a garage or bedroom, or you have limited mixing experience, do yourself a favor and buy the all-in-one monitors. It's hard enough to tune a room to a pair of monitors, let alone tune an amp to a pair of speakers. If you've been doing this for a while, you probably know where to look for great monitors, and you also know that a set of great monitors can cost more than the rest of your entire Cubase studio.

I've been using a pair of Yamaha MSP-5 amplified monitors (see Figure 2.10) for almost seven years, and I still love the way they sound. Before the Yamaha MSP-5s, I used some Tannoys and some Alesis monitors powered by a Peavey Studio reference amp. I've also mixed on some very nice Westlake BBSM-6 monitors. I have to admit that those Westlake monitors are probably the best I've ever heard, but

Figure 2.10   The Yamaha MSP-5 all-in-one reference monitors.

I'm still very happy with the $500 pair of Yamaha MSP-5 monitors. Whatever you do, don't just rush out and buy a pair of monitors without listening to them. If you live far away from a music store, make a special trip to a store where you can spend time listening and comparing several different types of monitors within your budget. I was a big fan of Genelec monitors, but the price of the Yamahas versus their sound quality made me choose them instead. If you plan to do a lot of mixing and recording in your studio, spend a little extra on the monitors. They will make a big difference to your Cubase studio working experience.

If you live in an apartment or a place where you can't record or mix music without affecting the lives of someone else around you, you need headphones. Years ago I was in a situation where using headphones was the only way I could mix. At the time, I was very frustrated because I'd found that headphones made it nearly impossible for me to achieve a good mix. There are a few who may have a different opinion regarding this issue, but I believe that most pros will agree that it's very hard to get a good mix using headphones. I finally decided I needed to look for some better headphones. I went to all the music stores, and a lot of consumer pro audio stores, and I couldn't find anything that I liked. Even the best studios in the world use headphones that are not well suited for mixing. That's because most of the time headphones are used for monitoring a performance. In a lot of cases, they just need to be able to get loud or prevent bleed-through when using microphones during a recording.

After a lot of demos, I finally found that the best pair of mixing headphones for me was a high-end pair of consumer headphones: Sennheiser HD590s (see Figure 2.11). At the time, using these headphones, I was able to get a mix to at least 95 percent so that I could finish the mix quickly using the reference monitors. These headphones are also great for monitoring while recording vocals. If you're serious about mixing and you have to use headphones, you shouldn't settle for headphones that color the sound in such a way that you can't distinguish parts clearly. On the other hand, if you plan on recording a lot of different bands in your Cubase studio, don't rush out and buy the most expensive headphones for the bands' monitors because you'll find that your headphones will become used and abused and you may have to replace them frequently. If you're recording live rock drummers, in a lot of cases you'll need headphones that are just plain loud.

Figure 2.11 Sennheiser HD590 headphones.

Another difference in using headphones as opposed to the all-in-one reference monitors is that headphones need amplification. You may own a sound card that has a headphone output, or even multiple headphone outputs. You can use headphone splitters to run multiple sets of headphones off one headphone output, but as you do this, you lose a lot of signal to your headphones. If you need to use multiple headphones (for instance, you'll be recording multiple musicians at the same time), you'll most likely need a headphone amplifier. The size of your headphone amp depends on the number of headphones you need to run at once. One of the great things about using a headphone amp is that most of them have volume controls for each output, which enables listening at whatever volume the user desires. A very simple and practical headphone amp available on the market today is the PreSonus HP4 (see Figure 2.12). The HP4 has been designed to work well with DAWs so that you can run your sound card's main output into the HP4 and then control the volume of both your reference monitors and four individual headphone outputs. The best part about it is the fact that it retails for around $100 and sounds fairly *clean* (doesn't color the sound going to the reference monitors or headphones).

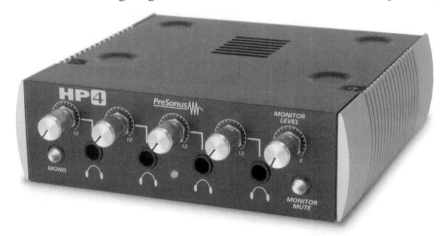

Figure 2.12 The PreSonus HP4 headphone amp.

Setting Up Your Monitors
Even if you are lucky enough to own a pair of the best-sounding monitors on the planet, if you don't have your monitors set up properly, you may as well be mixing on PC speakers.

Let's talk about *speaker placement* of what's known as *near-field monitors*. Most projects are mixed using near-field monitors. By using a good near-field monitor setup, you should be able to get a really good idea of what your mix will sound like in most other environments. Near-field monitors are the monitors you usually see in studios just over a console at the engineer's head level. For a Cubase studio, these monitors would probably be located at the same level as your computer monitors (head level), except on each side of your computer desk. Using speakers next to monitors used to be a major problem because speakers are huge magnets. Now that it's a more common practice, most manufacturers are producing speakers with *magnetically shielded* cabinets. Since we're also seeing more LCD flat-panel monitors as opposed to CRT (cathode-ray tube) ones, there's even less of a problem. However, if you insist on using an older pair of speakers or a CRT monitor, beware that you could have major computer-monitor issues.

Note: Since speakers *do* contain large magnets, you should try to keep your hard drives, tapes, and other magnetically sensitive objects as far away from your speakers as possible whether your speakers are magnetically shielded or not. Putting a magnet next to a hard drive could erase its contents.

When you're mixing in a small room, most of the time you don't have a lot of options for speaker placement. You need room in front of your desk to sit, and if you have a small room, there may not be much space *behind* your desk. Most people judge speakers by the way they sound when they're in front of them, but what a lot of people forget is that sound resonates throughout a speaker cabinet, and a lot of signal is moving from the back, sides, top, and bottom. The signals you normally have to worry about traveling from the back of the speaker are *bass* frequencies. If you have a speaker sitting right next to a wall, bass frequencies will most likely escape from the back of your speaker and resonate through the walls of your room. You may think this makes the speakers sound huge, but it's usually not a desirable effect. Your studio space was most likely not tuned by an acoustical engineer, so chances are it's going to create more problems with the coloration of your sound than you would like and you will not be able to get the best mix possible. Sticking some egg cartons behind your speakers will not resolve this issue. I will go over this and a few other acoustic solutions in Chapter 3, "Before You Record...."

As I previously mentioned, speakers resonate from all sides. This means that anything physically touching a speaker is going to resonate as well. Speakers have to be mounted somewhere, and mounting a speaker so that it doesn't resonate everything around it can be extremely tricky. Wall mounts are the worst choice you can make for mounting speakers because, as I mentioned before, the entire wall will become a part of your speaker cabinet. Sometimes speakers can be mounted on a pole stand. If the speaker was designed for this, this is a good option because the surface of the speaker where it connects to the pole is very small in comparison to a large shelf that may be attached or touching other objects. The key is to have the speaker rest on a surface that does not vibrate. Vibrations can often be handled by setting a speaker on a thick piece of polyurethane foam. There are manufacturers who make specially designed *speaker pads,* but even something as simple as putting a mouse pad under a speaker can help kill some vibrations. I have heard of people chaining their speakers to a beam in the ceiling. The idea is to contact the least amount of surface area and prevent the speaker from vibrating whatever it touches. Doing this will allow you to hear what the speaker's outputting and will eliminate your desk rattling every time a low–frequency note plays.

Compared to the woofers on your speakers, tweeters are usually pretty *directional*.

Note: Woofers are speakers that handle the low frequencies, and tweeters handle the high frequencies.

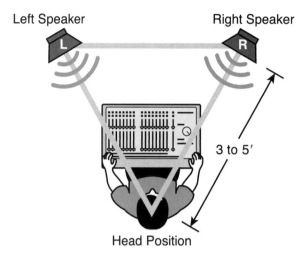

Left Speaker

Right Speaker

3 to 5'

Head Position

Figure 2.13 Angling near-field monitors toward a center point.

There are various opinions on which direction (angle) tweeters should point. I'm a big believer in angling your speakers to a center point (which is where the engineer's head should be when mixing). See Figure 2.13.

The shortest distance between two points is a straight line, and if a tweeter is pointed perpendicular to a wall, the sound will hit the wall and reflect directly back into the speaker. You always need to imagine the *flow* of a signal even as it flows from a speaker cabinet. If you have the speakers angled toward the center, for example, they will most likely hit the corner of a room at an angle and reflect to hit the other side of the corner. By the time the signal returns to the speaker, that reflection has already been *diffused* to a certain degree. I will discuss diffusion in greater detail in Chapter 3.

There are various ways to connect your speakers to your sound card. The easiest way is with analog or digital connections. If you can connect your speakers digitally, you should. Using a digital connection will create much less color in your sound than using an analog connection with dig-ital reference monitors. In order to make a digital connection, you need to have a digital output on your sound card (which most sound cards have), *and* you need to have a digital input on your speakers. Finding monitors with digital inputs is not as easy as finding monitors with ana-log inputs. All monitors have analog inputs because speakers produce analog waveforms. Analog vs. digital should not be your deciding factor when choosing a monitor system. The best speakers in the world do not have digital inputs. When using analog speaker inputs, you should keep in mind that the cable from the sound card to the amplified speaker plays an important role. Usually, when it comes to cables, the thicker the gauge, the better your sound quality will be. That 200-foot-long speaker cable from Radio Shack may be good for a home stereo system, but if you're serious about recording, you should explore other options. Monster and Mogami are names that come to mind for quality speaker cable. Westlake Audio makes a speaker cable that looks like a pair of heavy-duty jumper cables and costs around $600 for a pair! The Westlake Audio cable is probably overkill for your studio, but using quality cables will definitely make a difference in the sound of your monitors.

To get the *best* sound quality, you should direct the audio signal straight out of your audio interface into your monitors through a high-quality cable, but running the signal to a headphone amplifier that can also be used as a volume control (such as the PreSonus HP4 mentioned earlier) definitely has its benefits. The first benefit is, of course, having several headphone outputs. Having a volume control for your speakers is also a big plus. When using DAWs, you often get a loud audio pop when a system boots up. If your monitors are on when this happens, this startup pop can actually damage your speakers. If you have a volume knob, you can turn down your volume during startup to avoid this studio disaster. Also, even though you can control your volume in Cubase, sometimes it's easier and even necessary to adjust the level of the speakers themselves. The important thing to remember is that anything you put between your computer and your speakers can color the sound of your audio. You should be careful when doing this and possibly try setting up your system with and without these items to check the accuracy of the equipment in the signal path and make sure everything is working correctly.

Microphones, Preamps, and Outboard Gear

Whereas your speaker connection acts as the final stage of digital conversion back to an analog signal, we haven't even touched on all the possibilities you have when it comes to getting an analog signal into your Cubase studio. The easiest way to record an analog signal is to use an instrument that has an analog output. When an instrument has an analog output, it's just a matter of connecting the instrument to the analog input of your computer's sound card with an analog cable. There are various types of cables and connection types, but a fairly simple universal cable (also known by musicians as a "guitar cable") consists of a ¼-inch unbalanced male connector joined to another ¼-inch unbalanced male connector. If your sound card has this type of input, you should be able to interface most instruments that have this output with a standard guitar cable and nothing else in between.

Note: −10 and +4 are universal standards when it comes to analog inputs and outputs. −10 is more common with instruments. When you use a −10 input on a sound card or mixing console, the signal is amplified (by the input device) 10 db. When you use a +4 device, the signal is padded 4 db on input. This means that you should match −10 outputs with −10 inputs and +4 outputs with +4 inputs. Otherwise, you will likely have some distortion or noise in your system. Microphones tend to use +4 balanced because the signal carries better over long distances. If your instrument is not designed with a +4 output, you will need to convert it to a +4 signal before you can use a +4 input.

Most musical instruments should be capable of interfacing directly with a sound card's analog *instrument* (−10) *input*. There are companies that design convenient adaptors for guitars to plug directly into a computer, but be careful because often these devices do not have the analog-to-digital converters that better sound cards have. Throughout this book, I cover various recording scenarios in which you will be interfacing multiple instruments at once into your Cubase studio, including guitars. Sometimes it's necessary to premix the audio signal. Premixing instruments involves using a digital or analog mixer, and I will go over this in more detail in Chapter 7, "Recording a Whole Band or Multiple Tracks at Once." If you're interested in learning specific techniques and instruments for recording guitar or bass, please see Chapter 6.

If you will be recording vocals or acoustic instruments in your Cubase studio, you are going to need a microphone. Like speakers, there are a lot of choices when it comes to microphones. All good microphones are going to require a balanced connection with a +4 signal. For most home recording, a microphone that picks up signal in a *cardioid* (pro-nounced CAR-dee-oid) or *hypercardioid* pattern is what you're going to need. Any other sorts of microphones may pick up more noise than you'll want because they are super-sensitive and require very quiet atmospheres. The type of cardioid microphone you get depends on the type of instrument or vocal you wish to record.

For the most part, the only two types of microphones you're going to need are *dynamic* microphones (such as the Shure SM58) or *condenser* microphones (such as the AKG C414). Dynamic microphones are usu-ally fairly inexpensive and are designed primarily for live usage. Con-denser microphones can get expensive, are usually quite sensitive, and are designed primarily for studio vocals or acoustic instrument perfor-mance. Every instrument and vocal has its own unique sound, so it's impossible to say which microphone works best for a particular instru-ment. Dynamic microphones are great for capturing *loud* recordings. This means snare drums, kick drums, guitar amps, and screaming punk rockers. Condenser microphones are great for recording *soft* audio such as piano, acoustic guitar, and smooth vocals. Most profes-sional studios choose condenser microphones over dynamic micro-phones for most applications (even screaming punk rockers) just because they are better at reproducing the signal more accurately (without color). Yet there are famous vocalists with multimillion-dollar recording studios who sometimes prefer to use a $100 Shure SM58. There are no rules when it comes to microphones. There are other types of microphones besides the dynamic and condenser types, but these two types are the most common and practical for home studios.

Whether you use a dynamic microphone or a condenser microphone, chances are you're going to need a preamp to boost your signal before it goes through your sound card. Most mixing consoles have gain controls. These gain controls are essentially preamps. If you're running everything you do through an external mixer and you're using dynamic microphones, using an additional preamp will be overkill. You should be aware, though, that most of the time your mixer's preamps are cheap or poor quality. If you want a good clean vocal or acoustic instrument sound, the best approach would be to record with a condenser microphone, bypass the cheap mixer altogether, and plug a *mic pre* (microphone preamp) straight into the sound card of your computer. By doing so, you will give your microphone a much higher-quality preamp and cut out a lot of junk in the signal path that can color the sound. Mic pres can come with a lot of different and helpful features. Sometimes they use a *tube* in the signal path. Tubes are an old technology that is far from perfect but produces a warm, rich sound. Sometimes mic pres feature EQ and compression, which are tools commonly used on vocals or acoustic instruments during the recording process. Mic pres can really affect the tonality of a vocal or acoustic instrument more than anything. Some mic pres cost thousands of dollars due to pricey components such as ones built from vintage Neve consoles. PreSonus makes a budget-friendly mic pre for around $100 called the TubePre (see Figure 2.14). Your mic pre selection all depends on your budget and your individual needs. Try several before making a final decision.

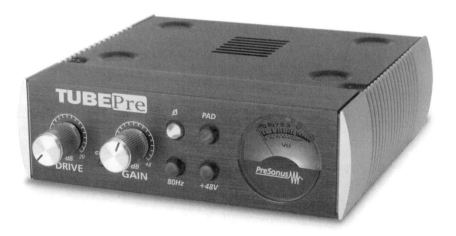

Figure 2.14 The PreSonus TubePre microphone preamp.

Note: Condenser microphones require something called *phantom power* to amplify the signal they're required to pick up. Sometimes a condenser microphone comes with its own phantom power supply. Other times it requires phantom power supplied from a mixing console or mic pre.

We've touched upon using external mixers, a great tool for recording multiple instruments or tracks at once. I will discuss that in more depth in Chapter 7.

Outboard gear refers to every piece of studio signal-processing gear that isn't a part of the mixing console. This equipment is usually found in a studio rack because it's normally rackmountable. A mic pre can be considered a piece of outboard gear. There are other types of outboard signal processors that can be applied either during recording ("pre-recording") or during mixing ("post-recording"). Compressors, EQs, de-essers, noise gates, and hardware auto pitch correction devices are usually used in pre-recording. Outboard gear such as harmonizers, reverb, delay, and other multi-effects processors are normally used during post-recording (but can be monitored as if they were being recorded during a performance). With technology continually improving by leaps and bounds for any process that occurs in the post-recording stage, most studios are simplifying their gear to using mostly outboard gear for pre-recording use. My advice on outboard gear is, unless there's a specific piece that you feel makes a valuable difference in the final recording, avoid it altogether. The more outboard gear you put in the loop, the more unwanted signal coloration and *signal loss* you get. Stick to outboard gear that benefits you in the pre-recording stage, and you'll be best off.

Optional Software and Plug-Ins

Cubase comes with a lot of plug-ins pre-installed (depending on which version you own). I find that the majority of plug-ins that Cubase has to offer are very good. I have a feeling that in the years to come, Steinberg will continue to develop new and exciting plug-ins for us all to enjoy.

Note: Plug-ins are like virtual outboard gear for your Cubase studio.

There are a few different plug-ins commonly used in recording that Cubase does not currently offer. One of these plug-ins is *auto pitch correction*. Even though you can correct pitch in Cubase, the program requires the use of a plug-in if you need to automate the process. There are several auto pitch correction software plug-ins on the market today. The leader in the auto pitch correction market is a company called Antares (http://www.antarestech.com). Auto pitch is such a handy tool because it can automatically tune mono instruments (instruments that can perform only one pitch at a time, such as a solo vocal or flute) to the proper note in a predetermined scale. This means that if notes fall slightly sharp or flat in the chromatic scale, it will automatically move the pitch to the closest pitch so that the instrument sounds perfectly in tune. This effect has been used a lot in today's recording (some argue that it's overused) and even in live shows. You have to keep in mind that this plug-in won't make you a good singer. It simply makes a *decent* singer sound on pitch and saves time in editing and retakes. There's no tool available for getting a good *performance* out of a singer, only tools to edit the performance. If you're looking for a plug-in that will make you sound like Celine Dion or Luciano Pavarotti, you may have to wait a few years. I'm sure someone's working on it!

Note: When using Cubase, you will be using plug-ins suited for VST (Virtual Studio Technology). There are several other types of plug-ins available, but this type works best with Cubase.

There are other vocal processes you can achieve through plug-ins not normally included with Cubase, such as *vocal modeling* (changing the character of a voice—from male to female, for example) or software *vocoders* (for that robotic vocal sound).

When it comes to recording guitar and bass, there are plug-in packages available that take the place of your entire rig (including the amp and speakers). There are software plug-ins that can even change the tonality of your guitar from an Ibanez Strat to a Gibson Les Paul or Ovation Acoustic. I will discuss this in more detail in Chapter 6.

There are plenty of other software plug-ins available today. A lot of them have the same basic functionality of the plug-ins that come with Cubase but take the quality even a few steps further than Steinberg. If you're not happy with the way a reverb or delay sounds in Cubase, try looking to higher-end processing-dedicated companies such as Waves or TC Electronic for some really high-quality processing plug-ins. If you do a Web search for "Cubase plug-ins," you can find some pretty interesting tools (like a plug-in that strips vocals from a recording to make karaoke tracks). You can even download some of these plug-ins for free. Try not to get too carried away with downloading free (unsupported) plug-ins, though, because they can cause system crashes, and the more plug-ins you have active, the slower your system can become.

Being a keyboard player/composer, my favorite type of plug-in is the VST instrument. Some versions of Cubase come with multiple VST instruments. A VST instrument can consist of either a software synthesizer or a software sample player. Cubase 4 comes with a simplified sample player called HALion One. HALion One's sample library is pretty impressive, but if you want to take it to the next level, you really need to get your hands on the current version of HALion. It allows you to import sample libraries from every known sampler, edit the sounds, create multis (groups of sounds, such as drums, bass, and guitar together), and create your own sample libraries. The best part is, it sounds better than any other sampler on the market. There are other sample players such as GigaStudio and Kontact that pretty much do the same thing in a different way. If you're a synth nut, Steinberg and Native Instruments are both great companies that have a lot to offer. Even though they're referred to as virtual instruments, Steinberg actually sells *virtual musicians* such as Virtual Guitarist, Virtual Bassist, and Groove Agent. These three programs contain actual patterns that play in time with your song, as well as sampled instruments, and can save a lot of time on programming parts.

Under the Device menu (located on the menu bar) in Cubase, you can select Plug-in Information to view a window listing plug-ins that are currently installed on your system (see Figure 2.15). This window displays version, type, and system-location information of all the plug-ins in your Cubase studio. You can deactivate certain plug-ins from displaying in the plug-in windows of Cubase by unchecking the boxes on the left side of the list of plug-ins. Unchecking them will not free up your system's resources (processing power) unless you also uninstall the plug-ins. In order to remove a plug-in from your system, you will have to remove it from the plug-in folder located within your system. For more information on this, choose Plug-Ins in the Help menu and look for more information on managing plug-ins. As you can see in Figure 2.15, I have several plug-ins that are not included with any version of Cubase.

Besides audio plug-ins and VST instruments, MIDI plug-ins can also be very useful when working with MIDI. You can select different tabs at

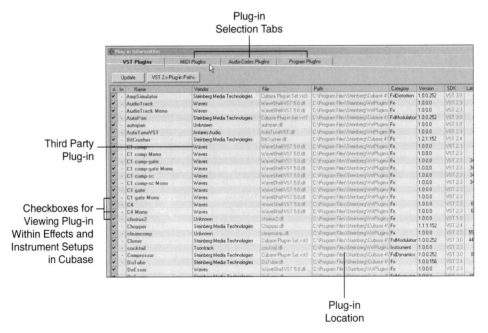

Figure 2.15 The Plug-in Information window in Cubase.

the top of the Plug-in Information window to view the different types of plug-ins available on your system. To learn more about the MIDI plug-ins that come with Cubase, I recommend reading my book *MIDI Editing in Cubase*. The MIDI capabilities within Cubase get very deep, and even though I cover some of the important areas of MIDI in Chapter 4, there's a lot that gets skipped over due to the fact that this book is designed to give you a better understanding of how Cubase interfaces with your overall studio.

Along with plug-ins, there are several other types of programs that can come in handy when working with Cubase. Even though Cubase covers a lot of territory, certain programs work better for applications depending on what your primary use of Cubase is.

Steinberg has been distributing a program called WaveLab for many years (see Figure 2.16). WaveLab was designed primarily as a stereo audio editor. Even though you can edit audio with Cubase, WaveLab takes editing audio to a very detailed and precise level. It can also be a great tool for mastering and finalizing a recording or CD and offers even more audio input and output formats than Cubase. There are other programs on the market, such as Bias Peak, that work similarly to WaveLab. Another great feature of WaveLab is *batch processing*.

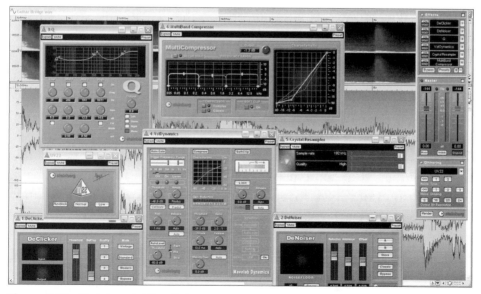

Figure 2.16 Steinberg's WaveLab.

Batch processing enables you to create similar edits on multiple files at once, saving you lots of time in the studio. For instance, you may want to convert the sample rate of 60 files from 48K to 44.1K and pitch shift up one whole step. I've owned and used WaveLab for about 10 years, and I can't imagine living without it.

At one point, Steinberg was working very closely with a company called Propellerhead. This is a great company to keep close tabs on. It first released Recycle and Rebirth. Recycle introduced us to REX files. A REX file can be used to map a loop, in what are referred to as audio *slices*, so that you can use each individual beat. For instance, in a drum loop, it allows you to remove beats 2 and 4, which could mean removing the snare hits. Using these slices also makes it possible to alter the tempos of loops without affecting the tonality of the recording. REX files are used a lot in music production and were even more popular before audio time-stretching became popular in programs such as Sony's Acid (another great program that takes some of the work out of making loops fit into a defined groove with tempo changes). Rebirth was one of the first VST instruments. It brought back a popular analog drum machine (the Roland TR-808) as a virtual instrument that you could use within Cubase.

Propellerhead's software uses the ReWire connection that Cubase offers. ReWire allows you to interface other programs into Cubase so that you can use Cubase's audio engine and bypass the other program's audio engine altogether. Propellerhead's latest and most popular program, Reason, uses this ReWire connection very well. If you're a Reason user, you will hear a dramatic improvement in sound quality when using Reason with Cubase through ReWire. To use ReWire, check the Reason manual, which is quite good. If you've never used Reason and you're wondering if it's something you need, the simple answer is that you don't need Reason if you already have Cubase. What Reason *does* have to offer that Cubase doesn't is a very handy GUI (graphical user interface). In other words, it looks pretty darn cool (see Figure 2.17). Using Reason's GUI comes in very handy for programming its included virtual synths and has a more old-school analog approach in the way it works (it displays virtual physical cables that attach the virtual synths to the virtual mixer and effects). Reason is

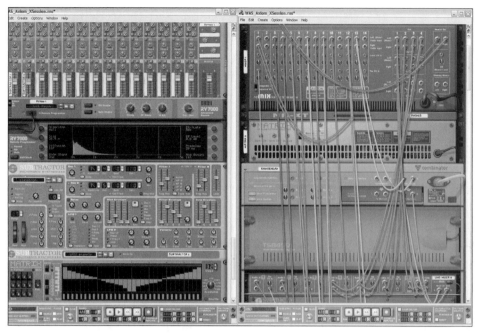

Figure 2.17 Reason's cool MIDI GUI.

exclusively designed to simplify working with MIDI, and in a lot of ways, it's much more limiting to work with than Cubase. But if the word MIDI scares you, Reason may help make your MIDI world a lot easier to live in. Also, if you're a big fan of synths, Reason is worth the purchase price for the included rack of synths alone. If you love working with audio loops, I recommend looking into using Sony's Acid. Even though you can easily work with audio loops within Cubase, Acid is set up to handle loops quickly and easily.

One thing you have to remember when purchasing and using other programs or plug-ins with Cubase is that, like Cubase, they need to be kept up to date. Also, the more software you have running on your system, the more likely you will have software conflicts on that system. Every time you add a plug-in, you should do system checks to make sure that things are running as they should. If you run into problems, you can always uninstall the plug-in that caused the problem. Buying plug-ins can be tricky. Because they are software, most retailers won't accept returns, and you can end up stuck with a program you can't use. An alternative is to download demos of plug-ins you're interested in from their Web sites. Even though these demos usually don't truly represent the full software, they can give you a good idea of what you're getting into before you bite the bullet. Another option is to try the software out at your local music store, but even that won't give you a true representation of how it will work on *your* system. You can refer to Steinberg's user forums for more help on conflicts and issues with existing plug-ins or programs.

If your main purpose for using Cubase is to record live instruments, you can get by using Cubase alone (without plug-ins), but I highly recommend owning a program such as WaveLab. If you're into MIDI and keyboards, you'll definitely want to explore more VST instruments. If you're new to MIDI but you'd really like to use it, you should probably start with Reason because it is easier to use than Cubase. If you're planning on recording a lot of vocals, you should look into pitch-correction software. And if you want to produce a CD that is ready to hand out to record executives, I really recommend using WaveLab, or, even better, a mastering service.

3 Before You Record...

By this time, you're probably really itching to do some recording. You have your computer set up with Cubase, and you have all the perfect accessories to make your Cubase studio work the way you need it to work. Unfortunately, though, the recording process requires just a little more than having the right equipment in place and the knowledge to use it.

A good recording engineer studies for years to understand the science behind sound. This engineer knows that to create a good recording, you must understand sound from where it's created to where it's mixed and put into a final mastered recording. Some engineers concentrate on only the final result, but it's important to begin where the sound *starts*. For a vocal recording, the sound starts with the singer. If a singer is uncomfortable with the surroundings, a recording engineer is not going to get the best performance. In some cases, it's a producer's job to be the liaison between the engineer and the recording artist, but in many cases (especially home studios) it's the guy who hits the Record button who is also partially responsible for capturing the best possible performance.

Another important job, which is usually a good engineer's responsibility before recording, is to eliminate bad, unintentional sounds: everything from squeaky chairs to ugly room reflections to your next-door neighbor's mower or a jet plane flying overhead.

The sole reason for this chapter is to help you avoid capturing these bad sounds so you can concentrate on just working with good sounds later on. Whether you are new to recording in a home studio or you have done this for years, you will find some valuable information in this chapter. It primarily focuses on home studios given that most professional studios are designed with all of these factors in mind and that people who design and build homes are rarely concerned with the way a room will sound.

Acoustics 101

Wikipedia says *acoustics* refers to the science of production, control, transmission, reception, and effects of sound. For most recording engineers, the term acoustics refers to the sound of a room. If you've ever looked at most digital reverb processors, you've noticed that the patches are sometimes defined by room names (such as small room, bathroom, cathedral, or large hall). That's because the sound of the room is mostly determined by its reverb, or the way it *reflects* sound. Some rooms have a lot of reflections, and some have very few. The important thing to understand is that every room has some sort of reflection.

Different types of recordings require different types of recording rooms. In a professional studio, the recording room is designed so that its reflections only enhance the acoustic sound. What makes a room sound good or bad can be different for different people. Often, the reason certain studios become popular is engineers find that a certain room in the studio sounds especially good for the type of recording they do. In these cases, the recording room itself becomes just as important as every other element in the recording chain.

If you're recording in a home studio, chances are it's a bedroom, basement, or garage. Each of these rooms can sound dramatically different for both recording and mixing. Several elements affect the way a room sounds acoustically: size, shape, and the materials used to create the walls, floor, and ceiling in the room. If you are recording outside (without a room), your problem will not be acoustics so much as sound isolation. It all starts with choosing the best place to record, but sometimes you don't get the recording room you want. Between the bedroom, basement, and garage, the best place to set up a studio is a bedroom, despite what you may have heard about garage or basement bands.

The two most important considerations for a recording room are size and surrounding material. Think about the length, width, and height of a room. A garage usually has a very high (and sometimes uninsulated) ceiling and a concrete floor: perfect for cars and trucks but horrible for sound. An unfinished basement is usually surrounded by concrete, except for the ceiling. This is great rehearsal space because sound will not travel through the concrete (in or out), but this means that some frequencies will get trapped in the room and muddy the sound (especially if you're recording loud instruments). Garages and basements can be turned into great places to record, but they require a lot more work than your average bedroom due to their structure and design.

Because a bedroom is a better and easier place to set up a Cubase studio, I will focus on this perspective. If you're forced to record in a garage or basement, you can use some of these principles to modify your space.

Not all bedrooms are created equal. The first thing to pay attention to is the floor. Concrete on any side of a room (inside or *outside* the room) will affect the sound. Concrete is great for isolation—blocking unwanted sounds such as passing cars or planes from coming through the walls—but it doesn't allow sound to resonate, or "breathe." Sound reflecting off concrete immediately travels in the opposite direction. In a basement, this means the sound travels upward and resonates through the whole house. Solid concrete floors prevent bass frequencies from escaping through the floor, so it's best if your bedroom floor is not solid concrete, including underneath the carpet. Before you completely write off concrete, I should mention that most pro studios have concrete or brick walls because they're great at blocking sound from entering the studio. At the same time, studios create a room that is completely suspended within the concrete structure so that sound can travel outside the room (see Figure 3.1 for a rough sketch of a studio wall). Unless you are building a studio from scratch, this is not an option.

Your standard floor has a plywood platform topped with wood, tile, or carpet. Because wood or tile can be very reflective, it's often a good idea to at least cover the floor with some sort of decorative rug. Carpet is more than just a soft surface to walk on with bare feet. It's excellent

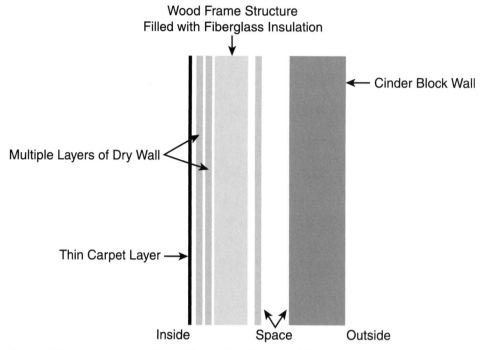

Figure 3.1 How concrete is used in studios for sound isolation.

for absorbing sound reflections and can also prevent annoyances like toe tapping, footsteps, and microphone pickup of floor vibrations. In most rooms, carpet alone can solve the problem of a room sounding "too live" (having a lot of unwanted reflections). In a Cubase home studio, you should always lean more toward achieving a "dead" room (having few noticeable reflections). To test a room's sound, clap your hands and listen for the sound *after* the hand clap. If you hear a lot of slapback, this is something you'll need to fix before recording and especially before mixing in the room.

After fixing the floor with a little carpet, examine the walls and windows. Walls vary a lot. Your standard wall consists of drywall (plaster board), which is excellent for sound isolation, as well as some sound absorption. Whether your walls are insulated will also make a difference in the sound of the room. Walls made of wood can be very resonant (warm-sounding) but have a tendency to create more reflections than you want. Wall hangings (such as paintings, gold records, or guitars) also change a room's acoustics. Most studios don't have windows because windows are bad for both reflections and sound isolation. If you do have windows, it's much better to have double-paned windows or glass brick windows. After spending many hours in rooms without windows, I personally feel that keeping a window or two is worth any extra effort you have to make.

Ceiling height is always an issue in your acoustic studio environment. I prefer the standard eight-foot-high ceilings, but higher ceilings can also work well. For me, a speaker should be located about the same distance from the ceiling as it is from the floor. Ceilings are usually constructed the same way a wall is constructed. In the 1970s and 1980s, it was popular to have "cottage cheese" ceilings. This acoustical ceiling treatment was designed to create quieter rooms, and it works. However, it's not usually necessary. Sometimes homes have suspended ceilings, like those in office buildings. I recommend avoiding this type of ceiling if possible. The space between the ceiling tiles and the actual ceiling can act as a bass trap and lead you to overcompensate on your bass frequencies (see Figure 3.2).

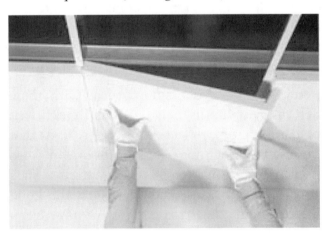

Figure 3.2 Acoustic ceiling tile as a bass trap—not good.

Before you spend too much money fine-tuning your room, you should also realize that everything you put in it (including yourself) is going to change the way the room sounds. This includes a desk, lamp, mixer, plant, curtains, CD collection, piano, drum set, and ceiling fan. There is no such thing as a perfect room because it is always changing depending on what is *in* the room. The most wonderful thing about using software such as Cubase is that you aren't limited to recording just at home. You can take your Cubase setup to most studios and finish a mix or record an 80-piece orchestra at another location. You can live in multiple worlds instead of one little bedroom in your house, and you don't have to worry about having the most perfect acoustic environment at home, just one that suits your basic needs.

Getting Rid of Unwanted Reflections

Because the sound of a room is always changing, it's important that you remain aware of your surroundings when you are recording. In a lot of Cubase home studios, this can be a difficult task because you're in the room where the recording is taking place. When I'm in this situation, I sometimes need to close my eyes and try to concentrate only on what I'm hearing in the headphones because that is what is being recorded.

Unwanted reflections can come from a lot of different sources. For instance, if a singer is using a music stand, he or she may be creating an unwanted metallic tone in the recording, or a guitar amp pointed toward a wall may be creating a "small room" sound. These are just two scenarios of an endless number of possibilities. As I go over recording techniques for guitars, vocals, and bands, I will also explain how you can get the best recording possible to avoid unwanted reflections.

You should have some key *tools* by your side to deal with these unwanted reflections when they pop up in the studio. As I mentioned before, carpet is great for manipulating reflections. Some studios that want a very dead room choose to carpet not only their floors, but also the walls and sometimes even the ceiling. This is a bit extreme; such measures are usually not desirable because they can suck the good sound from a recording along with the bad. But if you have extra rugs or carpet you can access as you need them (in moderation), you may be able to save a recording.

Blankets, towels, pillows, drapes, and curtains are also very handy to have. Like carpet, each of these items is very porous, sound-absorbing material. If you had to, you could even use your dirty gym socks to help kill some unwanted reflections. For instance, throwing a towel over a music stand will kill that metallic reflection, and hanging a drape on a wall may take away that small room reflection from a guitar amp. Pillows are great for kick drums, and blankets are great for pianos. Just don't put your dirty gym sock on the singer's microphone! Read the section "Studio Feng Shui and an Efficient Workspace" later in this chapter.

Most studios go the extra mile and use things that you can't find just lying around your home. For instance, instead of using a bedroom blanket as a piano baffle, you'd probably find a studio using a packing blanket (see Figure 3.3).

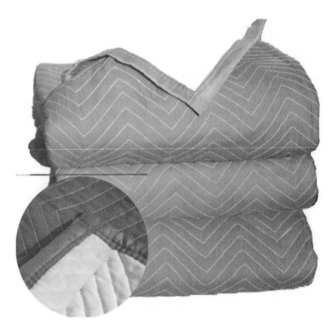

Figure 3.3 Studio packing blankets for troubleshooting acoustic problems.

In a studio, these packing blankets are useful for more than just moving furniture. Draping packing blankets over some chairs or tacking them to a wall can dramatically improve the way a room sounds.

Studio baffles are also a necessity, especially when recording multiple instruments at once. A well-constructed studio baffle not only can eliminate unwanted reflections, but can also provide some necessary isolation between instruments and amplifiers.

Acoustic foam is polyurethane foam that has been shaped to absorb sound. Because foam is usually thicker than carpet, it can be very good at capturing high-frequency reflections that are out of control. Two popular manufacturers of this foam are Sonex and Auralex. Even though these manufacturers strive for perfection in acoustical foam, you can also find similar, less expensive foam sold for packing/shipping or bed rolls. Egg cartons yield a similar result, but although they reflect sound in a less threatening way, they don't absorb sound nearly as well as polyurethane foam. Unless you're trying for a sound from 1956, I recommend sticking to the polyurethane foam (see Figure 3.4).

Figure 3.4 Auralex acoustic studio foam, great for high-frequency reflections.

Acoustic foam can be great for solving reflective corners in a room, a common problem. The foam scatters the sound and absorbs some itself. Some people think that covering a room in carpet or acoustic foam will eliminate any sound passing in or out of the studio. This is not at all true. Carpet and foam tend to control high-frequency reflections, which are very directional, as opposed to low-frequency sound, which is not so directional and much harder to control.

Isolation from Noisy Neighbors
Controlling unwanted reflections in a studio is a much simpler task than keeping unwanted noise out of a studio.

Unwanted noise can come from the guy who lives upstairs or next door, cars or planes passing by, a dog or bird outside, sirens from a passing emergency vehicle, and much else. If you're recording loud rock or pop music, a little outside noise may not be a problem, but if you're recording a soft vocal or acoustic instrument, these noises can become very frustrating. If you live in a brick, stucco, or concrete structure, you are less likely to have problems with noisy neighbors, but even then problems can come from windows and doors, or perhaps you live in an apartment where the outside walls are concrete but the floors, ceilings, and interior walls are made of wood.

Before you begin looking for a new place to live or start laying brick around your house, there are a few less complicated steps you can take to isolate sounds. As I mentioned before, windows are horrible for sound isolation. If you can stand to board up a window, chances are you'll have a quieter room. If you do take this step, you shouldn't just nail some plywood over a window. You should create a wall frame from 2 × 4s, insulate the wall with fiberglass insulation, and then nail drywall over the wall frame. After all this is done, you can also carpet or use acoustic foam over your homemade wall to go the extra mile.

If covering windows is not an option, you can build or even buy premade vocal booths that can fit inside a normal-sized room (see Figure 3.5).

Vocal booths can be great for sound isolation, but even though they're quite common, they're not always the best for singers, especially claustrophobic ones. Sometimes getting air in and out of these can be an issue. In some cases this may be your only option, though. A vocal booth will solve most issues you may have from noise that leaks from outdoors, but it may not fix sound leakage within the room. This means don't expect to set a loud guitar amp next to a singer whose singing softly in a vocal booth without some guitar bleeding over into the track. Another issue with vocal booths is the amount of space they require in a studio. I suggest using a vocal booth only as a last resort (before moving to a brick house) and, if you have ample room, constructing a vocal booth with ventilation (air conditioning)

Figure 3.5 A premade vocal booth.

and walls made out of drywall, similar to the window fix I described earlier. A professional vocal booth is simply another room close to the studio's control room with a double-pane window for easier visual communication.

Again, the type of music you're planning to record in your Cubase studio makes a big difference in what you will need for sound isolation. If you record soft vocals or acoustic instruments only 5 percent of the time, it may be a good idea to track your soft vocals or instruments in a nearby professional studio or another location. When it's said and done, you can always take the vocal track back to your Cubase studio and mix and edit it in the comfort of your own home.

If you must record multiple live instruments or vocals using mics, sound isolation is very important. I will go into more detail and offer some quick solutions in Chapter 7, "Recording a Whole Band or Multiple Tracks at Once."

Getting Rid of Hums and Other Unwanted Noises

Even if you win the battle of noise from bad sound reflections or noisy neighbors, you can still run into a lot of other noise issues with a home studio. Most of these issues have to do with how the electricity in your house is wired, the appliances and lighting in your home, and how much noise pollution you have in your neighborhood.

The most common type of electrical hum found in studios is known as a *ground loop*. Most of the time, a ground loop occurs when a device is connected to both a ground and to another device, thus forming a current that flows in a cycle. Modifying the connections on your equipment will usually solve this. The more equipment you are using in your studio, the more likely you will become victimized by the infamous ground loop.

Note: One common mistake a lot of people make is simply lifting the ground on a piece of equipment to solve the hum issue. This may solve the ground loop issue, but you could end up getting zapped and even killed if you aren't careful when you're working in an ungrounded studio!

You need to make sure that your electrical equipment is grounded for *your* safety. However, this does not mean that everything in your studio needs to have a three-prong plug connected to an outlet. As long as your equipment is connected (through audio cables) to one piece of equipment that is grounded with a three-prong power cord, you should be safe. In most studios, all equipment is grounded to the mixing console, and the mixing console is attached to the electrical ground. Having everything connected to the console ensures that it's grounded but free of ground loops. If you are using a mixing console in your Cubase studio and are experiencing a hum, try this setup. If you plan to just use your sound card and the mixer within Cubase, your computer should be grounded.

If you are using a lot of gear in a studio, here's a rock-solid way to find and kill any hum in your studio:

1. Turn off the power for everything in your studio except the speakers (and amp if necessary). Do you hear a hum? If so, you may have a ground loop in your amp, or you may have a bad connection. Try changing your cables and lifting the ground of your amp using a three-prong-to-two-prong adaptor (see Figure 3.6). If this does not solve the hum issue, it's most likely not caused by a ground loop (read more in the next section). If you aren't hearing a hum at this point, move on to step 2.

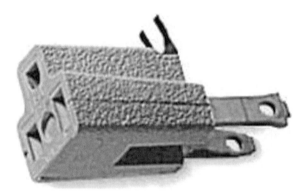

Figure 3.6   The three-prong-to-two-prong adapter.

2. Turn on your mixer (if applicable). If you hear a hum, unplug everything from your mixer one by one (except the speakers, amp, and power supply) and listen to see if the hum vanishes. Usually a good mixer will have a very low-level hum and a lot of hiss when turned up loud. If you're hearing a lot of hum with nothing plugged into the mixer, there may be something wrong with your mixer internally. Try removing the ground on the power cable as a test, but with your mixer still grounded for safety reasons. If everything sounds okay at this point, move on to step 3.

3. With your mixer, speakers, and amp on, turn on your computer system with it connected to your mixer and speakers as

usual. Your computer should be grounded, but if there is a hum, try removing the ground from the computer's power cable and listening for a difference. If the hum vanishes when the ground is lifted, you should either lift the ground of the computer or the mixer but leave one of these two items grounded. If everything sounds okay at this point, move on to step 4. If not, continue reading for other sources of hums and noises.

4.   Continue checking each individual piece of gear that is plugged into your mixer by turning on the power of each unit one by one. Pay close attention to any changes in sound as you power up each unit. If you run into a hum, remove the ground lift (if there is one), and if that doesn't work, try changing the audio cables.

Note: Don't be a knucklehead and rip the ground off of your power cord! You may need it someday. You can find these three-prong-to-two-prong adapters at any hardware store, and they cost less than a dollar each.

Even if your equipment is completely free of ground loops, electrical hums can come from other sources in your home. Here's a list of simple home remedies.

- Dimmer switches create some great mood lighting but usually cause hum problems in a studio. Try turning the dimmer all the way on or off to see if it makes a difference in your sound. If so, you may need to lose the dimmer switch and install a simple on/off switch, or else try to install a higher-end dimmer switch.

- Florescent lights are great for your electric bill and the environment, but they have a tendency to cause problems in a studio. If you have florescent lights, try turning them off to see if the hum goes away. If so, it may be time to switch out those light fixtures or use free-standing lamps.

- Refrigerators and AC units use thermostats, and sometimes the power kicks on and off, creating clicks, hums, and buzzes. Your best defense against this is an AC noise filter. These can usually be found on higher-end power strips and should be used on everything in your studio if possible.

- TVs (particularly ones with tubes) have been known to create hums. If you have TVs in your studio, try turning them off to see if they're causing any sort of noise.

- Almost all homes have appliances that can cause radio interference. Even your studio equipment can pick up radio signals from truck drivers CBs, wireless telephones, and kids' walkie talkies. If you live close to large towers or your building contains a lot of metal, you may be more vulnerable to this sort of thing. To research more on this type of interference and ways to report or avoid it, search online for "radio interference" or electromagnetic interference.

- The electrical ground to the outlet in your studio may not be wired properly. You can test outlets with a tester you can find at Radio Shack, but a ground is simply a copper wire connected to a metal pipe that runs into the ground. Usually the pipe is part of your home's plumbing. If you want to take it one step beyond the norm, you can buy a long piece of metal rebar (or copper pipe), drive it into the ground outside your home, and run a line from your console to the rebar. Make sure your wire is well connected to both the metal rebar and a metal part on the console with a Y fastener and screw.

- Sometimes lifting the ground to something that's connected to your mixer is not enough to kill a ground loop. In those cases, you can try connecting a thick piece of insulated copper wire from the gear that has the ground lifted to the mixer itself. Use a Y fastener to connect the wire to a screw that touches a part of the metal chassis on both the mixer and the offending piece of gear.

The combination of audio and power cables in a studio can be messy. Power cables often emit electromagnetic interference, and even though most audio cables are shielded, they can still be affected. Because of this, it's a good idea to *never run a power cable alongside an audio cable*. This means in a studio rack, try to run your power cables along one side of the rack and your audio cables along the other side. Try to keep your cables from getting too jumbled behind you computer as well because this could be another source for noise. You want to use the shortest cables possible in any situation. If you must mix your audio and power cables, try to keep them from running alongside each other for more than a few inches. If they need to cross each other, try to have the power cables cross the audio cables at only one point (see Figure 3.7).

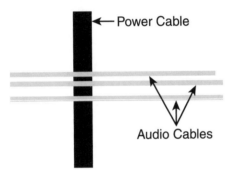

Figure 3.7 The way power cables should cross audio cables to minimize electromagnetic interference.

There are a few other noises that are pretty typical in home Cubase studios. The number one noise is the computer's CPU fan. I have heard of several methods of eliminating that noise. Some people surround the computer in acoustic foam; others simply put a baffle between the instrument they're recording and the computer. One of the more expensive but thorough ways of making a computer less noisy is by taking it out of the control room. Matrox makes a pretty handy device, called the Matrox Extio F1420, that's built for taking the computer completely out of the room. You can use the Extio F1420 as an interface to your computer. It contains FireWire and USB interfaces, keyboard and mouse hookups, and up to four monitor interfaces. If you're serious about getting rid of fan noise and you have the space and the budget, this could be your best option (see Figure 3.8).

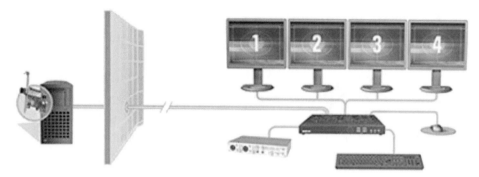

Figure 3.8   The Matrox Extio F1420 DAW setup eliminates CPU fan noise in your studio.

Apart from computers, there are lots of other types of studio equipment that require noisy internal fans, particularly amplifiers. It's not out of the ordinary to find a professional studio's amplifiers and tape machines outside the control room. If you have equipment with noisy fans, this may be an option to consider.

Squeaky chairs and doors can often be fixed with a little WD-40. Squeaky floor boards may require some extra help (usually a few extra screws in the floor can make a difference). I've even heard of crickets and other bugs being a noisy problem in a studio, but I'll let you figure that one out on your own.

Studio Feng Shui and an Efficient Workspace

After you've conquered the studio crickets, you're ready for the other side of the studio, which I consider to be as important as the acoustics for getting inspired and allowing creative energy to flow freely.

> **Note:** Feng shui (pronounced fung shway) is the ancient Chinese practice of placement and arrangement of space to achieve harmony with the environment.

Now, I'm not Chinese, but this makes a lot of sense to me, and the Chinese have been practicing it for thousands of years. My guess is that if this didn't work, they would have stopped doing it a long time ago.

I'm not going to get too philosophical here, so don't worry. It is important to understand that if you aren't *comfortable* in your workspace, you'll have lower odds of creating something that you are going to be *happy* with in your Cubase studio.

By being comfortable, I mean when you walk into your studio, are you filled with inspiration, or would you rather spend more time in the living room watching TV? Your comfort and the comfort of everyone you record are important in the studio. Some professional studios have pool tables, hot tubs, and lounges for artists to relax and unwind before they jump in front of a microphone. Sure, some of these things sound excessive, but artists have different needs, and whatever helps them create their art is very important. I've heard of famous artists who have had rooms in studios designed specifically for them (and their animals!). I've also heard of artists who hire models to stand around and others who like to ride their motor scooters in multimillion-dollar studios. When you're making a lot of money, I guess you can get a little carried away, and top-dollar recording studios don't really care what you do as long as you're paying your inflated studio bill.

You don't have to have a lot of money to practice some great studio feng shui. All you really need to do is figure out what inspires and motivates you. This can be anything from having a poster of an exotic island to filling a room full of instruments. If you like a particular color, decorate your studio in that color. Don't be too afraid to let yourself go. If there are several other people that use your Cubase studio, it's important to get their take on the décor. The more *they* are comfortable, the better *your* recordings will be. If your guitar player has a fear of snakes and musicians have to walk over a snake pit to get to the studio, chances are that the guitar player is going to have other things on his mind besides delivering the best musical performance. Studio feng shui is a delicate balance of everything in your musical world coming together in one room.

The reason I have three walls of windows in my control room is that sunlight inspires me. As I mentioned before, windows are horrible for sound isolation. For me, it's much more important to have a creative atmosphere than it is to have a quiet room. If plants make you feel comfortable, you should add some plants. If you feel more comfortable in a room that is painted black with no windows, so be it. Obviously, my point here is that even though the sound of a room is important, your comfort is equally (and sometimes more) important.

Just remember that no matter how much you love your first piano, that leather couch, or that giant lava lamp, everything you put in your studio is going to affect the way your studio sounds. The line between a good-sounding studio and a creative atmosphere is never completely clear. Only *you* can decide where to draw that line. For those who are very serious about sound, there is no other way to live than to have the best-sounding room no matter what the cost. That being said, a good performance is magical and requires more than good studio chops, a good ear, and a great-sounding room.

Studio efficiency is slightly different from feng shui, though both are subjective. Most people feel more comfortable in a well organized space, whereas some artists feel that organization takes away from their creative energy.

Here are some basic organizational tips to help you balance your studio and make it a more efficient workplace without crushing anyone's vibe. All of these tips are things to do *before* you start a recording session.

- Keep your computer, speakers, external hard drives, and monitors all on one simple workstation desk (see Figure 3.9). Your computer should be off the floor so you can easily access the back of it at any time.

- Manage your cables. Use cable wraps (or even tape if necessary) to group cables together so that they don't turn into a large pile of spaghetti behind your desk.

- Use power strips. Keep all your power coming from one place. There is no reason to use four different wall outlets in your typical Cubase studio.

- Organize your CDs and DVDs. Keep all your computer system's programs on one CD spindle, keep all your music on another spindle, and keep all you Cubase projects on another spindle. Store more projects on hard disk than on CDs or DVDs.

Figure 3.9 A very efficient Cubase computer workstation studio desk by Omnirax.

- Keep all your programs' manuals and documentation in one place. When you're in the middle of a session, it's good to know where your manuals are when you run into problems.

- When working with multiple monitors, try to keep it simple by using the same type of monitor, and make sure you have enough room on your desk for all of them. Using different sizes of monitors arrayed haphazardly around you is going to make things a lot more difficult.

- If you're running multiple programs that require USB security dongles, try to combine multiple programs on each dongle. You shouldn't need a dongle for every program you have.

- Keep instruments that you don't use often (and aren't a tremendous inspiration) stored away so that you have more space when you're working on your computer.

- Keep printers, fax machines, answering machines, paper, blank CD/DVDs, and other standard office supplies and equipment away from your main computer desk. If you need this stuff close by, use an extra shelving system that is separate from your desk. Try to keep everything that isn't directly related to recording away from your desk.

- Mount guitars (or other instruments that require stands) on the wall. This will save you some space and keep you from knocking over your instruments when you're shuffling everything around during a recording session. You can buy fancy guitar mounts, but if you want to go cheap, your average hardware store sells tool hooks that usually cost less than a dollar and work well.

- If you've got old gear that you never use lying around in the studio, get rid of it. eBay is great for that sort of thing. That old gear (or, as a friend of mine calls it, "space junk") will just sit around and haunt you forever. If you have a fear of letting something go, just remember that if you miss it later, you'll probably be able to find it again on eBay when you need it.

- Make sure you have adequate space for people to stand or sit, including yourself. Chairs are very important in a studio because you could be sitting for hours at a time. A lot of professional studios spend a lot of money on comfortable chairs (see Figure 3.10) because it really makes a difference to the comfort of the producers and recording engineers who put in 14-hour days in the studio.

Figure 3.10 The comfortable Herman Miller Aeron studio chair.

Your Cubase studio budget is obviously going to have some effect on how comfortable your recording environment is to you, but you should *consider* everything, from the type of computer to the color of paint for your studio walls, because everything will have some sort of effect on your final recording.

4 Recording MIDI

Now that you know all the ingredients that make up a great Cubase studio, you're ready to start recording. When Cubase was first introduced to the world in 1989, it was a software MIDI sequencer. If you weren't playing keyboards, there was little chance that you even would have known what MIDI was. Even today, if you aren't a keyboard player, you may disregard it, thinking it's something only keyboard players need to worry about. MIDI is for more than keyboard players, however. It's a powerful tool to create and edit music in Cubase in multiple ways, and it's important that you have at least a basic understanding of MIDI.

Understanding MIDI

The explosion of computers among recording engineers and studios can be credited in large part to the development of MIDI. Short for "Musical Instrument Digital Interface," MIDI (pronounced mid-dee) was invented in the early 1980s by synthesizer manufacturers to enable various synths and hardware sequencers to talk to each other, regardless of who manufactured the device. Put another way, MIDI was developed as a universal language for synths.

Undoubtedly, a lot of musicians frowned on MIDI when it came out. After all, this new technology put some musicians, such as string players, drummers, percussionists, composers, and even keyboard players, out of a job. Where were those jobs going? To the guys who embraced the MIDI technology. Some composers, music producers, keyboard players, and programmers just couldn't get enough. In fact, it was MIDI that inspired two guys in Germany to form a small business in the early 1980s and design a software MIDI sequencer that would one day become one of the most powerful tools in music creation. Today that company is known as Steinberg, and the software is Cubase.

Nowadays, MIDI isn't just for synth-pop dance bands or nerdy-looking guys with ties. MIDI is now used in just about every style of music: pop, rock, heavy metal, rap, hip hop, country, dance, classical, jazz, Latin, polka—even reggae! You name it, and MIDI has been there, and will continue to be there for a good while longer. This explains why, today, most music producers and composers need a professional understanding of MIDI technology.

Why MIDI? As I mentioned, MIDI is a universal platform and is more flexible to work with than audio. Almost every cell phone, computer, and video-game system plays MIDI files. Moreover, in addition to being supported by all pro music software, as well as hardware such as synths, MIDI files are used on the Internet, with video applications, and more. In short, MIDI is everywhere.

So what makes using MIDI in Cubase so attractive? First, Cubase can do absolutely anything that is possible in a MIDI sequencer. Second, the program's platform, essentially unchanged since its creation, makes musical sense. Plus, you can use Cubase to seamlessly integrate your MIDI with high-quality professional digital audio, to interface with other musicians through the Internet, and to export MIDI files. Using the program's virtual instruments and third-party software, you can pretty much carry around an entire laptop studio capable of creating any of the top-40 songs out there today.

A lot of people get confused when recording MIDI because they think that once they record a MIDI part, they've actually recorded the *sound* of the instrument they are playing. This is not at all accurate. What in fact happens is that when you press a keyboard key, it sends numeric values determined by *which* key you pressed (pitch info), how *hard* you pressed it (velocity info), and how *long* you held it (length info). There are a few other variables, but these three are the main ones. This information travels from the MIDI keyboard to Cubase, and Cubase records this as MIDI info and sends the MIDI signal to a synth. The synth then responds to the MIDI info and creates an audio sound based on that synth's settings. It sounds like a very complicated process when you look at it, but it's actually quite simple.

MIDI is like typing a letter and having your friend read it aloud as you do it. The words you type don't make the sound—your friend does.

You could send that letter to another friend to read, and it would sound different because that friend has a different voice. The letter is the *MIDI info*, and your friend is the *synth*. Using this analogy, you should be able to understand why editing MIDI is important. With MIDI you can change the words spoken in the letter and also tell your friend how loud to speak while reading it. If you were to record your friend reading the letter, you would be recording your friend's voice, which would be based on the words you wrote, similar to recording an audio track from a MIDI track.

Using a MIDI Keyboard

In Chapter 2, "Accessorizing Your Cubase Studio," I walked you through setting up a MIDI keyboard so that you could get a MIDI signal into Cubase. The reason you didn't hear anything was you weren't directing the MIDI information to a synth. As I mentioned before, you don't have to own a MIDI keyboard with a built-in synth to record MIDI and hear a synth in Cubase. Most versions of Cubase come with VST (Virtual Studio Technology) instruments, which are either synths or sample players exactly like the synths you may find sold with a keyboard at a music store. The difference is that these VST instruments use your computer to handle the processing. This in turn diminishes its processing power. A synth sold with a keyboard (or as a rackmount module) contains its own processor and does not burden your computer at all. External synths cost a lot more than VST instruments because of the hardware they require.

Being a music producer and a keyboard player, I prefer VST instruments over external hardware synths. There are many advantages to using VST instruments besides their being less expensive than hardware synths. As much as I like VST instruments, however, I also understand the need for external hardware synths. In this chapter, I discuss how to record MIDI using a VST instrument and an external hardware synth because their recording methods differ.

Using VST Instruments

As I mentioned before, Cubase comes with a set of VST instruments that depend on the version. At this time there are three main types of VST instruments: virtual synths, virtual sample players, and virtual musicians. Cubase 4 comes with a few different virtual synths and one virtual sample player called HALion One. One of the great things about VST instruments is that you can use *multiple instances* of each instrument. This means that you can use your single HALion One VST instrument to play, for example, 16 different samples at once, or as many as your system can handle.

Virtual samplers work by playing a digital recording stored on your computer. In some complex sample programs, each note on a keyboard can actually trigger several samples at once, creating a layered sound that changes depending on how hard a key is pressed. These virtual sample players use your hard drive more than they do your RAM or CPU by quickly accessing stored audio files from the hard drive upon demand. Most virtual sample players also include a synth filter (or multiple filters), which can be used to process the sample in a variety of ways. For example, this synth filter could be used to change the attack or decay of the sample, or it could send the sampled sound through a virtual oscillator to change its tonality. These synth parameters can be controlled with automation using Cubase to create some complex sound textures. The more synth parameters used in a virtual sample player, the greater the load on the CPU (because the synth portion of a virtual sampler requires processing power).

Virtual synths come in many varieties. Some start with a sampled wave and allow you to manipulate and combine samples to create unique textures. Other virtual synths start with a simple waveform type and allow you to manipulate it in a variety of ways. Programming synths can become quite an art in itself and requires a lot of understanding of each synth component. Most synths come with a variety of *presets* (or patches) that allow you to play around without getting in over your head with programming.

Virtual musicians are usually a combination of samplers, REX file players, and MIDI files and actually play prearranged parts on an instrument in time with your MIDI sequence. These VST instruments allow you to program chord/time changes to the MIDI track without spending a lot of time recording individual parts. Even though this type of VST instrument can be limiting, it's amazing what you can do with these when you apply a little extra MIDI and digital recording knowledge to the mix. Steinberg offers several virtual musician-type plug-ins, such as Virtual Guitarist, Groove Agent, and Virtual Bassist.

Loading VST Instruments and Setting Up MIDI Outputs

1. First, make sure that your MIDI keyboard is set to transmit MIDI and that Cubase is set up to receive MIDI, as I described in Chapter 2 for preparing to record on a MIDI track. You should be able to see a flashing MIDI In indicator just to the right of the track display.

2. From the Devices menu, select VST Instruments. A window should appear containing a virtual empty rack of VST instruments. To select a VST instrument from your Cubase arsenal, click where it displays the words "no instrument"; a pop-up menu appears with a list of choices of VST instruments in your system. Since Embracer is a Cubase synth that comes with Cubase 4, I have chosen it for this example (see Figure 4.1).

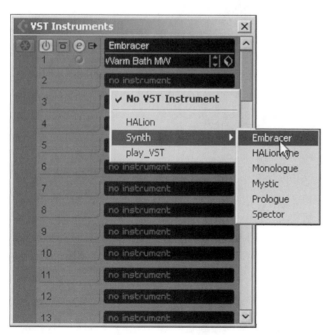

Figure 4.1 The VST instrument rack displaying Embracer, a synth that comes with Cubase 4.

Once you have selected your VST instrument, activate the VST instrument's power button if it isn't already activated.

3. Once you've chosen your VST instrument and loaded it into Cubase, you need to direct the MIDI track you are recording on to play back the MIDI through that VST instrument. Using the Inspector on the left side of the display (make sure that your Show Inspector button on the toolbar is enabled so that you can view the Inspector), locate the MIDI In and MIDI Out for the MIDI track you are working with (see Figure 4.2). From the MIDI Out, choose the VST instrument you would like to use to play back the MIDI from your MIDI track. (I have chosen Embracer in this example.) Now that you've established your MIDI In and MIDI Out, you should be able to hear something

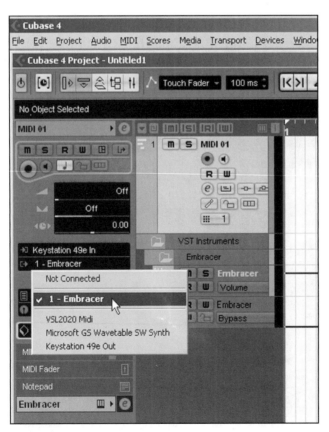

Figure 4.2 Setting up the MIDI Out to direct the MIDI signal to the VST instrument.

from your VST instrument when you hit a key on the keyboard. If you are not hearing anything from your VST instrument, make sure that a sound (patch) has been loaded in the instrument (see step 4). If for some reason you are still having difficulty, double-check your sound card's audio output and your speaker connection, or continue reading the next section, "Setting Up a VST Instrument's Audio Output."

4.   In some Cubase versions, the instrument control panel will appear when it's opened, but by clicking on the *e* on the virtual instrument you're working with in the rack, you can access its control surface no matter what. From here, you can edit or change the instrument's patch (see Figure 4.3).

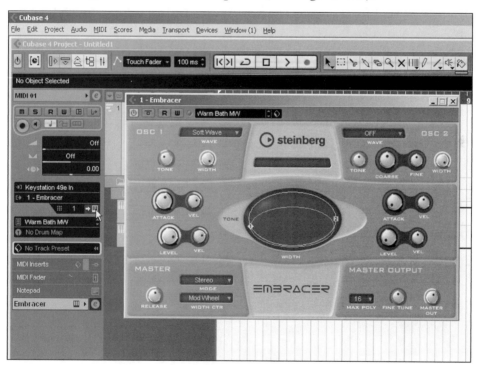

Figure 4.3 The VST instrument's control surface displayed.

Setting Up a VST Instrument's Audio Output

The MIDI output that you set up in this walkthrough directed the MIDI signal from your MIDI controller to the VST instrument *through* Cubase. What we didn't set up in the walkthrough was the *audio output* of the

VST instrument. By default, Cubase automatically assigns a VST instrument to an audio output. In certain cases, you may want to make changes. As discussed in the previous chapter, if you can understand signal flow (*how* the signal moves from being a MIDI signal sent from a MIDI controller to the audio signal of a VST instrument), you will be better off, because when Steinberg decides to change the look of Cubase several years from now, you'll know what to look for when you need it.

The Audio Out of the VST instrument can be found in multiple locations, and each can be useful depending on your needs. If you simply want to see the audio signal of the VST instrument, look in the particular VST instrument's folder (in this example, Embracer), located in the main VST instrument's folder within the track display (see Figure 4.4). From this instrument output track, you can control the audio as it leaves the VST instrument and enters Cubase's "internal" mixer. You can

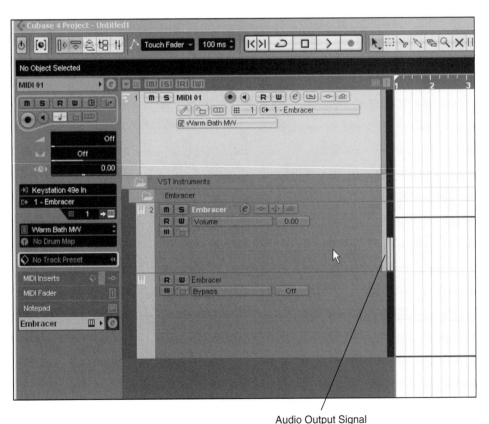

Audio Output Signal
for VST Instrument

Figure 4.4 The VST instrument's audio output track.

mute, solo, or automate the volume of the VST instrument's output *before* its audio signal is actually recorded as an audio file. I will go into more detail on this in Chapter 9, "Mixing It Down."

To get an even closer look at where the VST instrument's audio is going, click the *e* in the VST instrument's audio output track. A window appears that includes not only an instrument audio output signal indicator but also a volume control, an EQ section, and a virtual effects rack where you can apply processing to the VST instrument's audio output (see Figure 4.5). You should also be able to locate the main *bus* where the output signal is routed within Cubase. In most cases, Cubase's

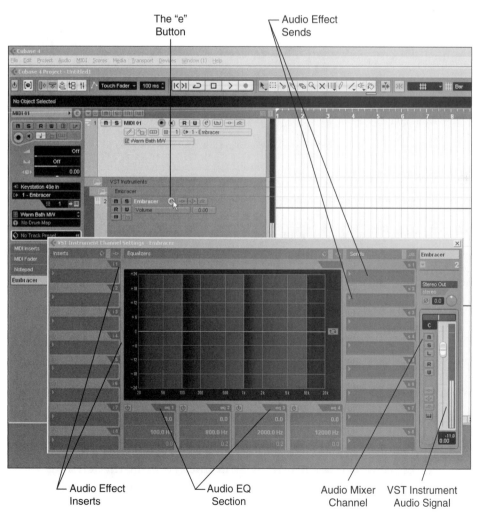

Figure 4.5 The VST instrument's individual audio control settings display.

default output for VST instruments will be the master bus (your main stereo output), but you can assign this output to another bus to group it with others and control multiple instruments' outputs simultaneously without affecting the rest of a mix. Again, I will go over more on this scenario in Chapter 9. For now, as long as you can hear your VST instrument when you touch a key on your controller, you should be in good shape for the rest of this chapter.

Recording MIDI Using a VST Instrument

Take a moment to play around with your VST instrument by striking keys on your MIDI keyboard. If you are not happy with the sound, go ahead and change it in your VST instrument. (If you need help with this, refer to your VST instrument's manual, or open Cubase's Help menu a Documentation, Plug-in Reference). Remember that you're getting ready to record MIDI, not audio. This means that if you decide you don't like this sound later on, you will be able to change it. When you've found a sound you're happy with (at least for now), read on.

Note: If you notice a delay between the time you strike a key and the time you hear a sound from your VST instrument, you may be experiencing either a slow attack from your VST instrument or latency. If changing your sound does not solve this, it's likely a latency issue. Try lowering the Latency setting within your sound card's control panel, as discussed in the "Setting Up Your Pro Sound Card with Cubase" section in Chapter 1, "Setting Up Cubase on Your Computer." If you need help, refer to your sound card's manual.

Whether or not you have any musical keyboard skills, you should be able to record something using the following walkthrough.

1. First, you need to set the boundaries of the part you would like to record. To set up the part boundaries, set the left locator at the start position and the right locator at the end position on the *ruler*, which is just above the part display, below the

toolbar, and to the right of the track display in the Project window (see Figure 4.6). Once you find the locators, you can move them on the ruler with your mouse using the click-and-drag method. Set the locators to start at measure one and end at measure eight. The ruler should appear shaded in blue where you are set to record. If the ruler is shaded red, you have the left and right locators reversed, and Cubase will not record.

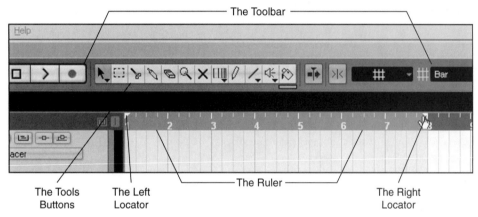

Figure 4.6 Setting the locator points on the ruler.

Note: If your toolbar is not set up to display in bars and beats, you can adjust this under the Project menu's Project Setup window by selecting Bars and Beats under the Display Format setting. Alternatively, you can right-click on the toolbar to change the same setting.

---

2.   Next, you need to determine a tempo and time signature. Cubase defaults to 120 BPM in 4/4 time. Those settings will work fine for this example. Cubase gives you the option of using a tempo *track*, which allows you to program tempo changes throughout the song, or a *fixed* tempo, which maintains a constant tempo throughout the song. To keep things simple for this example, we will use a fixed tempo. All of these settings can easily be adjusted by using the *transport* (see Figure 4.7). To get the most out of the transport, make sure that you are displaying

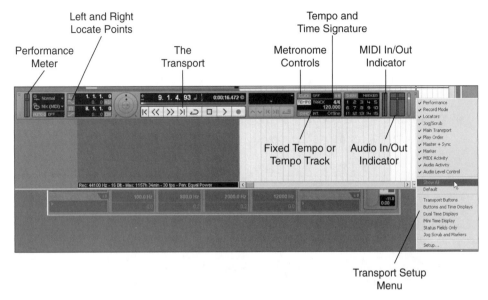

Figure 4.7 The transport showing all the display options.

all the features by right-clicking on the right side and ensuring that all the display options are checked, as in Figure 4.7. To toggle between a fixed tempo and a tempo track, click on either Fixed or Track (only one type is displayed depending on which type is currently active). If you would like to adjust the tempo or time signature, click in the field and type in a new setting.

3. This last step is one you don't always have to perform before recording, but it makes working with Cubase a lot easier. On the transport, there is a metronome (identified on the interface as *Click*) that can be turned on or off by selecting the word *Click*. If your metronome is set up properly, you should be able to hear it playing four beeps per measure when you click Play. To assign a standard two-measure count-in before you start recording, you need to set up a preclick. To do so, open the Transport menu (on the menu bar at the top of the screen) and open Metronome Setup. A window appears giving you a lot of different options to adjust your click (see Figure 4.8). At this point make sure that the audio click is activated, the MIDI click is deactivated, the metronome is activated in Play and Record, and your precount

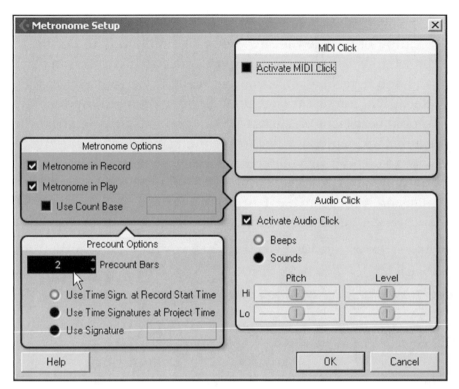

Figure 4.8 The Metronome Setup window.

bars field is set to 2 (measures). If for some reason you didn't hear a click when you clicked Play previously, you should hear one now. Close this window and select the symbol that looks like ||*(the *activate precount button*) next to the metronome (Click) control on the transport. When this button is enabled, your two-bar preclick is ready to go.

4. Now that you've set your recording boundaries on the ruler, set your tempo and time signature (in Fixed Tempo mode), and set up your metronome and preclick, you are ready to record. Later on, when you're recording audio, you'll notice that these initial steps usually need to happen before you record anything in Cubase, whether it's MIDI or audio. If your click is still playing from the previous step, select Stop on the transport. Make sure that your MIDI track is still active (selected), the track is receiving a MIDI signal, and your VST instrument is playing back as you strike a key on your MIDI keyboard

controller. It's a good idea to move the cursor to the start location of your left locator point. A simple way to do this is by selecting the *L* on the transport. Once your cursor is in place and you're feeling confident and ready to perform, select the Record button on the transport. Upon selecting the button, you should hear eight preclicks to count you in. When you hear the ninth click, Cubase will start recording every bit of MIDI info that you send it via your controller keyboard and recording will continue until you select Stop on the transport. Congratulations on recording your first MIDI part in Cubase with a VST instrument (see Figure 4.9)!

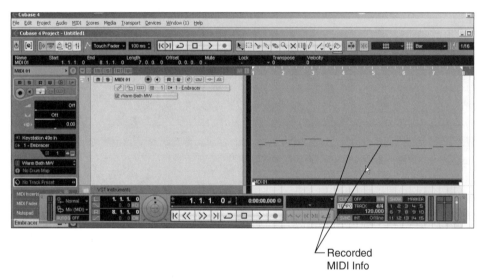

Recorded MIDI Info

Figure 4.9 A recorded MIDI track!

5. To make sure you have successfully recorded a MIDI part, select the *L* from the transport to move the cursor back to the beginning and then click Play on the transport to hear what you've recorded. If you can't hear it, try steps 1 through 4 again. When you have verified your recording, try switching the sound (patch) on your VST instrument during playback to another sound to verify that you have recorded MIDI and not audio. Being able to change the sound *after* your part has been recorded is one of the greatest benefits of recording with MIDI.

When it comes to recording VST instruments, you should be able to apply the previous section of the chapter to any type of VST instrument, whether it's a virtual sample player, synth, or musician.

To add additional MIDI tracks, open the Project menu, select Add Tracks, and then select MIDI. When using VST instruments, you usually don't have to worry about setting up a MIDI channel because most VST instruments allow only one sound to be played at a time. The full version of HALion allows you to load up to 16 MIDI channels at once (meaning you have the ability to use 16 patches at once). When using this, you need to assign your project MIDI track's MIDI Channel setting to correspond with the patches MIDI channel in the VST instrument you would like to use on that particular MIDI track.

Note: Still confused about MIDI channels? Imagine that you have one TV cable service provider (HALion) that provides you with 16 TV channels. You have 16 TVs (MIDI tracks) in your home and you want to watch all 16 TV channels at once. So, you tune each TV to a separate channel (1–16). Now stop watching all that TV and get back to recording MIDI!

As I mentioned before, you can create several *instances* of the same VST instrument. When you record another MIDI track, try using another instance of the same VST instrument you used in the previous example by loading an identical VST instrument in the virtual rack. You can have this other instance play a sound completely different from its twin. If you want, you can create several more of these instances. Some VST instruments do get maxed out by too many instances, but this varies from instrument to instrument.

As I mentioned before, VST instruments use your computer's processing power. Since these VST instruments usually require a lot of processing, they can burden your system's CPU. To monitor this, Cubase has designed a CPU/hard drive–performance meter (see Figure 4.10) that you can view from your Transport bar or by selecting VST Performance from the Devices menu. VST synths will show up a lot on your CPU (ASIO)

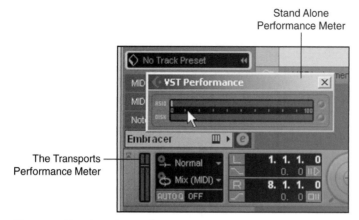

Figure 4.10 The VST performance meter.

meter, whereas VST sample players will cause your hard-drive meter to rise. It's important that you pay close attention to these meters as you are recording so that you don't crash your system. You can save valuable system resources by bouncing your MIDI tracks down to audio tracks or by *freezing* your VST instrument tracks. I go over bouncing and freezing MIDI tracks in Chapter 9.

Finding Missing VST Instruments and Plug-Ins

Many times, after you've installed VST instruments or plug-ins (other than the ones that came with Cubase) and gone to select them from the virtual rack, you find out they aren't there. This is a common problem and not one to get too upset about. All of these plug-ins must be copied to a subfolder in Cubase's Program folder called VstPlugins. You should be able to locate this subfolder within the Steinberg folder, which is on the main drive of your computer in the Program Files folder (see Figure 4.11).

A VST instrument is a plug-in. Not all plug-ins are VST, but since that has become a standard, Cubase has dropped support for most other types of plug-ins. The file for a VST plug-in usually ends with a .dll extension. If the .dll extension for the plug-in you are looking for is not in this VST plug-in folder, the plug-in you've installed might not be a VST plug-in, or its DLL file could be copied to the wrong location on your hard drive. If the DLL file is in the wrong location, check your

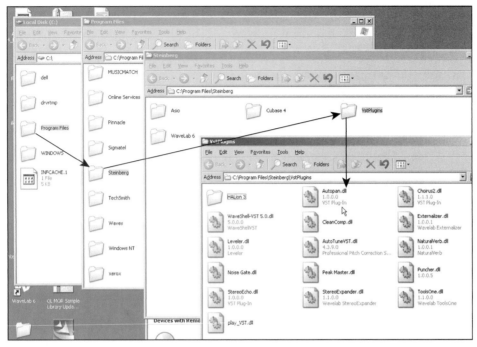

Figure 4.11   The VstPlugins subfolder on a Windows computer.

Program Files folder for a folder from the plug-in's manufacturer, and look for the correct DLL file. If you happen to find this file, drag it into the VstPlugins subfolder, located in the Steinberg folder. Unless you have a strong computer phobia, this is a fairly simple procedure. If you need help, call or e-mail the manufacturer of the VST plug-in for support.

Note: Deleting a DLL file could be a big mistake! If you move a DLL file and experience errors afterward, remember its original location so you can return it there if you need to.

Recording MIDI Using External Synths

A lot of MIDI keyboards include sounds, and if you own one, you'll probably want to use these sounds instead of a VST instrument at some point, especially if you're a keyboard player. You may be using a MIDI keyboard as a controller in Cubase (which means it will be hooked up as described in Chapter 2), but even if you aren't using it as a MIDI controller, you can hook it up to play back your MIDI track through the external synth's sound source.

Note: Anything that can generate an audible sound can be considered a *sound source*. In MIDI, the sound source is where audio signal is generated and processed. It's the source that translates MIDI info into actual audio you can hear. You'll usually find some sort of audio outputs on a sound source.

There are several types of keyboards on the market. The first step is making sure that your keyboard actually has MIDI. Next, you will need to locate a MIDI In on your keyboard. The final step is to make sure that your sound card has a physical MIDI Out. In some cases you may be using a simple MIDI interface as opposed to an audio interface with MIDI capabilities. If you're running a MIDI controller into a computer via USB, the MIDI Out could be on the MIDI controller. Once you have verified these three simple steps, you can get down to business.

Making Connections to an External Synth

Recording MIDI with an external synth works the same way as recording MIDI with a VST instrument. The only difference is that in order to hear the external synth, you need to wire both the MIDI and audio of the sound source to your system. There are several ways to achieve this, but I will show you the simplest and most direct way in this chapter. To keep matters even simpler, I will *not* display the MIDI Out of the keyboard connected to the MIDI In of the computer as I described in Chapter 2. I will assume that either you already have your keyboard connected that way or you are using another MIDI controller to actually play and record MIDI as you hear the sounds played back on your external synth. This example of the external synth is basically a hardware substitute for a VST instrument.

1. First, run a MIDI cable from the MIDI Out of your sound card/
    MIDI interface (or USB MIDI controller) to the MIDI In of
    your external synth.

2. Next, run either one audio cable (or a stereo pair) from the
    audio outputs of the external synth to the audio inputs of your
    computer's pro sound card. Your setup should look similar to
    Figure 4.12.

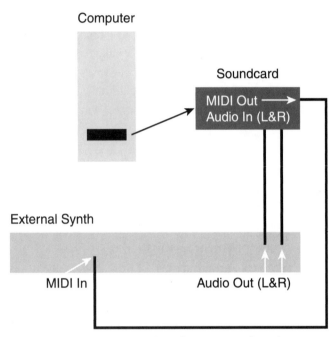

Figure 4.12 Basic connections from a sound card to an external synth.

Next, you have to make sure that your MIDI Out, as well as your
Audio In, are set up properly in Cubase. You also need to make sure
that your MIDI In is set up properly for your external synth.

1. Select the MIDI track that you wish to record to in Cubase and
    open the Inspector so that you can see the MIDI In and MIDI
    Out as you did when setting up MIDI Outs for a VST instru-
    ment in the previous exercise. Change the MIDI Out so that the
    sound card's MIDI output is selected (if you have multiple
    MIDI outputs, make sure that the one that is connected to your
    external synth is the one you select).

2.   Set the MIDI channel on the MIDI track to match the external synth's receiving MIDI channel. (The Receive MIDI channel is sometimes called the Rx channel # on a synth.) You may need your synth's manual to guide you in the right direction.

Note: Some common synth terms are "Tx" (transmitting MIDI channel), "local" (within that particular synth), and "global" (everything the synth is connected to). For the most part, in this section, you'll be dealing with Rx (receiving MIDI) channels and global settings, and if there is a MIDI menu on the synth, that's usually a good place to start in your search to make the right connections. Also, when you're recording MIDI in Cubase using an external synth that is also your MIDI controller, you should set your local keyboard to off.

---

3.   Once you've matched your MIDI channel in Cubase to the MIDI channel in your synth and your output is properly assigned in Cubase, you should be able to receive MIDI on your external synth. If not, the problem is most likely within your synth's MIDI setup (refer to your manual). Even if your synth *is* receiving MIDI, you may not be able to hear it because you still need to configure the audio. Unless your synth has some sort of MIDI input indicator (like a flashing LED), you may not be able to tell at this point if you're receiving MIDI at all. To make sure, select VST Connections from the Devices menu and select the Inputs tab. Check that the audio inputs (where the external synth is connected) are selected (see Figure 4.13). Next, create an *audio* track in the track display by selecting Add Track from the Project menu and adding an audio track. Use the Inspector to examine your audio inputs and outputs for the audio track. Make sure that the audio inputs for your external synth connection are selected, and also make sure that the audio outputs are the ones you wish to monitor through. Lastly, select the button that looks like a speaker on the audio track you have

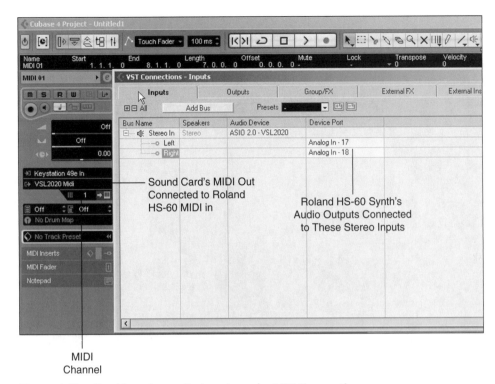

Figure 4.13   Checking the audio inputs under VST Connections.

created (see Figure 4.14). Make sure that the MIDI track on which you wish to record is still active, and strike some keys on your MIDI controller. You should be able to hear your external synth.

Note: Keep in mind that monitoring your external synth through your sound card and Cubase is not required. It's very possible to monitor your external synth through an external mixer, headphones, or keyboard amp. This method is ideal for those who wish to transfer the audio of their external synth to Cubase later on.

Even though using an external synth may sound complicated, this is one of the easiest ways to prepare to record MIDI for an external synth (using an audio track in Cubase as a monitor). If you notice a delay

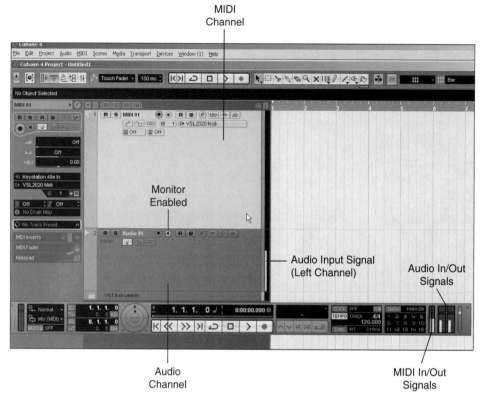

Figure 4.14 Setting up an audio track to monitor the audio of your external synth.

between the time a key is struck and the time the sound is heard, try adjusting the latency in the sound-card setup as you did in Chapter 1.

Cubase also offers a more complex way of handling external synths. Using the External Instruments tab (located in the Device Setup window) can be a very neat and organized way to interface with external synths. This tab allows you to not only name your inputs to match your synths but also to set up detailed MIDI maps. I think it's great that Steinberg has gone to such lengths to organize all of these things, but this is more for someone who uses one or two synths all the time than for someone who occasionally interfaces with an external synth. Also, if you're using multiple synths, you're best off premixing your synths with an external mixer before sending the audio signal back into Cubase. By using a premixer, you don't tie up so many inputs on your sound card, and by muting inputs on a premixer, you can also record the audio of each synth separately (at different times), as opposed to mixing the audio signal of all your synths together. Using this same method of premixing, it's also possible that you won't need to set up your Cubase audio inputs every time you record. Still, remember that the best possible connection you can make to Cubase is a direct connection (bypassing any sort of middle man, such as a keyboard mixer), and if you have the option of connecting the digital output of an external synth to the digital input of a sound card, your audio quality will be even better yet.

One of the best benefits to using VST instruments instead of external synths is that Cubase saves all your VST instrument settings along with the project. When you're using external instruments, you usually need to reset all your external instrument preferences when you reload a Cubase project, and this can be a time-consuming pain. If you make modifications to your external synth, you should save the patch on the synth as a new patch because Cubase will not remember your changes. Cubase does offer ways of helping you keep track of your settings on your external synths. One is to record program-change and system-exclusive data from your synth to Cubase. To learn more, I suggest referring to the Cubase manual or *MIDI Editing in Cubase.*

Another option is to leave yourself notes about your setup information. Notes can be typed for each MIDI track in Cubase within the notepad, which is in the Inspector (see Figure 4.15). Something else you can do, and that I highly recommend, is bounce your external synth tracks down to audio files. Once you have recorded an audio file, your synth part can be saved along with your project. The only downside to recording your synth part as an audio track is that you can't edit the audio track the same way you can edit a MIDI track; however, you can keep your MIDI track within Cubase and refer to it later on. It's possible that later on you will want to change not only a MIDI part but also the synth for that part, so there is no downside to bouncing a MIDI track down to an audio track as long as you don't *delete* your MIDI track from the project.

If you want to push your external synth to even greater limits, Cubase can store premade control panels (see Figure 4.16) you can use to

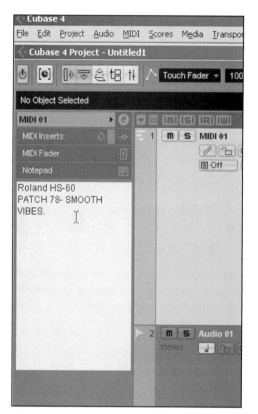

Figure 4.15 The notepad.

make automated changes to your synth's parameters (much in the way you can with VST instruments). Since there are tons of synths out there, Steinberg can't create these control surfaces for all synths. Cubase does offer several premade control surfaces you can find by opening the MIDI Device Manager via the Devices menu. You also have the option of creating your own control panels or importing them from another source. If you do a Google search for your synth and "Cubase instrument user panels," you may get lucky and find someone who has created one that you can download, or the manufacturer of the synth itself may have one available. For more information on setting up and using these panels, look in the Cubase Help menu for the Acrobat PDF documentation file called *MIDI Devices and Features*. The information is quite helpful, although it may be a little difficult for some.

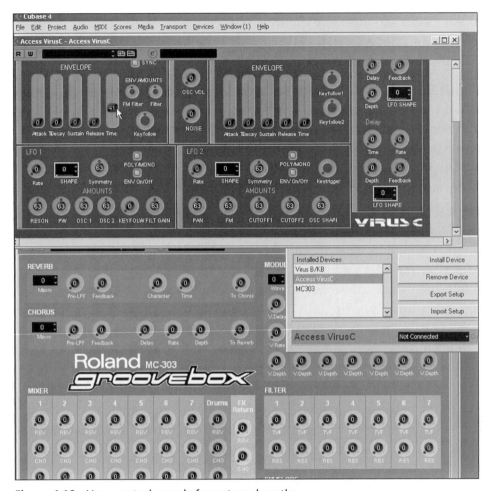

Figure 4.16   User control panels for external synths.

Note: To see all the available tabs in the Inspector, you have to set up the Inspector's display accordingly. To do so, right-click somewhere at the top of the Inspector and select Show All in the Inspector's Setup menu.

Recording MIDI Drums

Recording all types of MIDI instruments (MIDIfied guitar, MIDI sax, etc.) can be done the same way as MIDI keyboards in the previous walkthroughs. MIDI drum kits are no exception. However, because

MIDI drum kits don't really deal with pitch or note length so much, there is another editor in Cubase called the Drum Editor designed specifically for working with MIDI drum parts.

A MIDI drum kit is usually set up more like an external synth than a MIDI controller using a VST instrument, because a MIDI drum kit usually comes with its own "brain." The MIDI drum kit's brain is used to translate the hits on the individual drum pads to MIDI info consisting of MIDI note numbers, MIDI velocity, aftertouch, and MIDI lengths. Without this brain, the drums would simply output low-level audio noise. In most cases, the drum brain is not only the source for acquiring this MIDI info but also the sound source (much like an external synth outputs audio along with MIDI information). Because most drummers prefer the feel of a real acoustic drum kit to a MIDI kit, they sometimes don't really understand how MIDI works and assume that the sounds in the drum brain are the only sounds they can work with. Even though these sounds are usually very good, it's possible to trigger any type of MIDI drum kit sample from another source. This means that instead of simply recording, for instance, a snare drum part on an audio track in Cubase, you could actually record a snare drum MIDI track and later assign it to whatever instrument you feel necessary. If you really liked a snare sound from a particular recording, you could sample it with a virtual or hardware sampler and trigger it with your MIDI drum kit by using the same sample player along with Cubase. Like a MIDI keyboard, when recording with a MIDI drum kit, you can change the sounds, edit the timing and dynamics, and change drum parts *before* any audio is even recorded. If you were recording acoustic drums and wanted to change the snare drum after the part was recorded, you would have to re-record the entire drum part. With MIDI, you simply need to change to a different patch or preset on your sound source or change the sound source altogether.

Setting Up and Recording a MIDI Drum Kit with Cubase

As you can probably guess, there are many benefits to using a MIDI drum kit in a home Cubase studio. Not only can you save loads of time, but you're also probably going to get the best-sounding recording because getting good drum sounds hinges on so many variables.

In this short walkthrough, I explain the easiest way to interface a MIDI drum kit with Cubase. Since there are several different types of kits and brains on the market, I use general references that every drum brain should have.

1. First, connect the MIDI drum kit to the drum brain as instructed by the kit's manufacturer.

2. Run a MIDI cable from the drum brain's MIDI Out to the MIDI In of your computer's sound card/MIDI interface.

3. Run a MIDI cable from the sound card of your computer's MIDI Out to the MIDI In of your drum brain.

4. Run some audio cables from the stereo output of the drum brain to two analog inputs on your sound card. If the drum brain has a digital (SPDIF) output, run that output to your sound card's SPDIF input (for better sound quality).

5. Follow my walkthrough in the section "Making Connections to an External Synth" earlier in this chapter to make sure your audio is connected and monitored through an audio track in Cubase. Make sure that your global MIDI transmit channel is set to the same MIDI channel on the MIDI track you're recording to in Cubase. Also make sure that your global MIDI receive channel is set to the same channel you're working with. Because drum sounds are usually set up on different note numbers (as opposed to using separate patches), you should only need to use one MIDI channel to record an entire drum part. Refer to your MIDI drum kit's manual for help on proper settings.

6. Set your drum brain to Local Off (refer to your drum kit's manual). That way you will only be able to hear the sound from the drum kit as the MIDI has passed though Cubase. With Local On, you would receive a doubled sound: the sound of the MIDI as it is generated with the brain and the sound as the MIDI is regenerated in the brain when it reenters the brain from Cubase.

7. If you are experiencing a slight delay between a drum hit and the drum sound, try adjusting the latency of your sound card. This is a common problem when working with MIDI because MIDI definitely doesn't travel as fast as sound normally travels from a drum to a drummer's ear. No matter what your settings are, this MIDI delay may take some time to get used to before recording. Because of the way the MIDI is set in this example, it may create a slightly longer delay. If this is unbearable, try disconnecting the MIDI In on the drum brain and recording with the drum brain's Local On setting activated while recording. Then, when you're finished recording, reconnect the MIDI cable so you can listen to what you've recorded.

Note: When recording MIDI or audio, it's important to always make sure the red Record button is enabled on the MIDI track you will be recording on. There is also a button that looks like a speaker that you can use to monitor your MIDI signal without recording.

---

8. Continue recording as in the walkthrough in the section "Recording MIDI Using a VST Instrument" earlier in this chapter. If your MIDI is connected properly from the MIDI Out of your computer to the MIDI In of your drum brain, you should be able to replay your recording and change the drum kit within the drum brain as you listen back. See Figure 4.17 for a basic configuration.

Many MIDI drums kits' brains have multiple outputs for each individual drum sound. While these are great for monitoring and mixing a live performance, they aren't really necessary with a Cubase studio. If you have recorded the MIDI info from the MIDI drum kit properly, when it comes time to record the audio of each drum separately, you should be able to mute or solo drums during playback, which will allow you to record a solo audio track in one pass of the entire song. After this track has been recorded, you can then solo another

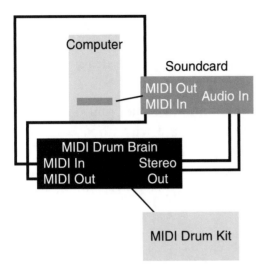

Figure 4.17 A basic configuration for a MIDI drum kit using Cubase.

drum and repeat this process until every drum in the drum part has been recorded. Keep in mind that this should all happen *after* the MIDI drum track has been recorded. Using this simple method will not only allow you to record drums individually for each pass but will also allow you to record groups of drums or other drum sounds using the same MIDI track. For more on muting drum sounds within your MIDI drum brain, refer to your drum kit's manual. You can also mute individual notes and sounds using Cubase's MIDI Drum Editor, as I will show you in the next section. Check out Chapter 9 for more information on bouncing down MIDI drum tracks to an audio track.

Working with the Drum Editor and Drum Maps

Drum parts don't really follow the pitch grid like a bass or keyboard part. That's because it would be unusual for a drum kit to be tuned like a piano or a guitar. Even though drums do have a pitch and can be tuned, you wouldn't normally tune a drum or percussion kit to a chromatic scale.

When you're dealing with MIDI drum kits, you have to stop thinking about pitch and start thinking about MIDI note numbers. Another difference between a note played on a chromatic instrument (such as a guitar) and a drum is that *holding* a note on a drum doesn't sound much different from playing a staccato (short) note on a drum. Length almost becomes a moot point, especially when you're dealing with a MIDI drum part.

These two differences—the use of note numbers rather than pitch, and the demotion of note length in importance—are why Cubase decided to incorporate a special editor for drum parts: the Drum Editor (see Figure 4.18). The Drum Editor can be opened in Cubase by selecting Drum Editor from the MIDI menu when you have a prerecorded MIDI track selected.

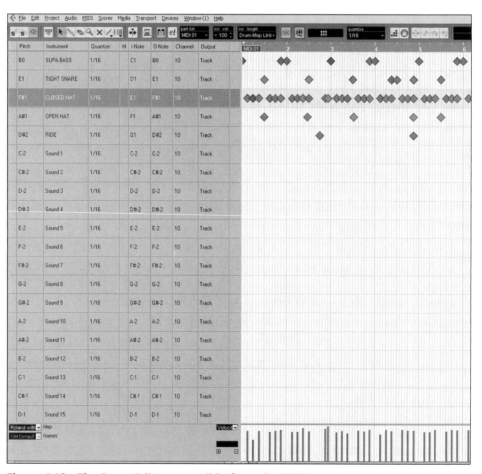

Figure 4.18   The Drum Editor, accessible from the MIDI menu.

The single most important aspect of the Drum Editor is its ability to work with drum maps. A *drum map* determines which drum sound is playing on which note number, as well as how the notes will be displayed in the Drum Editor's note display.

Drum maps were created because MIDI instrument manufacturers were setting up drum kits on their instruments with no regard for how their note numbers related to those used in other manufacturers' drum kits. That is, the note numbers were not *standardized*. This made things difficult for the programmers like you and me when it came to experimenting with various instruments and drum sounds for songs.

For example, you might record a song with your Yamaha drum machine but later decide that it sounded better on your Roland drum machine. But when you switched instruments, you'd find that the kick part was playing on the Roland's crash cymbal and the snare part was playing on the Roland's cowbell. Of course, this would sound like garbage, so you'd grudgingly go back to using your Yamaha drum machine because at least it *worked*.

In time, manufacturers got together and came up with General MIDI to control default instrument settings, so that switching from, say, one synth to another would not be a big issue with prerecorded parts. General MIDI brought MIDI to the next level, defining the note number on which each of the default drum kit's instruments would fall as well as which instruments were active on each of the 16 MIDI channels. (General MIDI is also the reason a MIDI file will sound one way when played on your cell phone and another way when played on your computer, but with the same musical arrangement—that is, it doesn't play a harpsichord sound when it should be playing a marimba.)

With the advent of General MIDI, *some* people's headaches went away— although General MIDI didn't put an end to drum kit–setup problems. For example, although it allowed for some standardization in note numbers, it didn't enable you to customize the drum-kit setup. We all want our setup to be as easy and efficient as possible, but what's easy and efficient isn't the same for everyone. Setting up your own drum map, as opposed to working with a General MIDI drum map, can help make you more comfortable and productive. Even though it takes time to set up a drum map, like naming a track, it will save you time when you decide to make changes later on.

Note: A drum map is a more advanced version of what Cubase calls a *name list*. I won't go into detail on how to create a name list at this point; if you know and understand drum maps, there's no point in learning the name list. On each controller lane is a small menu for the currently loaded drum maps and for the currently loaded name lists. When using drum maps, you will only need to use the Drum Maps menu.

Cubase is set up to use the Drum Editor strictly as an *editor* (meaning that you can work in it only *after* a drum part is recorded). However, it is possible to override this and record in the Drum Editor by first creating an *empty* part in the Project window where you would like to record your drums. To create an empty part, simply use the Draw tool accessible from (a button featuring a pencil icon, found on the toolbar) to draw a part (which looks like a box) between the left and right locator where you wish to record you drum part. Once this is created, it should look similar to Figure 4.19. You can also create an empty part by double-clicking between the locators just to the right of the track.

Now that you have an empty part, you can easily select the part and then select Drum Editor from the MIDI menu, and the Drum Editor

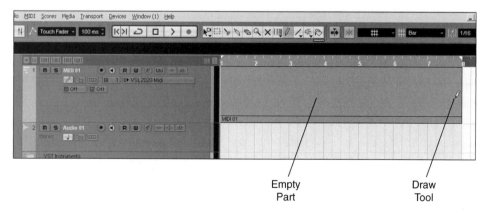

Empty
Part

Draw
Tool

Figure 4.19 An empty part has been created in the Project window with the draw tool.

will open. When the Drum Editor first appears, it appears as a drum list, which is an abbreviated form of a drum map. Change the setting in the small Map menu at the bottom of the Drum List from No Drum Map to GM Default, and use the pointer to select the dividing line between the drum list and the note display to expand the view of the drum map (see Figure 4.20).

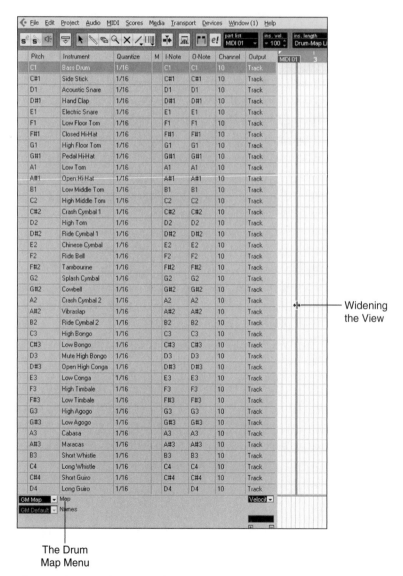

Widening the View

The Drum
Map Menu

Figure 4.20   Setting up a drum map.

There should be 11 columns visible in your drum-map display. In Cubase 4, two of these columns are unnamed. Just to the right of the first unnamed column is the pitch column (which should really be called the *note number* column), the instrument column (which defines the sound you hear on that note number), the quantize column, the M (mute) column, the I-note (MIDI input note) column, the O-note (MIDI output note) column, the channel (MIDI channel) column, and output (MIDI output) column. The last blank column is just to the right of the output column.

As much as I love Cubase, I have to say that this drum-map display isn't set up in the most logical way. The way they name these columns is confusing enough, and to make matters worse, they didn't even name the first column, which is not a blank column at all—it's an *audition* column. Clicking the column next to the note number will reveal the audio sound of that note number (the same way that playing that note number on a MIDI controller reveals the sound). Try clicking in the audition column next to some of the sounds until you hear one of the sounds.

When you create a drum map, you create a translation program that works between the notes you have recorded (or are playing with a MIDI instrument) and the sounds in your synth or sampler. In most cases, you won't be using all 128 note numbers in one drum track. Most of the time you'll be doing pretty good to use more than 10 note numbers (10 separate drum sounds) on a basic drum kit. To begin creating a drum map, you must first open the Drum Map Setup dialog box (see Figure 4.21), accessible from the MIDI menu. You can also open the Drum Map Setup dialog box by selecting it from the drop-down menu found on a controller lane. You can resize the Drum Map Setup dialog box by dragging the bottom-right corner of the box, just as you would a window.

Even though you can use the default GM drum map and make modifications to it as needed, I recommend building a drum map from scratch. By doing this, you can save your drum map and use it for future projects with the same setup. Create a new drum map by selecting this feature from the Function menu in the Drum Map Setup dialog

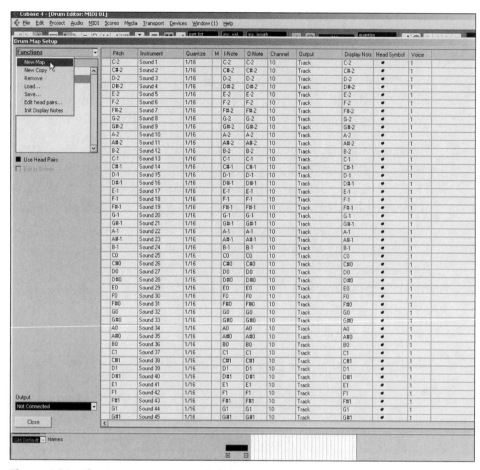

Figure 4.21   The Drum Map Setup dialog box with its Functions menu open.

box. Once you have created a new drum map, rename it to something you'll recognize later on by clicking and typing in the new drum map's name field. I have renamed this drum map "Roland with Halion One Hip Hop Kit" in this example. I have decided that I would like to trigger some samples from the HALion One VST instrument with my Roland MIDI kit. Here's how to set up a drum map you can use over and over again:

1.   First, select the proper MIDI output, the instrument you would like to trigger the drum sounds (the sound source). Since HALion One is a VST instrument, I have selected it as my

output source. If you were outputting back to your drum kit's brain, you would select the MIDI output connected to your MIDI drum kit's brain. Once you have the output configured, you should be able to use your mouse to click within the (unnamed) audition column to hear some drum sounds from your sound source.

2. By using the audition column, I can determine that B0 is the note number for the kick drum sample I would like to use in the HALion One. Since this drum is unnamed, I call it "SUPA BASS" in its name field and proceed to find the other sounds I want using the same method. Once I've found and named the five sounds I want to use, my Drum Map Setup dialog box looks something like Figure 4.22. As you can see, it's still a mess, containing the five drum sounds I want to use and 123 sounds I don't.

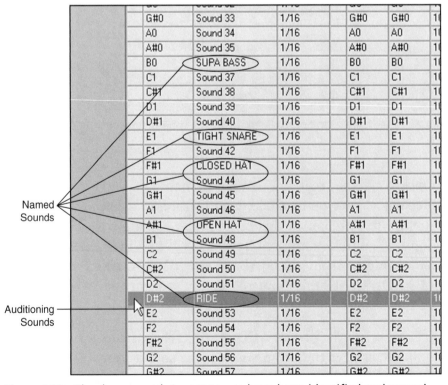

Figure 4.22 The drum sounds I want to use have been identified and named.

3. Unfortunately, you can't remove all of those unwanted sounds from the display, but you can at least organize the sounds so that the ones you want are all in one location. To do this, select the row of the desired drum sound within the note number (pitch) column and drag the row up and down through the rows until you find a good location. A green line should appear as a guide to help you find the right location. When you have arranged the drum sounds you would like to use, your drum map should appear more like mine, shown in Figure 4.23.

Sounds Moved to
the Top of the List

Drum Map Setup

Functions	Pitch	Instrument	Quantize	M	I-Note	O-Note	Channel	Output	Display Note	Head Symbol	Voice
Drum Maps	B0	SUPA BASS	1/16		B0	B0	10	Track	B0	•	1
GM Map	E1	TIGHT SNARE	1/16		E1	E1	10	Track	E1	•	1
Roland with Halion One Hip Hop	F#1	CLOSED HAT	1/16		F#1	F#1	10	Track	F#1	•	1
	A#1	OPEN HAT	1/16		A#1	A#1	10	Track	A#1	•	1
	D#2	RIDE	1/16		D#2	D#2	10	Track	D#2	•	1
	C-2	Sound 1	1/16		C-2	C-2	10	Track	C-2	•	1
	C#-2	Sound 2	1/16		C#-2	C#-2	10	Track	C#-2	•	1
	D-2	Sound 3	1/16		D-2	D-2	10	Track	D-2	•	1
	D#-2	Sound 4	1/16		D#-2	D#-2	10	Track	D#-2	•	1
	E-2	Sound 5	1/16		E-2	E-2	10	Track	E-2	•	1
	F-2	Sound 6	1/16		F-2	F-2	10	Track	F-2	•	1
	F#-2	Sound 7	1/16		F#-2	F#-2	10	Track	F#-2	•	1
Use Head Pairs	G-2	Sound 8	1/16		G-2	G-2	10	Track	G-2	•	1
Edit in Scores	G#-2	Sound 9	1/16		G#-2	G#-2	10	Track	G#-2	•	1
	A-2	Sound 10	1/16		A-2	A-2	10	Track	A-2	•	1
	A#-2	Sound 11	1/16		A#-2	A#-2	10	Track	A#-2	•	1
	B-2	Sound 12	1/16		B-2	B-2	10	Track	B-2	•	1
	C-1	Sound 13	1/16		C-1	C-1	10	Track	C-1	•	1
	C#-1	Sound 14	1/16		C#-1	C#-1	10	Track	C#-1	•	1
	D-1	Sound 15	1/16		D-1	D-1	10	Track	D-1	•	1
	D#-1	Sound 16	1/16		D#-1	D#-1	10	Track	D#-1	•	1
	E-1	Sound 17	1/16		E-1	E-1	10	Track	E-1	•	1
	F-1	Sound 18	1/16		F-1	F-1	10	Track	F-1	•	1
	F#-1	Sound 19	1/16		F#-1	F#-1	10	Track	F#-1	•	1
	G-1	Sound 20	1/16		G-1	G-1	10	Track	G-1	•	1

Figure 4.23 The drum sounds have been arranged for easier viewing.

Note: For simplicity, I will not be discussing the quantize, display note, head symbol, or voice columns in this chapter. They are not necessary for most applications. For more in-depth coverage, refer to the Cubase manual or my book *MIDI Editing in Cubase*.

---

4. Now we get down to the real nitty-gritty when it comes to making your Roland drum kit communicate properly with the HALion One VST sample player. This involves using either the I-note or O-note column. The I-note is the MIDI input note

number. If your I-note is C0, then when using a MIDI keyboard controller and playing C0, you would trigger that sound, listed in the Drum Editor, from your sound source. The problem with a MIDI drum kit is that C0 really doesn't make any positional sense. The letter C refers to a chromatic pitch, which a drum does not normally play. When it comes to C0, your MIDI drum kit views it as just a number. Therefore, drum kits can be set up to output different drum pads with different note numbers according to *your* specifications. Even though the drum-kit manufacturer usually has a standard setup formula, you should be able to adjust the output note number of each of your individual drum pads from your MIDI drum brain. The good news is that it's easier to adjust the I-note in Cubase so that you don't even have to start digging around within your MIDI drum kit's brain. To assign the right I-note to the right drum sound, simply record a few notes using the pad you would like to identify. Once you have recorded the note, identify the note number by scrolling through the 128 note numbers listed and determining where the note you played is located. Even if you're hearing the wrong sound for the drum you are hitting, by simply changing the I-note on the correct *sound* to the note number that you previously recorded, your drum pad will match your HALion One VST instrument's patch. Voilà! Once you've changed the I-note on the five drum sounds to match the pads on your Roland Kit, you're done.

This walkthrough should also work for setting up your external sound source (such as your MIDI drum kit's brain). Once you have your MIDI drum kit talking to your MIDI sound source, you may decide that you would like to change certain sounds in your kit. Changing the O-note will result in routing the MIDI signal to a source other than the original note number. By adjusting the data in the output or channel columns, you can even route the drum sound to a completely separate sound source. (For example, you may want to use the kick and snare from your Roland kit but the hi-hat from the HALion One's Hip Hop kit.) As you can see, using a drum map can be quite a powerful tool for managing your drum setups, especially if you are using multiple sound sources.

As I mentioned before, when you monitor an external drum sound source through Cubase using either the stereo or digital outputs of your sound source, you can bounce each individual track down as its own audio file by simply muting the rest of the drums as you bounce the track down in real time. This is easy to do using the mute column to mute the drum sounds you don't want to record to audio or using the Solo Instrument button from the toolbar and selecting the instrument you would like to bounce to audio. (All other instruments will be muted in the process.) See Figure 4.24.

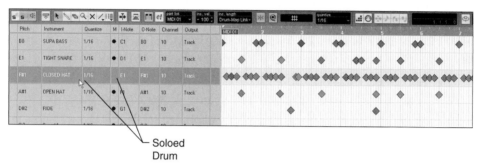

Soloed
Drum

Figure 4.24 The drum sound has been soloed and is ready to be bounced to a solo audio track.

Setting up drum maps is just a small part of what you can do when you're working with MIDI drums within Cubase. I will touch on some basic MIDI editing techniques in Chapter 8, "Basic Editing." Unfortunately, since this book covers both basic MIDI *and* audio editing in Cubase, I won't be able to go into great detail regarding editing within the Drum Editor. I will, however, touch on quantizing MIDI and some basic MIDI editing within the Key Editor. Most of that info should translate to the Drum Editor as well. For a more detailed approach to the Drum Editor, please explore the Cubase manual or my book *MIDI Editing in Cubase*.

Using MIDI Sliders, Buttons, and Knobs with Cubase

Apart from using MIDI instruments, you can also use other MIDI devices while working with Cubase. As mentioned in Chapter 2, there are a few devices that offer mixing control surfaces, such as the Mackie HUI. These types of devices are referred to by Cubase as *remote-control devices*.

Setting up a remote-control device is usually accomplished from the Device Setup window (found by clicking Device Setup in the Devices menu). By clicking on the plus sign (on the top-left side of the window), a drop-down menu appears with several available remote-control devices (see Figure 4.25). As long as you are using a remote control that's listed in Cubase, you're ready to start using your device. If your remote-control device is not listed in the menu, then technically Steinberg does not support it, but you can set it up via the Generic Remote setup screen (see Figure 4.26). Manufacturers such as M-Audio usually provide remote device maps that you can import via the Generic Remote setup screen's Import function. (This includes MIDI keyboards that have MIDI sliders, buttons, and knobs on them.) You can also import what's called a *mixer map* (a MIX file) or a *MIDI device* (an XML file) from the MIDI Device Manager (see Figure 4.27), which is accessible from the Device menu. If you have this option, I highly recommend it. Otherwise you will have to manually create the map you need, and this is not one of Cubase's more user-friendly panels.

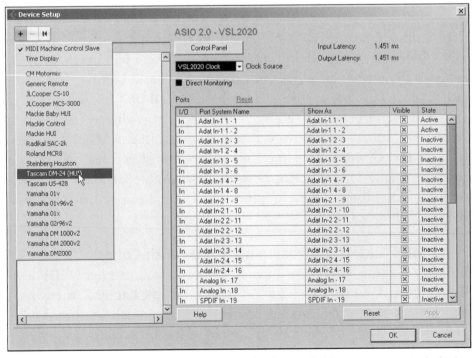

Figure 4.25 The Device Setup window with the available remote-control devices displayed.

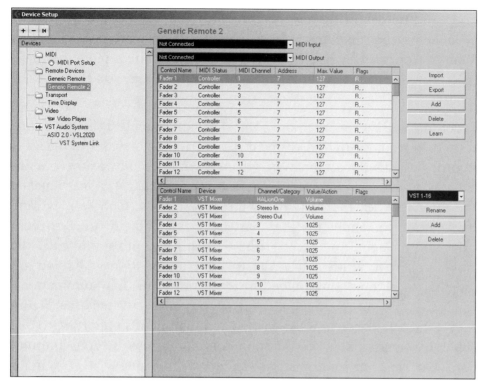

Figure 4.26   Cubase's Generic Remote setup screen.

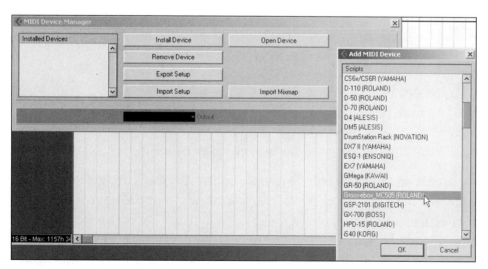

Figure 4.27   The MIDI Device Manager.

You can find details on how to configure your remote-control device by opening the Help menu and selecting Documentation and then Remote Control Devices. Even though it's not quite a plug-and-play-type procedure, this guide is pretty good at walking you through the process.

Recording MIDI from a remote-control device is handled slightly differently than from a MIDI instrument. Usually, a remote-control device is recorded using write automation, which is symbolized by a box containing a *W* within the internal mixer's channels, tracks, VST instruments, and effects. When the W (write) button is selected, Cubase is writing every move you input for that particular function. In order to hear what you've input, you activate the R (read) button to play back the moves you have written. In order to write automation while you are listening to automation you've already written (reading automation), you need to have both the R and W buttons activated (see Figure 4.28). Once you have finished writing automation, it's important to disable the W button so that you don't continue to rewrite your automation. Working with automation can get a little messy if you aren't careful and takes some practice to get the right result.

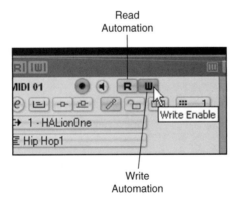

Figure 4.28 The R (read) and W (write) automation buttons.

As I mentioned in Chapter 2, remote-control surfaces are great for those who like the classic feel of sliders, knobs, and buttons, but you should also remember that these same moves can all be performed using a mouse and the Cubase GUI (graphical user interface). Even though I will not go over writing automation in depth, I will demonstrate ways in which you can automate Cubase with only your mouse and the GUI in Chapter 9.

5 Recording Vocals

When it comes to recording an audio performance in Cubase, one of the most common and basic types is a vocal performance. This chapter walks you through the basics of recording a vocal, whether you're recording an opera singer, a rapper, or a robotic voice. Recording a vocal requires a fairly simple setup but can get very complex depending on your specific needs. Besides your computer and Cubase, you will need at least some sort of microphone to get the most out of this chapter and your vocal-recording experience.

There are many microphones to choose from. I recommend that you spend a great deal of time exploring them before you make your decision. Most studios keep several types of microphones on hand because each offers specific advantages for certain kinds of vocal work. Even though the standard for vocal recording is a cardioid condenser-type microphone, you can apply the same basic principles to all microphone types. You could also apply some of the techniques in this chapter to recording acoustic instruments, such as guitar. I will go into more detail on how to record instruments in later chapters.

Preparing to Record Vocals

There are several key ingredients to getting a good vocal recording. First is choosing the right microphone for your singer. Second, you need to interface the microphone to your computer's sound card properly. Third, you need to make sure the singer can hear properly during recording. If a singer is not comfortable while recording a vocal part, you probably won't get the best performance. The most important element to capture in a vocal is the performance, our focus in this chapter. If a singer has slight problems with pitch and timing, the art of digital editing in Cubase can come in very handy and is commonly used with today's vocal performers—even with the best singers in the world.

Microphone Placement 101

All microphones belong on a mic stand in a studio environment. Even if vocal performers are used to singing with a handheld microphone, rip it out of their hands and put it on a stand. Handhelds tend to pick up a lot of vibrations and low-frequency noises when bumped during recording. If a singer is strongly opposed to this, you may not have a choice, but when you tell singers it will make them *sound* better to sing into a microphone on a stand, most quickly change their tune.

There are many types of mic stands and several ways to mount a mic. The standard studio vocal mic stand is a *studio boom stand*. Studio boom stands work much better than other types because they're not only easy to adjust to the proper height but also offer singers the freedom to move without fear of touching the mic stand. Touching a mic stand can create as much noise during a recording as using a handheld mic. Some choose to *hang* a microphone as a cheap alternative to a studio boom stand. This can work in a pinch, but keep in mind that if the microphone swings while you're recording, you may get an undesirable result. I've been in situations where vacuum cleaners or floor lamps with duct tape were used for mic stands—and I don't recommend *those* methods either!

Some microphones come with their own clips or mounts. If that's the case, I recommend you use that hardware. However, the best type of vocal mic mount (for studio mic stands) is a *suspension shock mount* (see Figure 5.1). There are several different types of shock mounts available, but the idea is that the microphone is suspended by elastic bands within a ring, which in turn prevents noise from traveling up the stand and into the microphone when recording. If you have a good cardioid/condenser mic with a boom mic stand (ideally a studio boom) and a suspension shock mount, you have already saved yourself a lot of headaches.

Figure 5.1   A suspension shock mount, the best type of vocal mic mount for studio mic stands.

Depending on your microphone and vocalist, you may need to use a *windscreen*. Usually microphones come with some type of windscreen that fits over the diaphragm of the mic. If your mic doesn't come with one, you should be able to find some universal windscreens at your local music store. Windscreens can cut down a lot on noise from lyrics that start or end with a P or K sound. They can be especially useful for rock vocalists or rap artists who sing or rap loudly into a mic. Another alternative for extremely loud vocals is called a *popper stopper* (see Figure 5.2). A popper stopper is fastened to an additional mic stand so that you can achieve the best sound from a mic and screen the troublesome consonants long before they're close to the mic. This further decreases your chances of noise interfering with a recording. I have heard of loud rock singers who required several popper stoppers at one time. Even though windscreens and popper stoppers can clean up a loud, enthusiastic performance, they can also get in the way of a soft, smooth performance by taking away some of a mic's crystal-clear sheen. If you're recording a softer vocal part, you might bypass the windscreen altogether.

A microphone should be level with a singer's head while he or she is standing or slightly higher so that the singer has to project slightly upward. Standing upright gives good singers better use of their lung

Popper
Stopper

Figure 5.2 A popper stopper can be used to screen out harsh consonants.

capacity, though this may seem awkward for singers who have not been professionally trained. But the most important thing is that the singer is comfortable, even if this means sitting down. A singer should stand not more than one foot (30 cm) and not less than six inches (15 cm) from the microphone. Getting too close can cause something known as the *proximity effect*, an undesirable increase in bass frequency in the voice. Radio DJs and interviewers love to get close to the mic and use this effect to their advantage, but it's usually not desirable on a sung vocal part. Don't take the six inch/one foot guideline too seriously. The best way to judge is by ear. Good singers are always using their ears, along with the vocal and microphone, to get a great recording. This is called *mic technique*. Usually singers will adjust their distance while singing into the mic (much like a compressor controls volume peaks and dips). If the vocal part is too loud, the singer moves a little farther from the mic. If it's too soft, the singer moves a little closer.

One thing to remember is that when you are recording a vocal performance (or *any* type of performance) with a mic, you're probably recording a lot more than you intend to. There is simply no way to prevent recording the studio environment when you're using a microphone. The more sensitive your microphone is, the more studio environment you will capture. Anything you record unintentionally because of the room's acoustics is called *ambience*. Different rooms have different ambience. Most engineers approach ambience as noise that should be reduced as much as possible. The ultimate goal is to have a much greater signal from your source than from noise (in this case, ambience). The difference between the audio level of the source and the noise is referred to as the *signal-to-noise ratio* (SNR). Your noise level should be almost undetectable, and your signal should be as loud and clear as possible without distortion, which occurs when the level going into or coming out of the microphone is too loud.

If you're working with a loud singer, it may be in your best interest to use mic pads. A *mic pad* reduces the signal as it enters the microphone to prevent distortion. Mic pads usually come with microphones as attachments or as simple switches and can pad the signal in various increments (see Figure 5.3). If the singer is not very loud, avoid using any type of mic pad because this may reduce your SNR.

Figure 5.3   A mic pad switch found on a cardioid condenser mic.

Using Microphone Preamps

Before you can record the signal from a microphone, the signal must be audible. That requires amplification from what's known as a *microphone preamp*, or *mic pre*. Mic pres come in many varieties. Some are found on sound cards. Some are external devices that work alongside sound cards. Most audio mixers have gain knobs that can be considered mic pres. Their most basic functionality is to boost the signal of the mic, but they work in different ways. The largest difference is in technology. The two main choices are *solid-state* mic pres and *tube* mic pres. Solid-state mic pres deliver a very clean and accurate representation of the audio. A good tube mic pre can offer a more vintage, or warm, edge to a recording. Both types have been around for a long time, but every manufacturer has its own take on what makes a good solid-state or tube mic pre. This means that your choice of mic pre is another ingredient in the sound you want to create and can make or break the vocal recording almost as much as the microphone itself.

Some sound cards, such as the M-Audio Fast Track Pro (see Figure 5.4), come with built-in mic pres, very handy for those who just require a simple microphone connection to a computer.

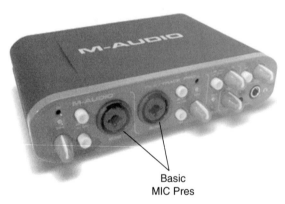

Basic
MIC Pres

Figure 5.4 The M-Audio Fast Track Pro with built-in dual mic pres.

For those who want to take their vocal experience to higher levels, you can get external units that offer not only premium microphone preamplification but also audio compression and equalization. An example of such a device is the Avalon VT-737SP (see Figure 5.5).

Even though Cubase can handle equalization and compression, these steps are often completed before the signal is converted from an analog to digital to ensure the best SNR. If you're looking for the secret to most major record producers' full vocal sound, it's mostly in the

Figure 5.5 The Avalon VT-737SP mic pre also offers compression and equalization.

microphone, the mic pre, the compression, and the EQ, and it's all done before the sound even reaches the computer. Of course, you also need to know how to use this equipment. The same principles for using Cubase's internal plug-in compressors and EQ can be applied to the external processors, and I will go over these a little later in this chapter.

Mic pres usually have at least one control, the *gain* control, for the loudness of the microphone. Fancier mic pres have a loudness level indicator (the *meter*), which helps in selecting proper gain settings. The professional choice in meters is a VU meter (see Figure 5.6). It may look a little old-fashioned compared to the flashier LED meters available on other makes, but VU is a favorite because of its speed and accuracy in determining audio signal peaks.

Figure 5.6 VU meters, popular for their efficiency in determining audio signal peaks, are commonly found on mic pres.

Note: When using any type of external meter to determine audio levels, it's always good to make sure the signal peaks in the red. However, if a signal is in the red a majority of the time, you will probably end up with distortion. If the signal is too far below the red, however, you may have too much ambient noise. A vocal recording can have a wide range of dynamics in any take; make sure you use a gain setting that works for both the loudest and softest points of a performance.

Capturing a Vocal Recording in Cubase

Once you have your microphone set up with the proper preamp (whether you decide to use outboard compression and EQ or not), you're ready to record your vocal. The microphone should be attached to the preamp with a mic cable, and if you're using an external mic pre, it should be connected to an audio input on your pro sound card. Now you can select your record and monitoring settings within Cubase.

The first priority is setting up your audio inputs within Cubase. Most sound cards offer multiple inputs, and Cubase allows for complex input configurations. But to record, you need to direct the proper input to the proper audio track. Setting up a mono vocal recording is easy in Cubase.

Note: Most vocal recordings can work with a mono audio signal (single audio track). Recording in stereo is always an option, but unless you're using a stereo microphone for vocals, there's no benefit to recording to a stereo track. (You'll either be recording a one-sided stereo signal or what's called a *dual mono signal*: two channels of identical mono audio.) Recording vocal tracks in stereo or dual mono is not common, and to keep things simple, I will discuss the mono mic setup only.

After opening your Cubase project or creating a new one, locate and select VST Connections, found in the Devices menu in the menu bar.

Often, an audio input will be selected by default. More often than not, the default will be a stereo input. Your first step should be to select a mono input bus from this screen.

1. You should see several tabs across the top of the VST Connections window. Select the Inputs tab, on the top left side of the window.

2. Disregard any currently available inputs and create a new mono input by clicking on the Add Bus button. The Add Input Bus window appears, allowing you to configure your new bus (see Figure 5.7). Change the configuration to Mono and the count to 1, and click OK. A single new mono bus shows up in the VST Connections window (see Figure 5.8). As I mentioned before, you may have other busses also available, but this will not make a difference.

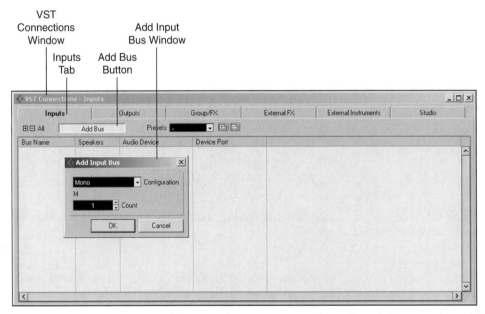

Figure 5.7 The Inputs tab of the VST Connections window after clicking on the Add Bus button.

3. Now that you've established a routing point within Cubase, you need to set up the bus to use the proper audio input from your sound card. Select the proper device port on your sound

card. For instance, if you've plugged your microphone into the left Audio In channel of your sound card, you will need to select the relevant audio port within the device port column (as shown in Figure 5.8).

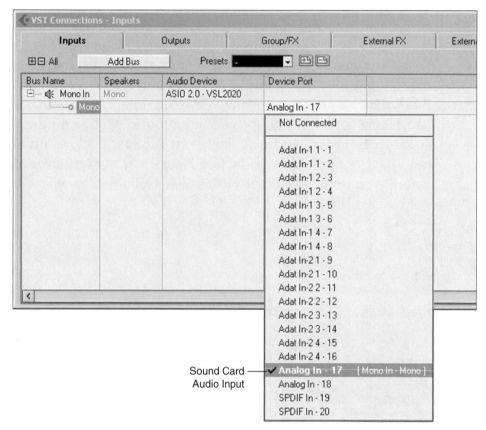

Figure 5.8 Setting the proper Audio In for the sound card to match a newly created mono Audio In bus in Cubase.

4.   Now it's time to route the signal to the audio track you would like to record on. You can either select a pre-existing mono audio track or create a new mono audio track for your vocal by selecting Audio from the Add Track submenu in the Project menu. After selecting Audio, an Add Audio Track window should prompt you to enter the type and number of audio tracks you would like to record (see Figure 5.9). Select Mono and at least one track, and click OK. If you may need to record several

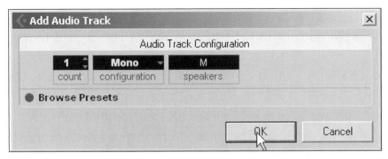

Figure 5.9   The Add Audio Track window set to add one mono audio track.

takes, you might want to create several mono tracks at this point, but you can always create more later if you need them.

5.   Once you have created an audio track, the last step in routing the incoming mic signal to the track is to assign the newly created input bus to the newly created audio track. This is easy to do with the Inspector (see Figure 5.10). If the Inspector is not visible, select the Show Inspector button on the toolbar.

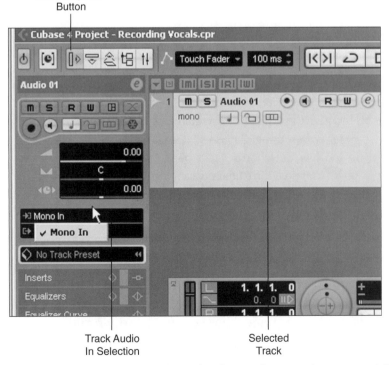

Figure 5.10   Setting the Audio In for the newly created mono track in the Inspector.

6. Now that the signal has been routed properly, select the red Record Enable button on the track on which you would like to record. You're ready to record. You should be receiving an audio input signal, which can be displayed on the transport (as shown in Figure 5.11). If you are not receiving a signal, make sure your mic pre is properly set, your cable connections are correct, and you are using the right input on your audio card. If for some reason you're not hearing your vocal or it sounds strange, don't worry. I'll explain more regarding this soon.

Figure 5.11 The audio input signal of the microphone on the transport.

Note: If you cannot see an audio signal on the transport, make sure that Audio Activity is selected from the transport's Display window, accessible by right-clicking on the transport. When recording, it's important to monitor the input signal within Cubase. Unlike using an external meter, when using Cubase's internal meter, the signal should not be too low but should *never* peak (hit the red) while recording. A signal that peaks in Cubase will create unwanted distortion and noise in your recording. To change your input level, adjust the gain on your mic pre.

After setting the proper recording levels, you're ready to make adjustments to the way you monitor the audio signal you're recording. Chances are that even though you might be receiving a proper audio signal, you may not be hearing what you'd like to hear. In fact, chances are you aren't hearing *any* audio signal, depending on the way your sound card works. If you are, it's probably a passive signal routed from your sound card's input to its output. If you're using the left or right input of a sound card's stereo input, you might be hearing sound on only one side of your stereo monitor setup (or in your headphones). You *can* record using this passive method. However, you may find it difficult to hear, and therefore monitor, the signal.

The proper way to monitor the mic's signal is through Cubase's Monitor section. This means that if you are hearing a passive audio signal, you should consult your sound card's documentation on how to disable it. This passive audio signal is usually referred to as *zero latency montoring* or *ASIO direct monitoring*. First, select the button with the speaker symbol on it, the Monitor button, within the track's display (see Figure 5.12).

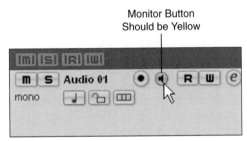

Figure 5.12   The Monitor button located on the audio track.

Note: When it comes time to play back a track you've recorded, you'll need to once again disable the Monitor button. The Monitor button should be active only on tracks you intend to record on.

After selecting this button, you should be able to hear your audio signal. The signal you will be monitoring occurs *after* the processing, which occurs between your sound card, Cubase, and your computer system. Because you're hearing the audio after it passes through this chain, you will experience latency (or a slight audio delay) within your monitors. It can be a nuisance for a vocalist to perform when you're monitoring with a lot of latency. For vocals, try adjusting your latency (as we went over in Chapter 1, "Setting Up Cubase on Your Computer,") to the lowest possible setting. This will reduce the annoying delay effect. If you encounter pops and crackles when you lower the setting, you may be forced to bypass monitoring through Cubase and use another source. If your sound card does not pass the audio signal, you can split the signal at input, sending half to your computer and half to your mixer, to blend with the output signal from Cubase (see Figure 5.13). The biggest drawback to monitoring using this method is that you won't be able to hear the actual sound being recorded until you play it back. The other drawback is that you will not be able to use Cubase plug-ins while you record. Using the plug-ins in Cubase (such as reverb, delay, compression, and EQ) during a recording can greatly enhance the performance of a vocalist without affecting the actual recording. This means that the singer will be able to hear the effect while he or she is singing, but you will be recording the unaffected (dry) signal. You can then change the effect later if necessary.

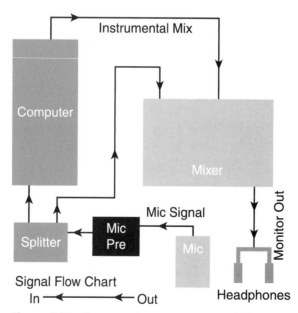

Figure 5.13 One way to reroute your mic input so that you can monitor the passive input signal.

Note: You may have already experienced this, but if you're trying to use a microphone in a control room where speakers are being used, you will need to mute the speakers and use headphones to eliminate the chances of getting *audio feedback.* Audio feedback occurs when the output signal (the amplified speaker) "leaks" back into the input signal (the microphone). Even if you don't hear feedback, using speakers around a microphone will also cause *audio bleed-through,* which means that you will most likely capture the audio coming out of your speakers while you're capturing the vocal performance. Recording audio bleed-through can create big problems during the mixing stage. Avoid this at all costs.

Using Effects While Recording Vocals

Using the steps you've learned so far, you should be able to start recording a vocal track just by hitting Record on the transport, but to get the most out of your vocal recording, there are still a few important steps you should take. One is to set up effects to use while recording your vocal part.

The typical way of monitoring effects during a vocal recording is through an audio track. Using this method, you can record a completely "dry" vocal take while hearing the audio the way you need to hear it during a vocal performance. Audio track monitoring should be available in most versions of Cubase, and I will discuss the details a little later in this section.

As I mentioned earlier, it's quite common to use compression and EQ while recording vocals. These effects can help you get the best SNR possible and enhance natural vocal qualities without causing major changes to the sound of the singer's voice. If you are using Cubase 4 or SX, you should be able to use an *insert* to access the input channel from the mixer and apply the effects within Cubase to the input signal directly. By using a compressor/limiter within an insert on the audio input, you can avoid clipping during loud vocal parts and increase the volume of softer vocal parts. A compressor/limiter actually reduces the dynamics in a performance, so use it sparingly if you want a dynamic performance. Often, obvious compression is undesirable in the end result. The ultimate goal is a signal that's never too loud or too soft, yet without the "squashing" of loud signals that compression sometimes causes.

To demonstrate setting up compression within Cubase, I will use the VST Dynamics plug-in, which comes with the program. If you do not have Cubase 4, you may opt to apply these effects to the input signal during recording with an external hardware compressor, such as the Avalon VT-737, shown in Figure 5.5, and with settings similar to those I use on Cubase's plug-in compressor in this demonstration.

1. Cubase recommends that you use 32-bit processing for internal effects. You can change your project's record format to 32-bit float in the Project Setup window (see Figure 5.14), which you access by selecting Project Setup in the Project menu on the menu bar. You can get by with 16- or 24-bit processing, but the 32-bit rate will lower your chances of clipping the live signal.

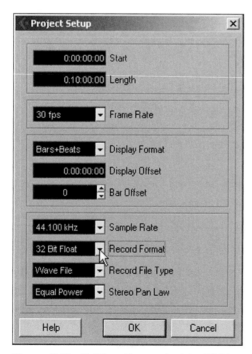

Figure 5.14 Setting the project to 32-bit processing to prevent clipping the signal.

2.   Next, open the Mixer panel by pressing F3 on your computer keyboard or choosing Mixer from the Devices menu. Depending on what you are working with in your project, your Mixer panel may look different. At the very least, you should see the input channel, the audio channel you're recording to, and the output channel (see Figure 5.15). All three of these channels should show a signal as you test the microphone. If you cannot find all of these channels, select Reveal All Channels. If you still cannot find the input channel, it's possible that the version of Cubase you are using does not offer this option.

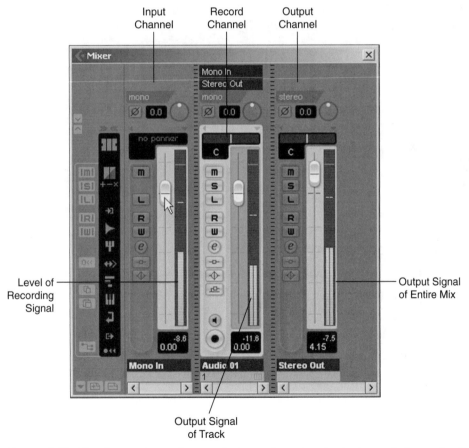

Figure 5.15 The input channel, record channel, and output channel shown in the Cubase Mixer panel.

3. Select the *e* button on the input channel. A window should appear giving you access to the input channel's settings (including the Inserts and EQ settings). Click in the first blank insert slot and locate the plug-in called VST Dynamics (see Figure 5.16).

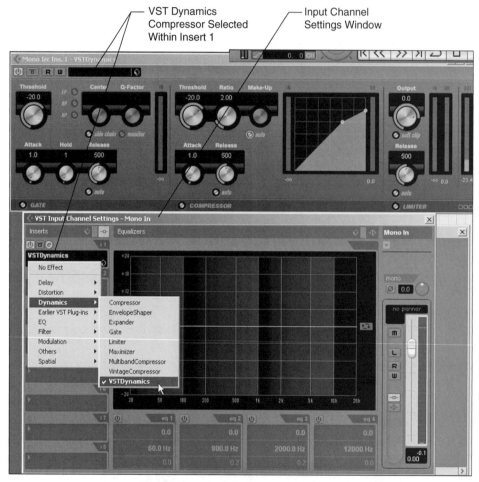

Figure 5.16 The input channel's Settings window with the VST Dynamics plug-in selected as an insert effect.

4. Now that VST Dynamics has been selected, it has been routed between the signal from your microphone and the signal to the audio track. Use Figure 5.17 as a guide to match your settings. The settings displayed are that of a soft compression, which

will prevent your signal from clipping no matter how loud the vocalist sings. Cubase offers several presets for this compressor, but they are often too drastic to yield great results. Feel free to experiment with the presets by loading them from within the compressor, as shown in Figure 5.17.

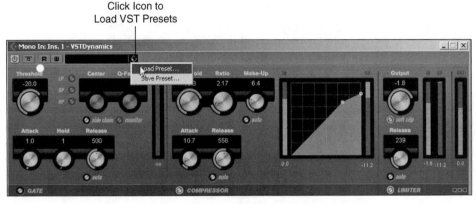

Figure 5.17 Applying the compressor to vocals during recording.

5.   Once you have your compressor set the way you like, you can add other insert effects as well. EQ can easily be adjusted from the VST Input Channel Settings window by clicking on the frequency you would like to boost or cut. When recording vocals, apply EQ sparingly. The EQ setting in Figure 5.18 is a high-frequency curve to add "air" to the recording. This is one of Cubase's EQ presets and is commonly used for recording vocals.

Using this method, you can add any plug-in effect within Cubase to the vocal track during recording. It's important to realize, though, that these effects are recorded to the track along with the vocal, and they cannot be removed later. In a sense, the effects are "married" to the vocal part.

Along with applying this basic compression and EQ during vocal recording, I will also show you how to apply some simple reverb to the vocal to make the singer feel more comfortable. It is uncommon to apply reverb to the signal prior to recording (as we did with EQ and compression in the previous walkthrough). The reverb in this example will be applied to the audio track instead of the input track.

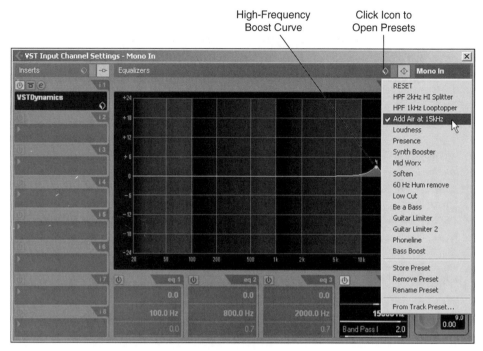

Figure 5.18 Applying the EQ to vocals during recording.

1. Using the same Mixer window as in the previous excerise, select the *e*, except this time select it within the channel you wish to record instead of the input channel. As an alternative, you can also select the *e* within the audio track in the Project window.

2. Next select a reverb within a blank insert as you did with the compressor in the previous walkthrough. I have selected the Roomworks reverb plug-in (shown in Figure 5.19). Feel free to scan through the presets while the singer tests the mic by singing. Have the singer let you know when one of the settings sounds good.

Even though you will hear this effect on this channel after the track has been recorded, the effect itself will not be recorded with the vocal. You can change the insert effect anytime during or after recording, and the original recording will remain unaffected.

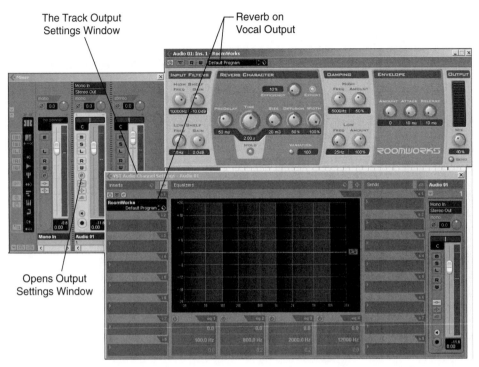

Figure 5.19 The Roomworks plug-in selected as an insert effect on audio channel one.

Setting the Vocal Monitor Levels During Recording

Making singers feel comfortable by using effects is one thing, but creating a mix they feel comfortable singing with is another. It's very important that singers can hear the music tracks or other vocal tracks in a way that doesn't *distract* them from their performance. While a singer is performing, the mix should *enhance* their performance. Singers have individual needs. This can make setting up a mix for them pretty tricky in itself.

Obtaining a great vocal tracking mix can be a delicate balancing act. Sometimes singers need to hear themselves more than the recording. A lot of singers remove one earpiece of the headphones so that they can hear both the mix and a true representation of their voice. For other singers, this is distracting. When it comes to controlling the levels of the entire mix (apart from vocals) without affecting the relative levels of the rest of the tracks, it may be necessary to group your tracks to increase or decrease the volume of several tracks at a time. This practice is known as *bussing*. By bussing within a mix, you can set up one fader that controls the entire background track mix, another that controls the background vocal levels, and another you can ride to get a great level for the lead vocal. In the following walkthrough, I will explain how to set up busses for use while tracking vocals.

Seeing as how this tutorial works best when you already have a lot of tracks, you may want to come back to it later. In the following example, I will group all the instrument background tracks together and all the background vocal tracks together to make sure the singer can always hear herself at the necessary level without affecting the rest of the mix or changing the input level of the microphone.

Cubase refers to its internal bussing channels as *group channels*. To achieve the ideal mixing setup for a vocal recording session including background tracks and background vocals, the first step is to add two separate group channels to the project.

1. From the Project menu, select Add Tracks and, from the Add Tracks submenu, select Group Channels. For this example, adjust the settings to create two stereo group channels, as shown in Figure 5.20.

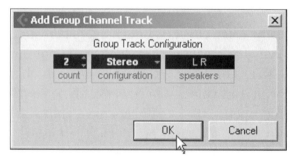

Figure 5.20 Creating two stereo group channels.

2. Open the Mixer panel as you have before, and make sure the mixer has been expanded so that it displays the routing at the top, as shown in Figure 5.21. The easiest way to expand the mixer is by using the arrows on the left side of the Mixer panel.

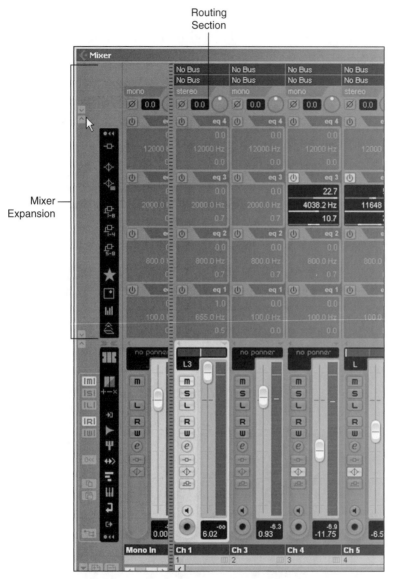

Figure 5.21   The Mixer panel has been fully expanded to reveal the routing at the top.

The channels must also be widened to their full size to reveal the routing.

3. Find the group channels you previously created within the Mixer panel. Rename group channel 1 "Background Music Tracks" and rename group channel 2 "Background Vocal Tracks" by clicking in the name field for the channel and typing a new name.

4. Change the outputs for all the instrument channels in the routing section above each channel to Background Music Tracks. You will need to select the VST instrument channels as well as the audio channels. MIDI channels do not need to be changed (see Figure 5.22 for an example). When you are

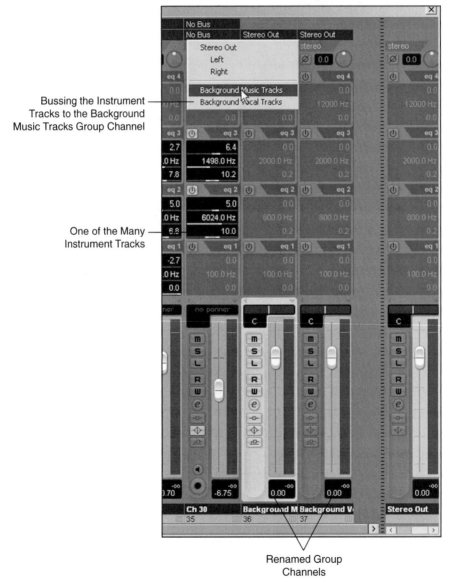

Bussing the Instrument Tracks to the Background Music Tracks Group Channel

One of the Many Instrument Tracks

Renamed Group Channels

Figure 5.22 Setting the channel to output to the proper group channel with the mixer channel's routing section.

finished with the instrument channels, change the same setting for the background vocals to output to the Background Vocal Tracks channel.

5. Leave the lead vocal channel assigned to the main mix output. Now you can control the level of all the instrument tracks and the background vocal tracks with the two new group channel faders, and you can control the lead vocal level with the fader of the audio channel you're recording to. You can also control the level of the entire mix with the main stereo out fader. Don't forget that you can control the entire level with your headphone amplifier. Make sure that none of the levels cause clipping. Sometimes using an external headphone amplifier can add signal boost without causing distortion. See Figure 5.23 for a closeup view of the four faders you can use to simplify your vocal tracking experience.

Recording Multiple Vocal Takes

As much as some vocalists would love to be considered "one-take wonders," the truth of the matter is that the perfect take is rarely captured from one recorded track in one pass. For a long time engineers mastered the art of something called *punching in*—replacing small mistakes during an otherwise perfect vocal performance. In Cubase you punch in by setting the location on the track for the punch in and using Record mode. Actually, since digital recording and editing have become so advanced in recent years, many engineers skip punching in altogether and just record another take that they can later edit as needed. This takes a great deal of pressure off both the engineers and the performers, saves time, and provides much better results for the final recording.

There are many ways to record multiple takes within Cubase, but the method I'm demonstrating in this chapter is the fastest and most painless way possible. First make sure that you have followed all of my previous walkthroughs. You should be set up so that you are registering the perfect sound and mix on one recording channel.

1. Record your first vocal take by setting the left locator at the start of the vocal part and the right locator at the end. Click Record

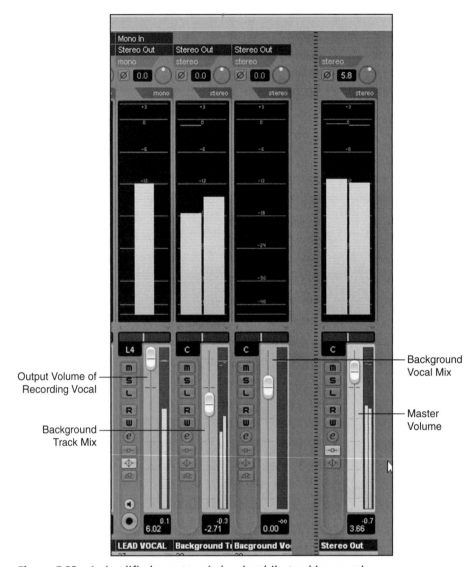

Figure 5.23 A simplified way to mix levels while tracking vocals.

on the transport. If a metronome or count-in is required, refer to Chapter 4, "Recording MIDI," for more details.

2. Select the recorded take by selecting the track you recorded to. From the Project menu, select Duplicate Track.

3. The track you have just recorded will be duplicated in its entirety. The fact that you have two of the same vocal take is

not really relevant. What's important is that you have two tracks with identical settings. The new track will be referred to as "Copy of..." (see Figure 5.24).

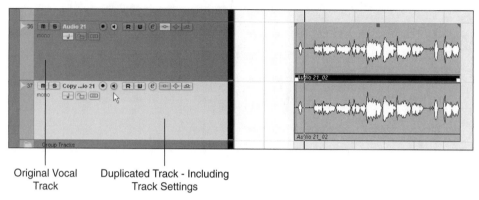

Original Vocal Track   Duplicated Track - Including Track Settings

Figure 5.24 A duplicate of the track you just recorded has been created.

4. Now *mute* the original track by selecting the yellow M.

5. Using the cursor, select the copied part(s) on the newly copied track (see Figure 5.25).

Mute Original Recording

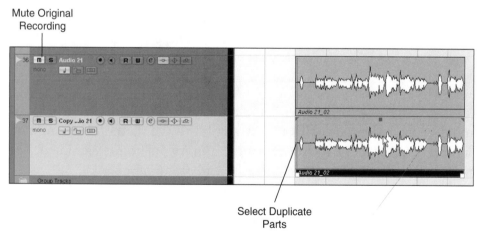

Select Duplicate Parts

Figure 5.25 Selecting the duplicate part on the duplicate track.

6. Now select Delete from the Edit menu, or press the Delete key or Backspace key on your computer keyboard (see Figure 5.26).

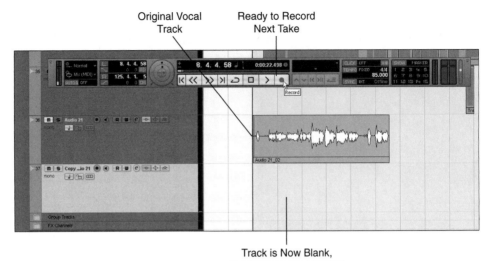

Figure 5.26 The copied part has been deleted, and the new track is ready to record the next vocal take.

7. Use this new blank track to record your next vocal take. When you need another vocal track, simply repeat these steps.

Note: To reduce these steps even further, you can duplicate the track before recording. This eliminates the need for deleting any parts that have been duplicated in the process.

Another way of working with multiple takes in Cubase is to record audio in stacked mode. This is very similar to the method I've outlined but can actually make the process more automated and streamlined. For more information on this, refer to the Cubase manual.

Experimenting with Vocals

What you've learned so far in this chapter should be enough to have you recording excellent vocal tracks. Even though a lot of recording engineers are very particular about their methods for recording vocals, sometimes you have to break the rules to achieve the best sound. If this means the singer holds the microphone during recording, yells into the microphone from across the room, or screams into the microphone at close range, then so be it. The studio should be looked at as a place to be creative and not just a place to accurately capture live sound.

Most studios have many different types of microphones at their disposal. You may not have that luxury, but keep in mind that changing the microphone is one of the standard ways to change the sound of a vocal recording.

Here are several other things you can try while recording vocals:

- Change the vocalist's distance from the microphone.

- Change the room in which the singer is being recorded. Add reflective or absorbent materials. You can even try recording the vocals outdoors or in the shower.

- Have the singer drink some warm tea with honey for a smooth vocal or smoke a cigar for a coarse vocal. Sometimes a little cardiovascular workout can get the singer's heart beating faster, adrenaline pumping, and lungs expanding. The physical state of the singer will make a huge difference in the sound of the recording. A singer with a cold will sound a lot different.

- Have the singer sing through a megaphone, a cardboard tube, a telephone, or another type of device.

- External effects processors can be used before the audio is recorded in Cubase. It's not uncommon to record vocals through guitar stomp box–type pedals if you're going for a grittier sound where high fidelity isn't necessarily the objective.

- A vocoder is the most popular way to achieve the "robot voice" effect. There are several types of vocoders, including software vocoder plug-ins you can use with Cubase. A MIDI keyboard is usually required to trigger the pitch of the note as it is spoken through the vocoder. Sometimes the best vocoder effect is done through an external synth before the signal even enters Cubase (see Figure 5.27).

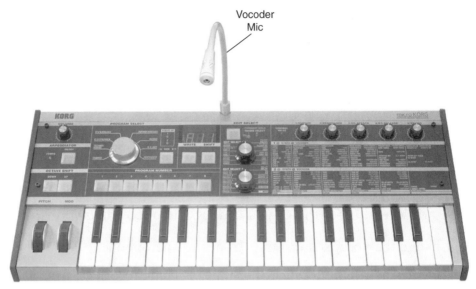

Figure 5.27 The microKORG keyboard synth with vocoder and built-in microphone.

If you really put some creative energy into recording your vocals, you will find some new and experimental ways to capture the best vocal performance possible with Cubase.

6 Recording Guitar and Bass

Obviously there are a lot of instruments out there besides keyboards. The most commonly used instrument besides keyboards and voice is the guitar. Guitars come in at least as many varieties as keyboards. Acoustic, electric, and bass guitars only scratch the surface. Because there are so many types, this chapter is dedicated to recording strategies only for these popular instruments.

Most guitar players can easily transition to a wide range of acoustic instruments: banjos, ukuleles, mandolins, 12-string guitars, high-string guitars, fiddles, pedal-steel guitars, nylon-string guitars, steel-string guitars...the list goes on. The sound of electric guitar can vary greatly by not only the type of guitar but also the type of amplification and effects used. When it comes to bass guitars, there are 5-strings, 6-strings, fretless, and upright acoustics, just to name a few.

A lot of what you have learned so far in this book can be applied to recording guitar and bass in Cubase, but there are specific, basic recording techniques you should be aware of to best record acoustic and electric guitars. Acoustic instruments and electric instruments should be handled in completely different ways. Because of this, I will break them up into two separate groups.

Recording Acoustic Instruments

Acoustic guitars—those that do not require amplification—vary widely. The most common type is the steel-string guitar (6-string), often used in country and rock music. Recording methods are very similar for all types of acoustics.

The amplification of an acoustic instrument is handled by the instrument itself. Most acoustic instruments offer what's referred to as a *sound hole* (see Figure 6.1) for amplification.

Figure 6.1 The sound hole on a 6-string acoustic guitar.

The sound hole on acoustic instruments is just the "output device." The sound is actually generated by several components, all within the instrument itself: the strings, fretboard (or neck), and body. Sound also depends on the method in which the guitar is played, e.g., using a guitar pick, steel slide, fingers, or a bow. Often, an acoustic instrument will offer what's called a *pickup* that's built into the guitar and usually located close to the sound hole (see Figure 6.2). The pickup is designed to capture the strings' vibrations and amplify them through an electronic output on the guitar, much like the output on other electric instruments.

Having a pickup on an acoustic instrument can come in very handy for live performances where amplification is necessary. If you plan on using a pickup in your Cubase studio, you should also refer to the section on recording electric guitar and bass in this chapter. Even though pickups can be very good at capturing the sound of an acoustic

Figure 6.2 The sound hole and pickup of a 4-string acoustic bass guitar.

instrument, most pickups cannot capture the full range of the instrument's sound. Most professional recordings of acoustic instruments use microphones with techniques similar to those covered in Chapter 5, "Recording Vocals."

Note: Sometimes when guitar players perform live, they not only use pickups to amplify their sound, they also use plugs that prevent sound from resonating through the sound hole. I highly recommend avoiding these sound hole plugs when working in a studio environment. They rob the guitar of its natural sound.

As with vocals, the most commonly used microphone when recording an acoustic instrument in a studio environment is a cardioid condenser microphone. You can use the same techniques as in vocal recording to find the best signal level without peaking. I recommend using mic pres, compressors/limiters, and EQ before the signal is actually recorded. Again, refer to Chapter 5 for specific instructions on these techniques.

Mic placement can also make a huge difference for a recorded guitar sound. The most common mic placement is close to the instrument's sound hole. A microphone that is too close to the sound hole, however, not only can get in the guitar player's way but also tends to amplify some frequencies more than others, particularly lower frequencies. Because of these two issues, the microphone is usually pointed toward the sound hole, but not placed directly over the hole, about a foot away. It should be pointed just at the sound hole's edge toward the neck of the guitar. The best way to experiment with sounds is to listen through speakers from outside the recording room while another person repositions the mic. When the right spot has been found, the engineer can inform the person placing the mic, and you can begin recording.

The position of the mic can change depending on the guitar player's style. If the guitarist is strumming loudly, sometimes the mic needs to be farther away. If the guitarist is playing a soft, jazzy solo, you might put the mic closer to the fretboard. Sometimes the only way to capture all the nuances of the performance is to use multiple microphones. Then you can mix the signals until you find the proper balance. There are two ways to go about recording guitar using this method. One is to blend the mics together and record the blended sound onto one or two audio tracks. The other way is to record each mic on a separate track and combine them during mixing. If the instrument also has a pickup, a lot of times the signal is also recorded from the pickup so that it can be blended as well.

Using multiple mics on one source can often cause an undesirable effect called *phasing*. Phasing occurs when two or more microphones adversely capture tonal qualities. Often the EQ and volume are affected by phasing. Sometimes it can be reduced by reversing the polarity of one of the microphones (possibly with a switch on the microphone or by using a mic cable wired with another pin configuration). Sometimes you can reduce phasing by switching microphones or changing the placement of the mic. Phasing issues are not always simple, and if you run into them a lot, your best option might be to revert to a single microphone.

Note: Nothing affects guitar sound more than the actual guitar itself. If the guitar player can't afford a very nice one, he or she should seriously consider renting one for the recording. This will make a world of difference to the sound. Also, new strings and tuning are both very important. The gauge of the strings will dramatically affect the sound as well. The heavier the string gauge, usually the fuller the guitar sound, but the more difficult the guitar is for some to play.

Recording an Acoustic Guitar in Cubase from Multiple Sources

First, place your mic and stand so that they are positioned appropriately. (Refer to the "Recording Acoustic Instruments" section earlier in this chapter for discussion of mic placement, and refer to Chapter 5 for guidance on setting up a mic stand.) Keep in mind that room noise (ambience) will be captured along with the sound of the guitar. This means you'll need to follow the same basic rules as if you were recording a vocal performance.

Next, follow the same setup procedures as described in Chapter 5. You can use the same walkthroughs to record acoustic guitar with effects or monitor the guitar with effects.

You can position several mics around the acoustic guitar during recording. There is no right or wrong setup when determining how many mics to use and where to place them. For the sake of simplicity, I will cover recording the guitar from its built-in pickup along with the microphone you should already have set up.

1. Set up another mono input in Cubase's VST connections with the same procedure you used to create the first mono input for the microphone. You can change the name of each input by clicking and typing in the name field as I have done in Figure 6.3.

2. Run a guitar cable (¼-inch male to ¼-inch male unbalanced audio cable) from the output of the guitar to another audio input on your sound card. Make sure that you match the device

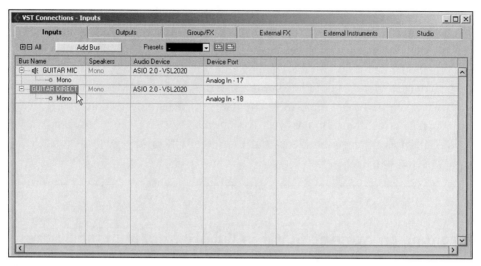

Figure 6.3 The names of the audio inputs have been changed to make them easier to identify.

port for the newly created audio input to the input of the sound card for which you ran the guitar cable. You should be using two separate device ports, as shown in Figure 6.3.

3. Create another mono audio track just below the audio track you created for your guitar mic. This time, change the input to reflect the newly created input, as shown in Figure 6.4. You can then apply effects to the input as you did with the other input channel and track.

4. Concentrate and modify the sound of each sound source by selecting and deselecting the Monitor button on the channel (see Figure 6.5). With both Monitor buttons enabled and both channels set in Record mode (i.e., with the red Record button enabled), you should hear both sound sources simultaneously. Also, make sure that your record levels are appropriate for both channels.

5. Make sure both tracks are record-enabled (i.e., their red buttons are selected), and click Record on the transport when you're ready. Both sources of the guitar will be recorded simultaneously.

Mic'ed Acoustic
Channel

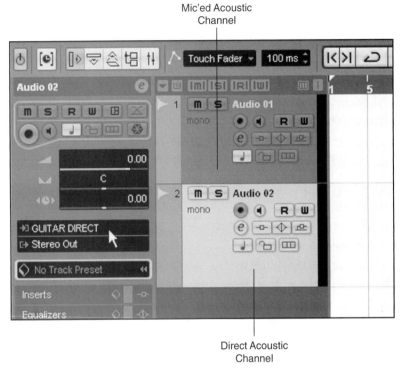

Direct Acoustic
Channel

Figure 6.4   A new audio track has been created and assigned to the new input.

Record Button   Monitor
Activated   Disabled

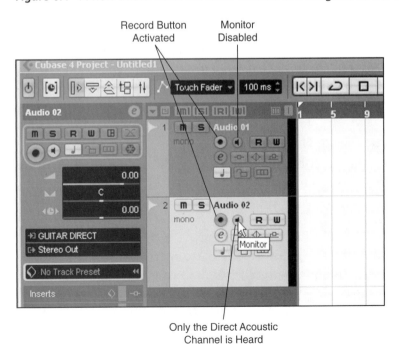

Only the Direct Acoustic
Channel is Heard

Figure 6.5   Toggle the Monitor buttons to isolate each sound source when making adjustments.

> **Note:** It's important to remember that whether you are using an acoustic guitar pickup or a microphone, it can capture ambient noise and feedback in the studio. You must monitor with headphones while recording, and the louder your headphone levels are, the greater the chance that you may still get feedback and bleed-through. It can be very tricky to record acoustic guitar without capturing bleed-through from the metronome, so be careful how loud you set the click. You may want to try a test run to make sure that you can't hear the click in the recording.

This simple procedure works with many instruments besides the guitar and can also be used with multiple sources, such as four microphones instead of the one in our example.

Most of the time you don't need to get too carried away with recording from multiple sources. The time to consider recording an instrument from multiple sources is when the instrument is the main focus of the musical arrangement. Otherwise, those little nuances you capture using multiple sources will generally be lost in the final mix. Most of the time the best-sounding recording stems from simply using a better guitar, a better microphone, a better guitar player, and possibly a better recording room. If the instrument doesn't sound good with one mic, don't expect it to sound better with two mics.

Preventing Click Bleed-Through

It can be difficult to record an acoustic instrument without getting bleed-through from the metronome in Cubase. Here are a few tricks you can try to prevent bleed-through yet still record the guitar playing in time during solo acoustic moments in the arrangement.

- First, record a "scratch" guitar track with a metronome. Once you've recorded the scratch guitar part, silence the metronome and record the second guitar part using the scratch guitar as a timing reference. This may not be as accurate timing-wise, but it will most likely greatly decrease the chances of having any click bleed-through on your track.

- Create your own click track by using a MIDI track and a VST instrument with a sound that will blend better if it bleeds through during a guitar performance. You can even create pauses where there could be bleed-through and change the audio level for each click so that it's still audible but less likely to bleed through to the guitar track.

- Use a visual metronome as opposed to an audible metronome. By selecting MIDI Click within the metronome setup, selecting a MIDI output (any you have listed), and deselecting the audio click, you can create a flashing metronome using the MIDI output indicator on the transport. This requires that the guitar player watch the computer screen during recording.

There are several other, more complicated ways to handle click bleed-through that involve more equipment, but the bottom line is that if there's a will, there's a way. Unfortunately, Cubase has not integrated a great visual metronome (such as one with numbers or a flashing light), but this may be something Steinberg develops in the future.

Even if a click makes its way to the final recording, there are ways to silence it using digital editing. I will discuss digital editing in more detail in Chapter 8, "Basic Editing."

Note: Hardwood floors and boots are not a good combination when recording toe-tapping, boot-wearing guitar players. If your guitar player has on hard-soled footwear, ask him to take it off, and put a rug or bit of carpet under his foot. Don't ask him to stop tapping his foot, because it may alter his performance.

Recording Electric Guitar and Bass

There are a lot of variables to consider when you introduce an electric instrument, but the good news is you're less likely to have feedback and bleed-through. There are two basic ways to record an electric guitar or bass: recording direct or using a microphone on the guitar or bass amplifier. Each method comes with its own guidelines, so I will explain them in separate sections.

Using a Microphone on a Guitar/Bass Amp

If you're recording heavy metal, rock, or blues (where the sound of the amplifier is a key sonic ingredient), you'll most likely want to record using a microphone on the guitar or bass amplifier. This setup is very similar to recording acoustic guitar except here the focus is on the amplifier, not on the guitar. Even though the amplifier is the output, as with acoustics, the guitar itself is the primary ingredient in a great recording. Guitar brands and types are not created equal. Even guitars of the same type vary depending on the year they were created and the way they have been maintained. Setup and string type also play a role. Guitar players who are serious about their craft spend a lot of time testing many guitars until they are comfortable with the way a guitar feels and sounds. Because of this, sometimes electric guitars have natural flaws such as hum or fret noise or slight intonation problems. Even though a guitar may have natural flaws, this does not mean that it's not a suitable recording guitar.

Most of the tweaking needed to get a great guitar sound when using an amp happens before the sound even reaches the microphone. If you aren't satisfied with the sound you are hearing from an amplifier, chances are you won't be satisfied with the sound of the recorded guitar. Finding the right guitar/amp combination can be difficult in itself. Often, guitar pedals, or stomp boxes, are used between the signal of the guitar and the amplifier. They can also greatly alter the way a guitar sounds. Sometimes these stomp boxes can be crucial to the guitar sound, but I highly recommend that guitar players remove the pedal from between the guitar and amp for song sections that don't require it. You can always capture the rest of the recording on another take. The best possible path of the guitar signal is directly from the guitar to the amplifier with a high-quality (shielded) guitar cable that isn't too long.

The hardest part about recording a guitar amp with a microphone is controlling the volume of the amplifier itself. To get a great distorted rock sound from a guitar amplifier, you need to push the amplifier so that it drives the speakers, which may even cause the speakers to distort themselves. Lower levels simply do not achieve the desired effect. The microphone needs to be placed near the amplifier's speaker cabinet. Guitar speaker cabinets usually contain anywhere from one to four speakers. A full Marshall stack actually consists of two speaker cabinets, which each contain four speakers. Even though you can use a full Marshall stack with one cabinet, the overall tonality of the guitar cabinet will be different using two cabinets. Using more speakers does not always mean that the cabinet is just louder. Guitar amps called *combo amps* are often used, and they usually consist of an amplifier and one or two speakers combined in one cabinet.

While I recommend cranking the volume on guitar amps to get the best sound from the amp/speakers, there are several things to be careful of when pushing the amp into the red:

- Many amps on the market are not perfectly designed. Sometimes, when an amp is playing at full capacity, certain notes (frequencies) will rattle parts of the cabinet. This can create an unpleasant sound. If this happens, try a different amp before recording at a lower volume. If that's not an option, you can also try recording direct, which has come a long way in recent years (see the next section, "Interfacing Direct Guitar and Bass").

- When guitar amps are cranked, they are usually very loud. Because of this, they are difficult to isolate when you are simultaneously using microphones to record other instruments. Sometimes the best way to handle this is by moving the amp to its own room, or sometimes to an isolation box that the guitar amp can be placed inside.

- Loud amps can really affect the way the environment around the amp sounds. They can cause stands, chairs, and a various other metal objects to rattle. They can also cause windows, light fixtures, wall paintings, and even the ceiling and floor to rattle. Although this sound is less likely to come across in a recording, it's possible it can affect the sound. If it does, try removing or padding the culprit, or changing rooms before changing the volume of the amp. You can also try moving or changing the position of the amp and/or possibly setting the amp on an elevated amp stand.

- Positioning a microphone over the amplified speaker for the best sound possible can be a deafening experience. Sometimes the best way is to wear ear plugs and adjust the mic, then journey back into the control room to hear how the amp sounds through the microphone. Popping ear plugs in and out can be a bit of a pain, but it may save your ears.

- The guitar player needs to hear the guitar and most likely some other tracks. You may need a somewhat long guitar cable to separate the guitar player from the amplifier, and the guitar player will need to monitor through headphones or through the studio control room monitors. You may find it tricky balancing the length of the guitar cable, the placement of the guitar player, and the guitar mix with other tracks. For more information on this, refer to Chapter 7, "Recording a Whole Band or Multiple Tracks at Once."

When positioning the microphone over the speakers of the amp, you'll often find the best sound by pointing the microphone just at the edge of one of the speakers in the cabinet. Since all speakers and speaker cabinets sound different, you should definitely try many configurations (various speakers and positions) before you commit to one for the recording. Sometimes it's easier to have another person adjust the microphone while you listen from the safety of the control room in the studio and relay to the other person whether it sounds good or bad. This can be tricky because when a guitar amplifier is cranking at deafening levels, it's hard for the microphone adjuster to hear through the headphones without going through a lot of pain. Visual signals and ear plugs for the microphone adjuster can save the adjuster some agony. For more information on using a *talkback*, which is an alternative communications system between control room and studio, check out Chapter 7.

The best type of microphone to place in front of a loud guitar or bass amp is a *dynamic cardioid microphone*, such as the Shure SM57. This microphone is excellent at handling loud volumes. Although it is fairly inexpensive and common, it is almost always the microphone of choice in world-renowned professional studios.

Note: While you are recording guitar, periodically check the microphone placement to make sure the microphone hasn't moved from its original position. Vibrations from high-volume amps sometimes cause microphone stands to loosen and turn or fall from their original position. A change in position can definitely affect your sound on the recording.

When it comes to actually recording electric guitar and setting up Cubase, you can do it the same way you would record an acoustic guitar or vocal (the only difference being you should adjust your input level on your mic pre and within Cubase so that the signal isn't always clipping). While the sound you're going for may be a gritty, distorted guitar sound, the best distortion is going to come from the amp and *not* Cubase or your mic pre. Any distortion or clipping in Cubase could actually result in an unusable recording down the road. If you want to add clipping as an effect in Cubase, it's easy enough to do after you've recorded the guitar at the right levels.

If the guitar part you're recording has a lot of parts that require sound changes, such as switching from a clean guitar sound to a distorted guitar sound or adding an effect such as wah-wah, I highly recommend that you record each part separately as an *overdub* so that you can make adjustments to each sound in order to achieve the best sound overall. Often, switching sounds can throw off the EQ and levels, and this can make a dramatic difference in the guitar sound. If the guitar player wants to play along with the band to achieve a live feel, then so be it, but most likely, every part should be re-recorded afterward.

Note: The term *overdub* refers to any track that is recorded after the original part has been recorded. These days, in the professional recording world, there's almost no such thing as a recording without overdubs. You shouldn't consider overdubs as "cheating" in the studio. Overdubs are very common and are just a way to go about getting the best sound possible and getting the most out of a multitrack recording studio.

It is very common when overdubbing guitars to double guitar parts in the studio. If you're wondering how a certain band achieved such a massive rhythm guitar sound in the studio, it might be because they recorded multiple tracks of the same part and mixed them together. Slight variations in performances can create larger-than-life guitar sound, and sometimes that's exactly what you need in a recording.

There are a lot of engineers who spend a lot of time finding ways to record electric guitar through various amps or processors simultaneously. Personally, I feel that you can add more to an electric guitar part in an overdub than you can by tracking multiple variations of guitar sounds simultaneously (as we went over with the acoustic guitar). If anything, you may want to try using two microphones on a speaker cabinet. Avoid splitting the signal from the guitar cable to other sources as this weakens the signal from the guitar source. There are no rules, and if you feel so inclined to tweak your guitars more, feel free—but remember that the sound starts with the guitar, and if the sound isn't right at the beginning, it most likely won't be at the end no matter how much you tweak it.

Interfacing Direct Guitar and Bass
Ten years ago it would have been hard to imagine that you could record heavy-metal guitar by plugging a guitar into a computer, but time and technology have changed things dramatically. It used to be that the only type of guitar recorded direct was a "clean-sounding" electric guitar, but these days there are programs that can make a direct guitar sound as if it were played through a Marshall stack, and it's pretty darn convincing. The bottom line is, if you can't afford a great-sounding guitar amp or you can't record at high volume, you *can* record direct to Cubase with a guitar or bass and it will sound good.

If you *do* have a great amp and guitar; are recording rock, heavy metal, blues, or country; and can record at high volumes, I recommend using the standard way described previously. No matter *how* you record, you should be aware of the potential that you have by recording guitar direct.

One of the most attractive features of recording guitar or bass direct to Cubase is that you can later completely change the sound of the guitar without having to replay the guitar part. This is similar to recording a

MIDI part and then changing the instrument later. If you are a person who doesn't really know what sort of sound you're looking for until you have developed the overall mix a little more, this can be a great tool. You can also automate your effects, which can take away some of the juggling a guitar player may have to do during a performance and offers possibilities that aren't available when not recording direct.

Even though you *can* simply plug a guitar into Cubase and record direct without any third party plug-ins or additional hardware, if you're going for a quality recording, you'll most likely want to incorporate some hardware and software plug-ins that don't come with Cubase. When it comes to hardware, you don't need much; however, there are quite a few possibilities on the market. As long as your sound card has an instrument input with some sort of level control, you can get by without using additional outboard gear. If your sound card doesn't have a good instrument input, you may want to look into trying one of these hardware interfaces.

- A company by the name of Tech 21 makes an interface called the SansAmp. This is a very popular direct box for guitarist and bassists. There are several models to choose from. The most basic model is called the XDI (see Figure 6.6), which acts as a signal amplifier and a way to convert your ¼-inch unbalanced guitar line into a balanced mic line. There are other models that provide distortion and overdrive effects that actually rival those of amplified speaker cabinets.

- A company called Line 6 uses a technology slightly different from that of SansAmp called *amp modeling*. One of the most popular interfaces available is the POD. There are several POD models available. The POD X3 (see Figure 6.7) not only works for guitar and bass but also for vocals. It has a USB output, which allows you to bypass your sound card altogether. You can also run the digital outputs directly to the digital inputs of your sound card for "better-than-analog" quality. Line 6 has quite an impressive variety of gadgets that can make your direct recording experience much more fun. For more info, visit http://www.line6.com.

Figure 6.6 The SansAmp XDI.

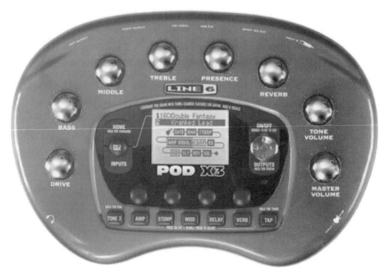

Figure 6.7 The Line 6 POD X3 amp modeling interface.

■ M-Audio may have the market cornered on most lower–cost, high-quality sound cards and MIDI interfaces, but they also have a guitar interface called the Black Box (see Figure 6.8), which is very similar to the POD.

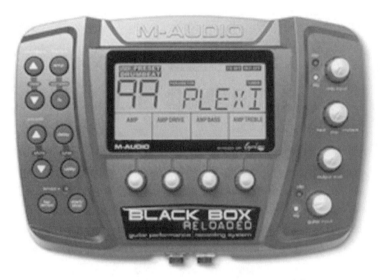

Figure 6.8 M-Audio's Black Box amp modeling interface.

- Waves is a company well known for its high-quality studio plug-ins. It has teamed up with guitar legend Paul Reed Smith to create a guitar interface that comes with a software plug-in package called GTR (see Figure 6.9). Unlike the POD and Black Box, the GTR is similar to the SansAmp XDI. By using your computer's processor, you can supposedly achieve better results in sound quality than with the POD or Black Box, but this is more for recording than live performances.

These are just a few suggestions. There are a lot of other possibilities. You can also use stomp boxes between the guitar and computer in a similar way to these interfaces. The only real way to determine whether the internal effects in Cubase are better than using a stomp box is to compare them while your guitar is hooked up to the computer and ready to go. You'll probably find that you have a lot more options using Cubase's internal effects, but if you're going for a more natural or live sound, you may want to revert to the guitar pedals.

Besides Waves GTR, there are several manufacturers that make software plug-ins specifically for recording direct guitar. Here are some of the more popular choices:

Figure 6.9 Waves GTR amp modeling software and hardware package.

- Native Instruments makes a lot of plug-ins that are compatible with Cubase. Guitar Rig is a very popular program that includes many amp simulations and effects. The Guitar Rig 3 Kontrol Edition comes with a pedal interface that has many useful inputs and outputs (see Figure 6.10). This package works similarly to Waves GTR but gives the guitar player even more flexibility on the interface. For more information, see http://www.nativeinstruments.com.

- AmpliTube, similar to Guitar Rig comes from a company called IK Multimedia. For more information, see http://www.amplitube.com. The same company also makes software specifically designed for bass guitar called Ampeg, which models the sound of the classic (and popular) Ampeg brand of bass amplifiers (see Figure 6.11).

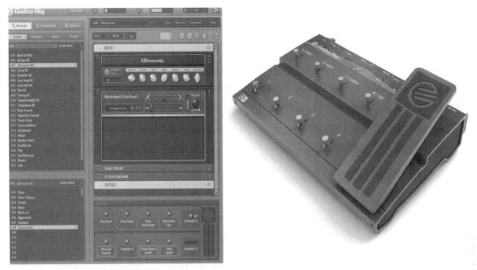

Figure 6.10   Native Instruments' Guitar Rig 3 Kontrol Edition.

Figure 6.11   IK Multimedia's Ampeg bass amplification modeling software.

- Another company, Izotope, offers a program called Trash that works similarly to Guitar Rig and AmpliTube (though Izotope does not have the variety of hardware solutions that other manufacturers do). For more information, see http://www.izotope.com.

Again, if you're on a strict budget the, amp simulator plug-in that comes with Cubase 4 can be used with a direct guitar and will work wonders in a pinch.

Even though these software plug-ins and hardware options are some of the most popular available today, there are always products in development. This technology is fairly new and is rapidly becoming important to have at your disposal.

Tips and Tricks for Recording Electric Guitar and Bass

Once you've decided which way you would like to record electric guitar or bass, there are ways to get the most out of each type of recording, whether it's direct or a miked amplified speaker.

Compression is commonly used on both guitar and bass when recording to get the best SNR and sustain out of each instrument without clipping the signal. Just like with recording vocals, compression is best used *before* the signal reaches the amplifier or computer. In this case, a hardware compressor/limiter is definitely the way to go. You can also use a compression plug-in to record guitar or bass direct. For the best results when using this type of compression, apply the plug-in to the input signal as I demonstrated for recording a vocal in Chapter 5.

Compression may be applied sparingly or liberally depending on the style of music. It is often tricky to find the right setting because the effect itself can be a little hard for some to hear. Here are a few settings for electric guitar you can experiment with:

- If you're looking for a chunky rock rhythm guitar sound, try setting your threshold around −15 dB, the ratio around 5:1, the attack around 10 ms, and the release around 100 ms.

- If you need some chimey, sustained guitar chords, try setting the threshold to around −18 dB, the ratio to around 10:1, the attack to around 150 ms, and the release to 950 ms.

- If you're looking for some Nashville chicken pickin', try setting the threshold to around −30 dB, the ratio to 6:1, the attack to 1 ms, and the release to 100 ms.

- For a clean jazz or R&B sound, try adjusting the threshold to around −28 dB, the ratio to 10:1, the attack to 50 ms, and the release to 40 ms.

- If you're looking for the perfect funk tone, try adjusting the threshold to −22 dB, the ratio to 7:1, the attack to 60 ms, and the release to 80 ms.

A lot of variables are going to affect how these settings perform (the type of guitar, the actual player, the compressor type, etc.), but this should at least get you started. Use your ear to help you the rest of the way. The same thing goes for bass guitar. When using compression on both electric guitar and bass, keep in mind that compression reduces dynamics and should be used only to enhance the sound, not so much to *color* the sound. If you're having trouble finding the proper setting, choose a low ratio (4:1 or lower) and make sure that your signal peaks at or below 0 dB by adjusting the limiter to 0 dB or lower. Try to train your ear to hear the slight variations in the settings of the compressor. If you need more help with compression, try Googling "compressor limiter."

One of the downfalls of recording electric guitar or bass in a studio environment is that players are probably used to standing directly in front of their amplified speaker cabinet. That can help them hear themselves better, and it can also improve their performance by changing the way they feel when they play at loud volumes. Unfortunately, the only way for them to achieve that feeling during recording is to play in the same room as the amp, which could mean deafness from the sheer volume of the amp. Feedback can get out of control. One substitute would be to have the guitar or bass player play in the control room while listening on the control room monitors, rather than headphones. By using the control room monitors, a performer can get a little more from the feel of the guitar and can also use the speakers to achieve effects similar to the feedback and harmonics they know from working in front of an amplified speaker. This technique should work whether you are using a guitar amplifier or recording direct into Cubase.

It's quite common for electric bass to be recorded direct in the studio environment. It's also somewhat common to record the direct signal along with a signal from the amplified speaker cabinet. A lot of times, these two signals can work well together when combined later in a mix. To do this, a *direct box* (see Figure 6.12) is often used for the bass guitar, and the signal is split from the direct box to the bass amp and to an input on your computer's sound card. The balanced signal usually runs into a preamp before entering the computer, as shown in Figure 6.13. This configuration is much like recording an acoustic guitar using a pickup and a microphone. Because it can handle loud signals and works well with bass frequencies, a popular microphone to use when miking a bass amplifier is the Sennheiser MD421 II (see Figure 6.14). This same microphone is often used when recording acoustic kick drums as well.

Figure 6.12 The Whirlwind Director direct box.

When using amp-modeling software such as Guitar Rig, there are two ways to process the signal. One way is to apply the effect to the input signal, similar to the way I demonstrated for applying compression to

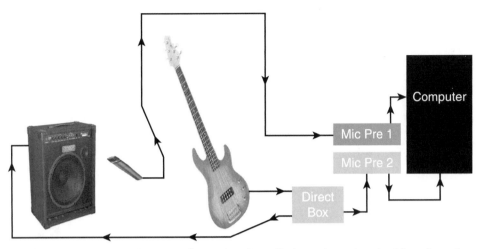

Figure 6.13 A possible basic configuration for splitting a bass signal with a direct box and recording from two sources.

Figure 6.14 The Sennheiser MD421 II dynamic cardioid microphone.

vocals in Chapter 5. The other is to apply the effect to the track signal, similar to my approach to a reverb effect with vocals in Chapter 5. By applying the effect to the track, you will be recording a dry signal from the guitar and monitoring through the distortion. This method is the opposite of the way an amplified speaker is recorded, but it has several advantages. The biggest is that you can completely modify your "amplified sound" anytime after recording (just as you could change your reverb setting after recording the vocal part in Chapter 5). This gives you the freedom to later make changes you would not be able to make if the amplified sound were recorded on the track along with the guitar part itself. Using this technique, you can actually double one guitar part with multiple instances of the effect, as if several different guitar sounds were played at one time. To do this, duplicate the track and change the guitar sound for the new track while keeping both tracks active in the mix.

When you're happy with the sound, bounce the dry guitar track along with the amplified sound so that the sound becomes its own fully processed guitar track. When you're done, the original dry track can be muted and saved (in case you decide to change the sound again later). There are several benefits to bouncing down the guitar effects to a single processed track. It saves CPU power for your PC, and it gives you a more finished version of what you are hearing. Sometimes software plug-ins tend to create errors when your system is not performing at its best. These errors include dropouts and digital noise. When you receive a dropout during processing, you may actually hear the dry guitar sound in the mix of the processed sound. Most of the time, this is not the sound you'll want to hear in the final mix. You can either try bouncing again or use some digital editing to fix the glitch before it makes it into your final mix. For more information on bouncing (or exporting audio), check out Chapter 9, "Mixing It Down." For information on digital editing see Chapter 8.

Stomp boxes (guitar and bass foot pedals) are fun to play with and great at achieving a live sound in the studio, but Cubase's digital effects and those that come with many of the guitar-effect plug-ins I've mentioned are far superior. There are several reasons for this. First and foremost, the digital technology of the software is usually far more advanced than that of a foot pedal, and that translates to higher-quality processing. Although pedals have characteristics that give them a certain charm, plug-in effects can also be automated so that your delays fall on the appropriate beats, the distortion increases or decreases, the chorus or flange speeds up or slows down, and the sound effects turn on or off without your having to jump up and down during a performance. For more information on automating effects in Cubase, refer to Chapter 9.

Note: Although it is possible to automate effects so that they change during a performance, I find that automating is easier after the guitar has been recorded. If you need to use several different types of effects during different parts of the song, it's easier to overdub a new guitar track with a different setup for each part than to worry about changing effects in the middle of a track.

If you have to run a long cable from the guitar (in the control room) and a guitar amp (maybe in a closet or another isolated room), it's much better to run a balanced cable than a regular, unbalanced guitar cable. Unbalanced cables tend to pick up more noise and lose their signal over great lengths. Unless the guitar amp has a balanced input, you'll need to convert the guitar's unbalanced signal to a balanced signal and then revert the balanced signal to an unbalanced signal once the cable has reached the amp's unbalanced line input. There are several ways to do this. A company by the name of Radial has made this simple by introducing SGI (Studio Guitar Interface) (see Figure 6.15). The SGI

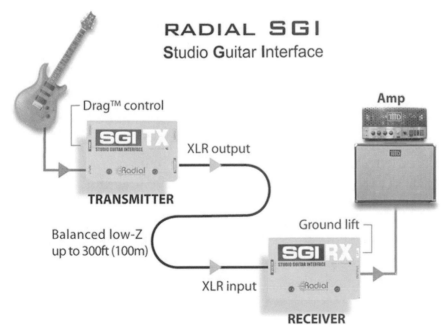

RADIAL SGI
Studio Guitar Interface

Drag™ control

XLR output

TRANSMITTER

Balanced low-Z
up to 300ft (100m)

Ground lift

XLR input

RECEIVER

Amp

Figure 6.15 The Radial SGI setup.

consists of input and output boxes you connect with a regular XLR (balanced mic) cable. Whatever you do, don't try to use a wireless system (such as a Nady, Samson, or Shure) to run the guitar into an amp in the studio. There are way too many complications with wireless systems, and you'll be asking for headaches.

It's important to check the guitar or bass tuning periodically while you record. Often, guitars and basses get out of tune while they're being played, and you may not be aware of it until you go to mix. Correcting the pitch of single bass notes in Cubase is not very difficult when using some pitch-correction tools or plug-ins, but correcting the pitch of a chord (multiple strings at once) can be next to impossible.

In Chapter 3, "Before You Record...," I mentioned how to get rid of hums, buzzes, and other noises. Guitars and basses are notorious for hums and buzzes. Make sure you kill any dimmer switches, fluorescent lights, and, most important, CRT monitors and TVs while you're recording. If you own a CRT monitor for your computer rig and you plan on recording a lot of guitar and bass, you should seriously consider buying an LCD (flat panel) monitor instead. You'll save yourself a lot of grief.

On a final note, a lot of guitar amps and bass amps have what is called a *direct out*, usually on the back of the amp. While it is possible to run a line directly from these outputs into the computer, it's not usually recommended. Although it may work with a lot of bass rigs, most of the time the sound quality is far below the quality of recording a guitar through a miked, amplified speaker or direct using plug-ins. The only possible exception to this rule is for amps with amp-modeling effects, such as those by Line 6, where using a direct out may not make any difference to the sound due to the nature of the amp-modeling technology. Bass players who are really happy with the sound of their bass head (amplifier) may wish to go directly out of the head for recording. Sometimes the built-in compression and EQ in a bass head is the ideal solution. If you have a choice of using a balanced XLR direct out and an unbalanced direct out line, always opt for the balanced output for a better recording.

7 Recording a Whole Band or Multiple Tracks at Once

Now you've learned how to record MIDI keyboards, MIDI drum kits, vocals, acoustic and electric guitars, and bass. With what you've learned so far, you can pretty much apply the same techniques to individually record almost any instrument on the planet! This is great news, but there is something magical about capturing the live performance of an entire band playing a well-rehearsed song. That magic can sometimes get lost when each instrument is recorded on its own. Now that you understand what each instrument requires for the best sound possible, it's time to explore your options for capturing an entire band or a section of instruments (such as acoustic drums) all in one take, yet on separate tracks.

Recording a full band or multiple tracks at once is most likely going to require a lot more equipment, accessories, and physical space out of your Cubase studio. The hardware for recording multiple tracks at once can be expensive and usually involves a great deal of knowledge in order to fully understand. In today's world, *most* professional music producers own DAW (digital audio workstation) studios with minimal equipment, and when it comes time for tracking, or for the final mix, they take their project to a professional, world-class studio. Doing this affords the producer the best sound, gives him ample tweaking time (from a home studio), provides amazing results, and costs a fraction of what the same record would have 10 years ago. My best advice for someone who owns a Cubase studio, but only occasionally records bands, would be to track the band at a professional studio. Whether or not the studio is equipped with Cubase isn't important. As long as you are able to transfer the audio tracks to a digital file format (such as WAV or AIF), you will have plenty to work with when you take the project back to your own studio.

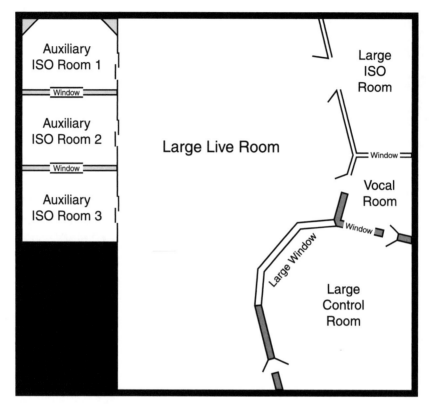

Figure 7.1 The layout of a large professional recording studio.

Even though the idea of using another studio (and probably paying an hourly or daily rate) sort of goes against the whole concept of owning a do-it-yourself Cubase studio, consider what you could be passing up by not using another studio:

- Most studios come with an engineer who knows and understands the studio and all the equipment that comes with it. Some studios even provide assistant engineers and runners who may be able to help you out during the session.

- Most professional studios provide expensive gear (such as a mixing console, microphones, mic pres, compressors, and baffles) that most home studios don't have.

- Most studios provide not only great-sounding recording rooms but also acoustically designed control rooms. The rooms sound better than most home studios, and they offer better isolation for multiple players.

- When you're paying someone else to worry about the technical issues with recording, you can concentrate more on actually making good music.

- The musicians get *real studio* recording experience.

- The studio atmosphere may actually inspire the band to perform better than they would normally.

- If you're lucky, you might even get free bagels, fruit, and coffee!

The idea of paying a studio may seem crazy to a lot of bands, but studio rates are pretty competitive in most cities. I've seen professional studios charge as little as $15 an hour (*with* a recording engineer)! A cost this low can be a lot more affordable for a band (especially if everyone's chipping in) than buying a lot of expensive equipment to use at home with Cubase.

Although the option to record at a professional studio may make sense for some, it's simply not a possibility or a necessity for *all* bands. For this reason, I will discuss the basics of how to record a band from a home Cubase studio. If you have already decided that taking your band to another studio is the right choice, you can skip to the end of this chapter for more information on working with another studio. If you've decided that your Cubase studio is the only studio you need, please read on.

When it comes to recording a live band or multiple tracks at once, each performer must be able to hear the mix the way that works best for them. This could mean that a separate monitor mix may be important for each member of the band. Also, as when recording individual instruments, each instrument must be captured in the best way possible. Communication can become very important and difficult when working with several performers at once. The most important piece of hardware to make your life easier on all of these levels is a good mixing console (also called a mixer or mixing board) (see Figure 7.2).

Figure 7.2 A professional-quality mixing console, the Midas Verona.

There are a lot of different mixing consoles on the market. You may already own one. It's important you understand how a mixing console works so you know what you need for recording.

Understanding an Analog Mixing Console

All mixers have two basic sections: the *input* and the *output*. Most analog recording mixers have another basic section known as the *monitor* section. Most mixing consoles appear very similar to the virtual mixer in Cubase. The most widely recognized section of the mixing console is the input section. The input section is where everything (instruments, vocals, tape machines, etc.) interfaces with the mixer. In this section each instrument receives its own channel of gain, EQ, volume, and pan. The output section is where the input's signal gets routed to its final destination within the console itself. The output section (of a console) includes master outputs as well as group (bus) outs. These outputs usually direct the sound to a recording source, in your case your computer's sound card and Cubase.

Note: Even though Cubase 4 allows you to record up to 256 tracks simultaneously, you will most likely be limited by the number of outputs on your mixing console, the number of inputs on your sound card, and your computer's overall capabilities.

The monitor section of a mixing console is strictly designed as a sub-mixer within the mixing console, and its sole purpose is to enable you to hear the inputs without using the output section. The monitor section was originally intended to enable you to hear the signal as it was coming from the recorder so you could hear what the *final* sound would be.

Because there are a tremendous number of possibilities for signal routing, I've used a popular 24-channel mixing console, the Mackie 24x8 (see Figure 7.3), and 24 channels of a popular sound card, i.e. three PreSonus FP10 FireWire recording interfaces chained together (see Figure 7.4), to demonstrate one of the most complex home-recording setups

Figure 7.3 The Mackie 24x8 recording console.

Figure 7.4 The PreSonus FP10 (8 inputs, chain enabled, rackmountable) FireWire sound card.

imaginable while simplifying it as much as possible. I won't go into great detail on how to operate the hardware. You'll need your hardware manuals for that. Instead I will go into great depth on hardware configurations for your Cubase studio. Most of these configurations will work with other DAWs as well, but I will address some points specific to Cubase.

The Mackie 24x8 is a somewhat large, lower-cost analog recording console. Most digital mixers (both hardware and software) have been modeled after the classic analog mixer. Using the following scenario, you should be able to compare how settings can be made with many other mixers available on the market, regardless of whether they're analog or digital.

I've told you about the equipment; now here's the scenario. You will be recording a seven-piece band: a singer, an electric guitar player, a bass player, a drummer, a percussionist, a keyboardist/pianist, and an acoustic guitar player. To make things more difficult, check out this nightmare list of things they require as they play live:

- The band will be playing with 12 prerecorded tracks that they must be able to hear.

- The drummer needs a loud click track, but the rest of the band will not be using a click, and they don't want to hear it in their monitors.

- The drummer will be playing an all-acoustic five-piece kit with a hi-hat and three other cymbals.

- The keyboardist brought a rack of seven synths (two of which have multiple outputs) and has prerecorded 18 MIDI tracks that the band will need to hear when performing live.

- The keyboardist will also be playing a grand piano and singing backup vocals during the take.

- The acoustic guitar player will also be singing backup.

- The electric guitar player brought a guitar amp that is wired in stereo and wants to hear and record both sides of the stereo signal.

- The singer needs to hear reverb on his voice when he sings but would like to record the vocal dry.

- The percussionist is using an electronic percussion pad and would like to record the MIDI live. At the same time, she will also be playing live tambourine and singing backup vocals.

- The bass player would like to record both a direct signal and a miked signal from the bass.

- Besides the control room in your home Cubase studio, you have a living room with a piano and a bedroom. Luckily, you also have a few closets, a portable vocal isolation booth, and a few homemade studio baffles.

First of all, don't panic. This is a complicated setup even in a professional studio, and hopefully you won't be doing anything this crazy. However, if you're recording a lot of bands, you will run into quite a few of these technical issues.

Connecting the Sound Cards to the Mixing Console

First of all, to keep things simple, you really shouldn't worry so much about mixing your session down on your Mackie 24x8. All the mixing can be handled internally within Cubase, and the quality will be much better than using the external mixer in this case. This means that those 12 prerecorded tracks the band needs to hear can be premixed and grouped to two outputs (for a stereo mix) out of the 24 available outputs you have on your sound card. This also means that you'll only need to run two cables out of one of the PreSonus FP10s to the Mackie console to hear this mix. Since you need an audio click from Cubase only for the drummer, you'll also need to run another mono or stereo line out from one (or two) of the PreSonus FP10s' outputs. Last but not least, you'll probably want to monitor the sound going to the computer. Since you can control all your monitoring levels within the Cubase mixer, you'll only need a stereo line out for the entire mix that's going to the computer. This means that out of the 24 available outputs on the three linked PreSonus FP10s, you're only using six total outputs max.

There are many ways you can patch these six outputs to the Mackie board, but this is a very complex session, and it's going to push the Mackie to its limits. On a mixer, *stereo returns* are very similar to inputs on a console. This Mackie has a special option to route the incoming signal to a stereo return so that it blends with the entire mix in the headphones or in the control-room mix, but does not necessarily get sent to the recording source. You can also control the level of the signal from the console itself. This is an ideal input for the pre-recorded tracks that the band needs to monitor because this is music that they will only need to *hear* (not record), and when using this input, you can turn those tracks on or off in two separate headphone monitors and the main control-room monitors.

The level of the click for the drummer can be controlled from Cubase, so the input needs to be something that is directed to the drummer's headphones. The external input on the Mackie is set up perfectly for monitoring this sort of application. By using the simple External Input button on either one of the headphone controls, the signal can be turned on or off in the drummer's headphones without a hitch.

Since you'll be monitoring the band's input signal using the Mackie, the output signal from Cubase (after the band's signal has been recorded) should not be heard at the same time. Sometimes it's a good idea to listen to what you've recorded and make sure it works. By bussing and connecting the entire mix from Cubase to the 2-tk (two track) input on the Mackie, you can toggle between the two signals to hear the difference between the pre sound and post sound. For more info on these inputs and this configuration, visit the Mackie Web site and explore the PDF manual of the 24x8 console at http://www.mackie.com. Have a look at Figures 7.5–7.8 for details on everything I've discussed so far.

Three Separate
Busses for Routing

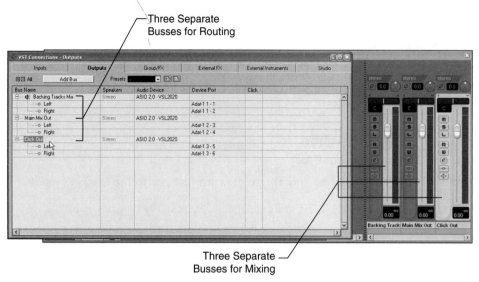

Three Separate
Busses for Mixing

Figure 7.5   A closeup of the Cubase mixer set up with three stereo output busses.

Deselect Click in the Fields of the
Busses You Don't Want to Hear the Click

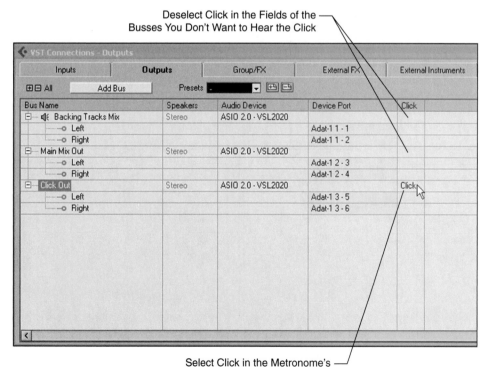

Select Click in the Metronome's
Click Field to Hear the Click on That Bus

Figure 7.6   Setting the click to its own output.

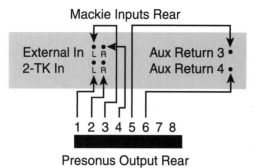

Figure 7.7 Basic connections from the sound card's output to the Mackie's inputs.

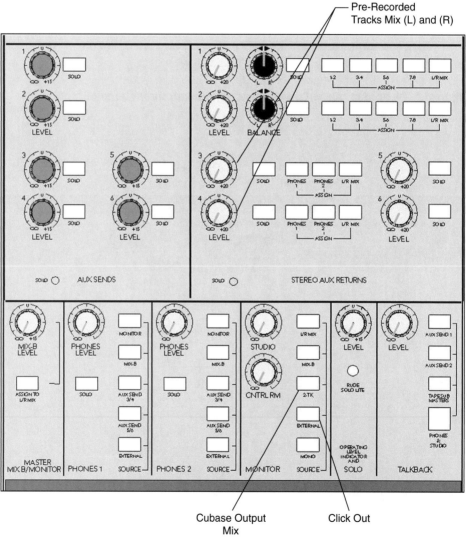

Figure 7.8 A closeup diagram of the Mackie displaying where the three separate signals will be mixed.

Note: Instead of patching your control-room reference monitors directly from a headphone amp or sound card, when using a recording console, you should patch the speakers to the control-room output of the console. This should enable you to hear both the prerecorded audio signals and postrecorded audio signals. This should also give you a volume control (for your speakers) that will not affect the recording levels. A headphone cue amp(s) will still be necessary for the band to use with their headphones.

Hooking Up the MIDI Devices for Recording MIDI and Monitoring

In our little scenario, the keyboard player has preprogrammed 18 MIDI tracks and brought a rack of seven synths. The percussionist will also be playing a Roland HPD-15 electronic percussion multi-pad and will need to record the MIDI performance as well as hear the Roland HPD-15.

Even though this may sound like a nightmare to non-keyboardists, recording the MIDI and dealing with MIDI tracks are really not major concerns. MIDI tracks contain only data. The data from the MIDI tracks must be played back through the keyboardist's rack of synths or the percussionist's MIDI percussion multi-pad. When it comes to the audio signal, the number of MIDI tracks is irrelevant. What *is* important is the number of synths used and the number of physical audio outputs they require. In our scenario, the keyboardist is using a rack of seven synths. Five of these seven require a stereo audio output, and two of the seven have been configured to use four outputs each. The percussion pad also needs to be hooked up in stereo. This means that the synth's combined outputs (counting stereo outputs as two separate output sources—left and right) total 20 (see Figure 7.9 for a visual breakdown). Monitoring signals from *20 separate sources* will be the largest obstacle we have to face during a live playdown.

The good news is you don't have to record the synth's audio at this time. The band simply needs to hear the synths during the performance. The only thing you'll actually need to record is the MIDI from the percussionist's electronic kit. There are many ways you can patch the MIDI to the synths. Your PreSonus FP10s are equipped with

SYNTH	OUTPUTS	TOTAL
GEM RP-X	STEREO	2
GEM GM-X	STEREO	2
MOOG MINIMOOG VOYAGE	STEREO	2
Akai MPC-4000	OUTPUTS 1-4	4
Korg Radius	STEREO	2
Alesis Andromeda	OUTPUTS 1-4	4
Nord Electro 2	STEREO	2
Roland SPD-20	STEREO	2
	TOTAL OUTPUTS	20

Figure 7.9 Calculating the total number of audio outputs from the synths.

one MIDI In and one MIDI Out each. You can use one FP10's MIDI In and Out exclusively for recording the percussionist (refer to Chapter 4, "Recording MIDI," for more information on setting up MIDI drums). For the rack of synths, you need to concern yourself only with using the remaining MIDI Outs on the FP10s because the MIDI has already been recorded. Since you have only two MIDI Outs left, you will need to connect the synths in a manner known as *daisy chaining,* which involves connecting the synths to each other.

Each MIDI Out is capable of outputting 16 MIDI channels of data. Using three MIDI Outs, you can output a total of 48 MIDI channels of data (16 channels × 3 outs). Since we've decided to dedicate our MIDI output to the percussionist, this leaves you with 32 output channels. Since our keyboardist has recorded 18 MIDI tracks, the maximum number of MIDI channels he can use is 18. This means that even though you have only two MIDI Outs, you actually have room for an additional 14 MIDI tracks assigned to their own MIDI channels. see Figure 7.10 for a breakdown of the MIDI tracks, MIDI channels, and MIDI Outs. see Figure 7.11 for an example of how you can daisy chain the MIDI within the rack of synths to make this scenario work out for you.

Now that we've solved the MIDI side of the scenario, let's concentrate on the real problem: how do we *hear* the 20 audio outputs while we're recording using a 24-channel mixing console? Fortunately, the Mackie 24x8 has been designed to handle this.

TRACK	MIDI CHANNEL	SOUND	SYNTH	OUTPUTS		TOTAL
MIDI 1	A1	Piano	GEM RP-X	STEREO		2
MIDI 2	A2	String Pad	GEM GM-X	STEREO		2
MIDI 3	A3	Lush Strings	GEM GM-X	STEREO	x	
MIDI 4	A4	Choir Male	GEM GM-X	STEREO	x	
MIDI 5	A5	Choir Female	GEM GM-X	STEREO	x	
MIDI 6	A6	Cello	GEM GM-X	STEREO	x	
MIDI 7	B1	Fat Synth	MOOG MINIMOOG VOYAGER	STEREO		2
MIDI 8	B2	Big Bang	Akai MPC-4000		1	1
MIDI 9	B3	Scratch	Akai MPC-4000		1	1
MIDI 10	B4	Electro	Akai MPC-4000		1	1
MIDI 11	B5	zap	Akai MPC-4000		1	1
MIDI 12	B6	Synth Choir 1	Korg Radius	STEREO		2
MIDI 13	B7	Synth Choir 1(2)	Korg Radius	STEREO	x	
MIDI 14	A7	Buzzy Synth	Alesis Andromeda		1	1
MIDI 15	A8	Tight Bass	Alesis Andromeda		1 x	
MIDI 16	A9	Funk Clav	Alesis Andromeda		1	1
MIDI 17	A10	Phased Out	Alesis Andromeda	STEREO		2
MIDI 18	B8	Juicy synth	Nord Electro 2	STEREO		2
MIDI 19	C1	Latin Percussion	Roland SPD-20	STEREO		2

MIDI CHANNELS A1-9= 1 PRESONUS MIDI OUT
MIDI CHANNELS B1-8= 1 PRESONUS MIDI OUT
MIDI CHANNELS C1 = 1 PRESONUS MIDI OUT
TOTAL MIDI TRACKS AND CHANNELS=19 *(including the new percussion track)*
TOTAL MIDI OUTS= 3 *(1 OUT FROM EACH PRESONUS)*
Note:each Presonus is capabale of outputting up to 16 MIDI channels
X= OUTPUT IS SHARED WITH ANOTHER OUTPUT

Figure 7.10 Calculating the total number of MIDI tracks, MIDI channels, and MIDI Outs.

The answer to this problem is something I've mentioned before: the *monitor* section of the console. When you're monitoring on the console, that audio signal is used only for monitoring. The signal you're hearing through the monitor section does not pass through to the recording device. This means that the monitor section works perfectly for the synths because we're recording and playing back MIDI, which has nothing to do with the Mackie board. We simply need to hear the synths while we record the other instruments.

As I also mentioned, not all boards are created equal, and a lot do not have an extensive monitor section. In some circumstances, you would actually have to use an additional mixer to blend the 20 inputs into a stereo mix and then run the stereo mix into an audio return on the console. This process is known as *submixing* and can be handled in many other ways. To use the monitor section on the Mackie, just connect the 20 audio outputs to the tape returns.

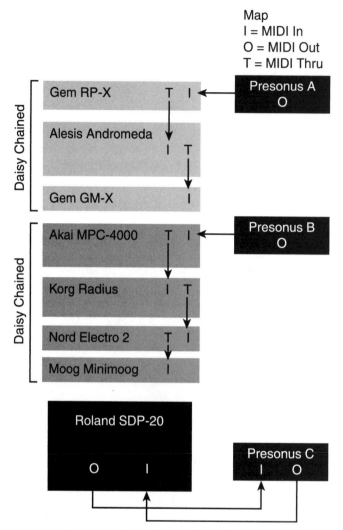

Figure 7.11 A possible MIDI configuration for this scenario using a daisy chain.

Note: Often, access to the monitor section of the mixing console is through what's known as the *tape returns*. In the good old days, people recorded on magnetic tape. To hear what they recorded, they played back the signal from the tape machine through the tape returns of the mixing console. Maybe they'll change the names on these monitor section inputs someday, seeing as how so many people record on DAWs now.

Mackie designed this mixing console so you can split the EQ section and use a portion on the monitor section and a portion on the input channel (the live instruments you'll be recording). This is a nice option when you need to get the mix just right for the performers. Sometimes getting a good headphone mix is better than having a lot of EQ available on a performer's instrument during recording, and since the audio on these synths is not running through Cubase at all, you cannot use Cubase to control their EQ (unless you're a master MIDI programmer and the synths have built-in EQ).

Note: The way the Mackie board has been designed, it may be in your best interest to monitor the prerecorded tracks through the tape returns instead of the aux returns. Again, since the tracks are premixed within Cubase, you will need only two channels of tape returns to monitor your entire mix within Cubase.

You may be thinking to reach for your professional studio phone numbers at this point already, but we've barely touched on the setup for this complex recording scenario. There's a little more to cover on monitoring these synths through the tape returns, but for now I will skip ahead to the band and getting microphones connected to the mixer so we can actually record the performers!

Taking Over the Closets, Living Room, and Bedroom

Push the furniture out of the way. You're going to need some space for this band.

Among instruments, the piano and acoustic drums will require the most room. Since you have three rooms to work with (living room, bedroom, and your chosen control room) and the drums can get pretty loud, I suggest you put the drums in the bedroom and the piano in the living room. The piano is much easier to control than an acoustic drum kit volume-wise. Along with the piano, I would put the acoustic guitar player and percussionist in the living room. The singer should be in the isolation booth, which can be in the control room or the living room, depending on the amount of space you have. You have two closets, one of which is in the living room and the other in the bedroom. Since the bass and drums are usually important to lock together, I would put the bass guitar setup in the bedroom closet and the guitar setup in the living room closet. The guitar player and bass player will probably want to perform with the other musicians in the living room.

Let's take a moment to look at what we've just done. We've taken a seven-piece band that is used to playing together and separated them in three rooms. In theory, this makes sense because it's the best way to get proper sound isolation. On the other hand, you have just "broken up the band." If a band is new to the studio, this could totally throw their performance out of whack. Sometimes you have to make sacrifices for the sake of the performance, and in this case the sacrifice is sound control.

Also, sometimes visual cues are more important than a good headphone mix. The drummer may really *need* to be in the same room as the guitar player to get into the right groove. Also, the bass player may need to *feel* the bass from the bass cabinet to get the right groove. Every player and band has unique personalities and characteristics that contribute to the band's sound. Working against those personality traits and characteristics is only going to make it harder for you to get a good take. Make sure that everyone in the band is comfortable with the setup. If they're not, you should rework it.

Note: Visual cues are very important. If you are using several rooms, doors with large glass windows or walls with windows can be invaluable. If there is no way to install windows between the rooms, try adding a video monitor setup so that performers can see what's happening in all the rooms as they play.

The worst thing you can do to a musician is make him or her feel unimportant: for instance, stuffing someone in a closet with no windows and then never talking to him or her during the session. No matter what the final compromise ends up being between the band and the studio, there is no such thing as a perfect setup. Sometimes it just takes time for the band to adjust to the environment by running though a few songs together.

See Figure 7.12 for a layout of our band and their locations throughout the home studio.

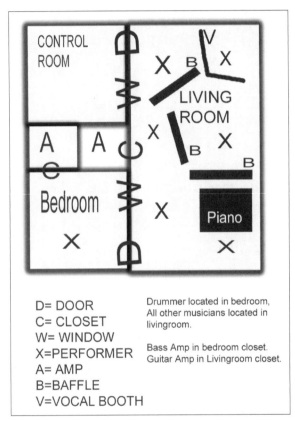

D= DOOR
C= CLOSET
W= WINDOW
X=PERFORMER
A= AMP
B=BAFFLE
V=VOCAL BOOTH

Drummer located in bedroom, All other musicians located in livingroom.

Bass Amp in bedroom closet. Guitar Amp in Livingroom closet.

Figure 7.12 The band is scattered throughout the house.

Warning: Mics and Cables Everywhere! Beware of Snakes!

Just when you thought things couldn't possibly get messier, it's time to break out the mic stands and start patching the mics into the mixing console.

One of the cleanest and tidiest solutions to interfacing multiple rooms to the control room is to run a snake from the console to each of the recording rooms. A *snake* (see Figure 7.13) is a collection of audio

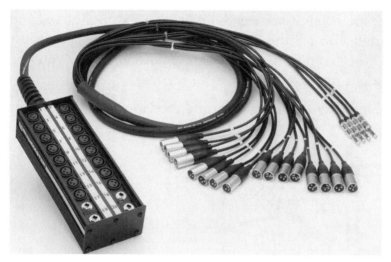

Figure 7.13 An audio snake.

cables that have been grouped together to simplify things when two patch points are far apart. All of the ends of the snake are numbered to match the inputs of an input box on the other end, which takes a lot of the guesswork out of patching cables from room to room.

Depending on your miking technique, acoustic drums can eat up a lot of mics and a lot of inputs on a recording console. Since this is a five-piece drum kit with three cymbals and a hi-hat, we will be using nine microphones on the drum kit: one microphone on the kick drum, one on each tom (three total), two microphones on the snare (top and bottom), one on the hi-hat, and two microphones overhead. Overhead mics capture the overall stereo image of the drum kit. Their main purpose is usually to record cymbals, but since it's impossible to prevent bleed-through from other parts of a drum kit, the overheads usually pick up frequencies from all the other drums as well.

Since the bass amp is in the bedroom closet, we'll also need one input for the microphone on the bass amp as well. The bass player would also like the balanced line out on his bass amplifier to go direct, so we will need to have one more mic input available.

This means that the bedroom requires a total of 10 microphones and 11 balanced mic inputs (located on a snake). Since the bass amplifier is in the closet and the doors will be shut between the rooms, there is no need to further isolate the drums.

In the living room, we've decided to do a simple stereo mic setup on the piano, which takes two microphones, one over the low strings and one over the high strings. Since the piano player is also singing, that makes a total of three microphones and three mic inputs. The acoustic guitar player would like to do a basic mic setup on his guitar but would also like to record the direct guitar signal from his pickup while he's singing. This will require two microphones and three mic inputs. The percussionist will be playing tambourine along with her electronic percussion kit, and she'll also be singing background vocals, so she'll need two microphones and four mic inputs (because her Roland kit needs to be patched into the studio as well). The guitar player would like to record his guitar amp in stereo, so this requires two microphones (one on each speaker side) and two mic inputs. Lastly, the singer will require one microphone and one input.

The living room, then, requires a grand total of 10 microphones and 13 balanced mic inputs. Since you have several different musicians all playing in one room, it would probably be a great idea to separate the musicians with homemade studio baffles and use some packing blankets on the grand piano. The closet door will be shut for the electric guitar, so most of the bleed-through between microphones will be fairly easy to control. The bleed-through between the musicians' vocal mics and instrument mics will be harder to control.

Now we know what we're going to need. You can run a 12-channel audio snake into the bedroom and a 16-channel snake into the living room from the control room. You'll also need 24 mic cables, 20 microphones, 20 mic stands, one direct box for the acoustic guitar, and two direct boxes for the Roland percussion kit. This also means that you'll be using either 22 or 24 input channels on your 24-channel mixing board depending on where you decide to patch the Roland drum kit. Considering that you're also using 18 to 20 tape inputs on your Mackie console, your board is almost maxed out.

Speaking of being maxed out, let's take a quick look at possible costs to add this type of setup to a home studio.

- Mackie 24x8 console $3,400

- PreSonus FP10 (3 @ $600 each) $1,800

- Shure SM57 microphones (8 @ $100 each) $800

- Sennheiser MD421 II microphones (2 @ $350 each) $700

- AKG C 414 microphones (4 @ $1,000 each) $4,000

- AKG C 1000 microphones (5 @ $350 each) $1,400

- Blue Bottle Cap microphone $5,000

- 16-channel audio snake $350

- 12-channel audio snake $275

- Baffles, packing blankets $300

- Video monitoring system $3,000

- Headphones (7 pair) $700

- Headphone amplifiers (2) $300

- MIDI cables, patch cables, and unbalanced cables $900

- Microphone cables (20) $400

- Mic stands (20) $2,000

- Direct boxes (3) $300

Not even counting the computer system, Cubase, the grand piano, special mic pres, or the cost of actual space, your cost has increased by more than $25,000. The good news is that most of this equipment doesn't lose its value over time, so if you're planning on recording a lot of bands or just recording one band a lot, this is a small investment compared to the thousands you could spend in studio time. On the other hand, you simply cannot compare the quality of a Mackie console and your bedroom to that of a professional recording studio.

I won't go into detail on how to connect these mics to the console, where to place them, and which ones to use for which applications. You can use what I've explained in my previous chapters, your manuals, and other sources for that information. There's still a lot of basic ground left for us to cover.

Note: Getting levels and setting EQ on an analog console is much the same as working on the Cubase mixer. I will go into detail on how to get the best sound for each instrument. I *will* say that you shouldn't worry too much about setting EQ during the recording stage. A lot of professional engineers choose to spend less time with EQ when tracking and more time with EQ when mixing. During the tracking stage, your focus should be primarily on microphone placement, sound isolation, and performance.

Setting Up a Monitor Mix and Using a Talkback System

Now that the band is patched into the console, you should be able to hear everything in the control room by bussing the entire mix to the master stereo bus on the Mackie 24x8. I'll go into more detail on bussing a little later when I discuss sending the audio signals from the band to individual tracks in Cubase. The task at hand right now is a great headphone mix for the band so that they can hear themselves and each other.

With the Mackie console, we're hard pressed to give the band members individual mixes. The maximum headphone mix combination on the Mackie is three stereo mixes; two mono mixes and two stereo mixes; or four mono mixes and one stereo mix. Also, depending on the number of mixes you need, you'll also need a separate headphone amplifier for each mix. The Mackie comes with two built-in headphone amplifiers and six sends. By using the sends on each channel, you can set up entirely separate mixes for monitoring. Unfortunately, the way the Mackie board is wired for aux sends 5 and 6 leaves you with some combination of aux send 1–4 or sends 1 and 2 and 5 and 6, thus giving us five monitoring options (counting the control room as another monitoring source).

The drummer has a few requests for his monitors. He needs to hear a loud metronome click in his headphones, and he need to hear the rest of the band with the bass being a little louder—but because his acoustic drums are so loud in the bedroom, he does *not* want to hear his drums in the headphones. The lead singer needs to hear his voice (with reverb) much louder than the rest of the band. Since the bass player is standing in a different room from his bass amp, he needs to hear a little more bass in his headphones. Fortunately, the rest of the band isn't as picky when it comes to a mix as long as they can hear everything.

It looks like we have four headphone mixes to set up: one drum mix, one vocal, one bass, and one for everybody else. I will be using two mono mixes and two stereo mixes. Here's what I think is the best way to work this on the Mackie 24x8.

- Aux sends 3 and 4 on each channel will be used to set up a stereo headphone mix for the drummer. Each knob will be balanced to create a mix in the stereo field (send 3 for the left channel and send 4 for the right channel). All the channels that include drum mics will be zeroed to cut the drum kit's signal running to the drummer's headphones. Once the appropriate mix is made (with the bass guitar slightly louder in the mix), the master aux send 3 and 4 knobs will be centered, and the Phones 1 module will have three of its sources selected: mix B (which includes the mix of the synths plugged into the tape returns), aux 3 and 4 send (which is the mix of the band we just set up), and external (the signal of the click routed from Cubase) (see Figure 7.14). The click level should be set in Cubase. The overall headphone level will be controlled from the Phone 1 module on the Mackie 24x8. Aux 3 and 4 should be set to Prefader on each channel so that the send is controlling the sound before the audio signal reaches the fader. This way, fader adjustments during the session will not affect the drummer's headphone mix.

- Aux send 1 will be used for the bass player similar to the way aux sends 3 and 4 were used for the drummer. The difference is that the bassist's mono signal will be routed to an external headphone amplifier instead of the Mackie's built-in headphone amplifier. The mono signal may need to be split into two separate mono signals before being patched to an external headphone

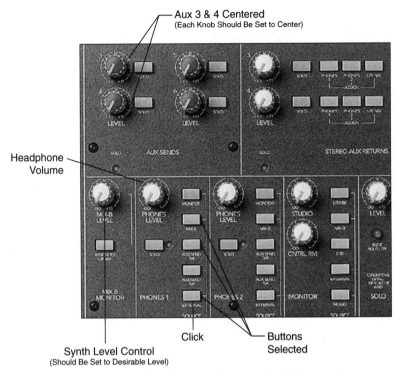

Figure 7.14 Setting up the drummer's stereo headphone mix.

amplifier (see Figure 7.15). One big difference when using aux send 1 is that there is no way to include the mix of the synths (through mix B). Because of this, you may want to route the Roland drum machine to a tape input to free up two more channel inputs on the console and then use a stereo-to-mono Y cable to route the stereo signal of mix B to a channel on the console (see Figure 7.16). By doing this, you can add the signal of mix B through the aux sends. The output signal of this send will need to be controlled from the external headphone amp. If you choose to use two channels to monitor mix B, make sure to disable the channels from the L/R master bus by deselecting the Routing button.

- The lead singer's mono headphone mix will be set up exactly like the bass player's. In this situation, the most reliable and easiest way to get the reverb setting the singer needs is through an external signal processor. Since we've used all the aux sends for monitors, we need another way to get the vocal to an effects processor. Try

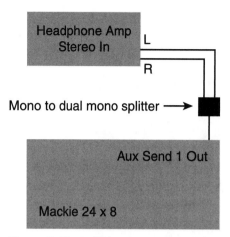

Figure 7.15   Splitting a mono signal to an external headphone amp.

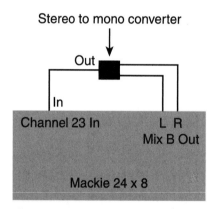

Figure 7.16   Sending the keyboard mix to a regular input channel.

using the Group Out to bus the vocal through its own group channel and then running the Mackie's bus output to the input of the effects processor. Once this is done, you'll need to run the output on the external effects processor back to the main board through the last remaining input channel (as you did with the mix B output of the console). That will allow you to control the mix level of the reverb in the singer's headphones using the Aux Send 1 knob (see Figure 7.17). Disable the reverb channel from the L/R master bus unless you need to hear the reverb in the control room, in which case you can do so using the master bus and controlling the reverb level with the Channel fader.

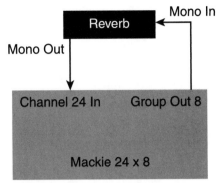

Vocal channel bussed to Group out 8
Group 8 out fader controls reverb input level of vocal

Figure 7.17   Patching in an external effect without using a send.

- Last but not least, the keyboard player, percussionist, and both guitar players all need to hear a group mix without a click or reverb. The only option that's really left is to send the rest of the band the same sound that you're hearing in the control room (the mix you have set up on the faders of the console). On the Mackie, this is done by either sending the signal from the Phones 2 module (with Monitor and mix B selected) or sending a signal from the studio out to an external headphone amp. I normally don't like to use a Studio Out as a band's monitor because changes you make to the sound while they're playing may affect the performance, but since this band is demanding and the mixer is limited, it's the only choice left. If you do use the Studio Out, you'll need to keep mix B selected as a source at all times so the band can hear both the synths and percussion. You will also not be able to switch back and forth to hear the sound actually being recorded (by pushing the 2-tk button) because it could throw the band off.

As you can see, setting up monitors for a band can be very tricky, especially when you have limited resources, but understanding signal flow will help you give band members a mix they can live with while they perform.

Note: It's a good idea to have one headphone jack for each monitor setting available in the studio control room. This way you can use a set of headphones to quickly make adjustments without changing your setup as you go. Dealing with four or more separate mixes at once can be a bit of a challenge.

One of the most important tools for a recording engineer/producer during a recording session is the talkback (see Figure 7.18). The *talkback* bridges the gap between the control room and the studio. The

Talkback Level and
Output Select

MIC

Figure 7.18 The talkback system on a Mackie 24x8 console.

system usually involves a cheap mic built into a recording console. When the engineer presses the talkback button on the board, the control monitors are muted, and the mic on the console picks up sound in the control room and routes the signal to various monitor sources. The talkback on the Mackie console can send the control mic's signal to aux sends 1 and 2; tape subgroups; and phones and studio. For our scenario, the talkback would need to go to aux sends 1 and 2 and the phones and studio in order for the musicians to hear the control room. If there is no visual (such as a window or video monitoring system) between the control room and the band, the talkback is indispensable. More advanced versions of Cubase, such as Cubase 4, allow talkback without using the console. For more information on this, see the section "Bypassing a Recording Console and Recording a Band" a little later in this chapter.

Note: When it comes to running a headphone signal from the control room to the live room, you can run the amplified signal from the control room or keep the headphone amplifier in the room with the performers. Sometimes it's nice for musicians to have the option of adjusting their own volume, but once a volume is set, it usually doesn't need to be adjusted. Sometimes you can run the signal (before or after amplification) through a line on a snake. Other times a long headphone-extension cable will work just fine.

Getting the Audio Signals to Cubase (Where They Belong!)

Now that you've got the band all patched in to the console and you have their monitors set up so they can hear what's going on in both the studio and the control room, you're finally ready to get the audio signals to Cubase!

Our main concern is getting the 22 channels of audio coming through the Mackie console into Cubase. You can continue to monitor the MIDI parts through the Mackie until we decide to bounce them to audio tracks later on.

Getting the signal to Cubase is the easy part. If you would like to record each channel on its own track, just connect the Direct Out on each channel of the Mackie console to 22 inputs on the PreSonus FP10s (see Figure 7.19). The biggest concern would be whether your computer can handle not only recording 22 tracks at once but also playing back 12 prerecorded tracks as well as 18 MIDI tracks. There's only one true test, and that's to cross your fingers and press Record. If you run into problems, you have a few options to free up your computer's resources, but they may also limit what you can do for a mixdown later on.

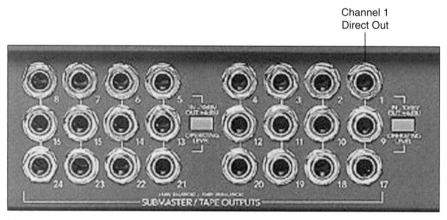

Figure 7.19 A direct output on the Mackie.

The first option would be to *bounce* the 12 tracks you are playing to one stereo track. For more information on bouncing tracks, see Chapter 9, "Mixing It Down."

The second option would be to blend the audio signal of several instruments *before* the signal is recorded. By doing this, you could cut down on the number of tracks you need to record at once. This is accomplished by bussing (or grouping) the audio signal in the mixture to shared outputs. For instance, instead of recording nine individual drum tracks, you could group your three toms together and three cymbals together into one stereo pair. That would move you from nine tracks of drums to five, saving you four tracks. The big problem with this is that those three drum and cymbal tracks would be *married* in the mix and could not be separated later. If you wanted, you could record the entire band on one or two tracks, but that would severely limit what you could do with the recording later on. Even though this method can be limiting, always keep it in mind. Some of the best-selling records of all time were recorded using only two to four tracks at once.

The Mackie mixing console in this example allows you to use up to eight busses at once (plus the left and right stereo master bus). Using these busses, you can create up to eight groups to record at once. If you mix in a few direct outs with the group outs, you can pretty much come up with an endless number of combinations for this scenario. For more information on bussing and grouping your outputs, refer to your mixer's manual.

Once the signal has entered the sound card, setting up each recording track in Cubase is very similar to the approach I described early in Chapter 6, "Recording Guitar and Bass," for recording multiple tracks of an acoustic guitar at once. See Figure 7.20 to see how Cubase's tracks and inputs should most likely be configured for this recording.

Bypassing a Recording Console and Recording a Band

In the previous example, the band was monitoring their performance directly from the analog Mackie mixer. There was no need to monitor from tracks they were recording. Because the band was monitoring from their input signal rather than their output signal, there was no noticeable latency in the monitoring process and the buffer could be increased to help your system perform better without worry of affecting the monitoring.

Though this style of recording and monitoring can be very useful, the best signal is the one with the least resistance. This means that bypassing the console and running the signal directly to the sound card can be better than running the signal through a console. The real problem with bypassing a console in the recording chain is latency and other monitoring issues. You can group and bus in Cubase just as you can with the Mackie mixer (see Figures 7.21 and 7.22). If you think about it, it makes perfect sense to bypass a recording console, especially when working with lower-end recording consoles.

TRACK	MIDI CHANNEL/AUDIO IN	SOUND/	SYNTH/INSTRUMENT	OUTPUTS		TOTAL
MIDI 1	A1	Piano	GEM RP-X	STEREO		2
MIDI 2	A2	String Pad	GEM GM-X	STEREO		2
MIDI 3	A3	Lush Strings	GEM GM-X	STEREO	x	
MIDI 4	A4	Choir Male	GEM GM-X	STEREO	x	
MIDI 5	A5	Choir Female	GEM GM-X	STEREO	x	
MIDI 6	A6	Cello	GEM GM-X	STEREO	x	
MIDI 7	B1	Fat Synth	MOOG MINIMOOG VOYAGER	STEREO		2
MIDI 8	B2	Big Bang	Akai MPC-4000		1	1
MIDI 9	B3	Scratch	Akai MPC-4000		1	1
MIDI 10	B4	Electro	Akai MPC-4000		1	1
MIDI 11	B5	zap	Akai MPC-4000		1	1
MIDI 12	B6	Synth Choir 1	Korg Radius	STEREO		2
MIDI 13	B7	Synth Choir 1(2)	Korg Radius	STEREO	x	
MIDI 14	A7	Buzzy Synth	Alesis Andromeda		1	1
MIDI 15	A8	Tight Bass	Alesis Andromeda		1 x	
MIDI 16	A9	Funk Clav	Alesis Andromeda		1	1
MIDI 17	A10	Phased Out	Alesis Andromeda	STEREO		2
MIDI 18	B8	Juicy synth	Nord Electro 2	STEREO		2
MIDI 19	C1/MIDI IN-PRESONUS C	Latin Percussion	Roland SPD-20	STEREO		2
AUDIO 1	PRERECORDED	Background Vocal 1	N/A	1 & 2		2
AUDIO 2	PRERECORDED	Background Vocal 2	N/A	1 & 2	x	
AUDIO 3	PRERECORDED	Background Vocal 3	N/A	1 & 2	x	
AUDIO 4	PRERECORDED	Background Vocal 4	N/A	1 & 2	x	
AUDIO 5	PRERECORDED	Trumpet	N/A	1 & 2	x	
AUDIO 6	PRERECORDED	Trumpet 2	N/A	1 & 2	x	
AUDIO 7	PRERECORDED	Bari Sax	N/A	1 & 2	x	
AUDIO 8	PRERECORDED	Tenor Sax	N/A	1 & 2	x	
AUDIO 9	PRERECORDED	Alto Sax	N/A	1 & 2	x	
AUDIO 10	PRERECORDED	Trombone	N/A	1 & 2	x	
AUDIO 11	PRERECORDED	Trombone 2	N/A	1 & 2	x	
AUDIO 12	PRERECORDED	Tuba	N/A	1 & 2	x	
AUDIO 13	Presonus 1	Kick Drum	Kick/Sennheiser 421	3 & 4		2
AUDIO 14	Presonus 2	Snare Low	Ludwig Snare/ SM57	3 & 4	x	
AUDIO 15	Presonus 3	Snare High	Ludwig Snare/ SM57	3 & 4	x	
AUDIO 16	Presonus 4	Hi Hat	AKG CS-1000	3 & 4	x	
AUDIO 17	Presonus 5	Tom 1	SM 57	3 & 4	x	
AUDIO 18	Presonus 6	Tom 2	SM 57	3 & 4	x	
AUDIO 19	Presonus 7	Tom 3	SM 57	3 & 4	x	
AUDIO 20	Presonus 8	Cymbals (L)	Overhead/ CS-1000	3 & 4	x	
AUDIO 21	Presonus 9	Cymbals (R)	Overhead/ CS-1000	3 & 4	x	
AUDIO 22	Presonus 10	Bass1	Amp/speaker- Sennheiser 421	3 & 4	x	
AUDIO 23	Presonus 11	Bass2	Amp/direct out	3 & 4	x	
AUDIO 24	Presonus 12	Piano Low	AKG 414	3 & 4	x	
AUDIO 25	Presonus 13	Piano High	AKG 414	3 & 4	x	
AUDIO 26	Presonus 14	Acoustic Guitar 1	AKG 414	3 & 4	x	
AUDIO 27	Presonus 15	Acoustic Guitar 2	Direct	3 & 4	x	
AUDIO 28	Presonus 16	Electric Guitar (L)	Fender Twin/Left side/SM 57	3 & 4	x	
AUDIO 29	Presonus 17	Electric Guitar (R)	Fender Twin/Right side/SM 57	3 & 4	x	
AUDIO 30	Presonus 18	Tambourine	AKG CS-1000	3 & 4	x	
AUDIO 31	Presonus 19	Tom Background Vox	Piano singer/ CS-1000	3 & 4	x	
AUDIO 32	Presonus 20	Tina Background Vox	Perc singer/ CS-1000	3 & 4	x	
AUDIO 34	Presonus 21	Todd Background Vox	Guitar singer/ CS-1000	3 & 4	x	
AUDIO 35	Presonus 22	Joe Cool	Lead Vocals/ Blue Tube Mic	3 & 4	x	
CLICK	CUBASE	Metronome	Cubase	5 & 6		2

PRESONUS IS USING 22 AUDIO INPUTS, 6 OUTPUTS, 3 MIDI OUTPUTS, AND 1 MIDI INPUT.
NO AUDIO IS BEING RECORDED FROM THE SYNTHS, ONLY MIDI.

Figure 7.20 A chart showing Cubase's final track and input settings for this recording scenario.

Cubase 4 is set up to deal with more monitoring issues in the studio than other Cubase versions. As technology develops, we'll have less of a need for analog mixers, but as it stands right now, the technology available is in a lot of ways inferior to the classic style of recording a band through an analog console. Signal flow with a physical analog mixer is a little easier for most people to understand than it is on a

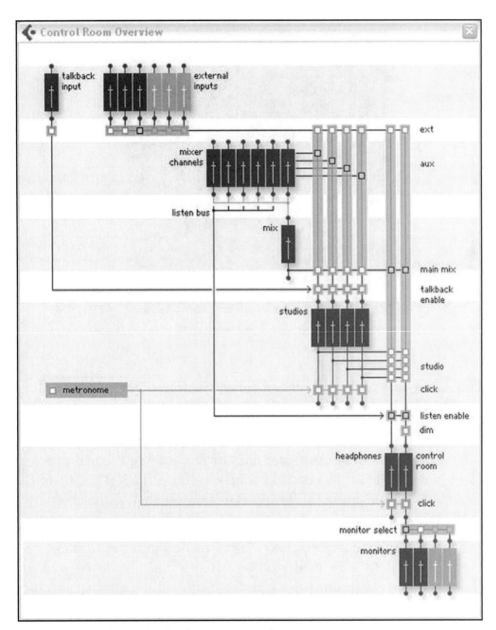

Figure 7.21 A schematic of Cubase 4's control room.

virtual mixer (such as the one found in Cubase) that hides buttons and contains drop-down menus for routing. But both the analog and digital worlds can be difficult to understand if you don't understand signal flow.

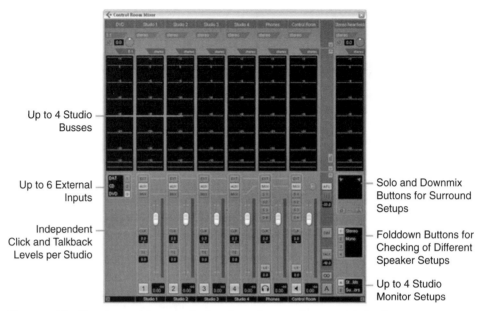

Up to 4 Studio Busses

Up to 6 External Inputs

Independent Click and Talkback Levels per Studio

Solo and Downmix Buttons for Surround Setups

Folddown Buttons for Checking of Different Speaker Setups

Up to 4 Studio Monitor Setups

Figure 7.22   The Control Room window in Cubase 4 shown with its features.

Cubase 4 contains several analog console features that take recording directly into the computer to new levels.

- The control-room features completely separate output busses for control room and headphone monitoring, leaving the main mix output untouched by control room–specific settings. This is similar to bussing and using the Master Outs on an analog console.

- It also features four user-definable monitor setups, similar to having a headphone jack for every monitor mix in order to make adjustments to individual monitor mixes. This allows you to hear each setup as it sounds from the monitor.

- Six external inputs (for external sources such as DAT, tape, CD, or DVD) are also available and can be played through any studio, track, headphone, or control room bus. This is a nice feature, but keep in mind that it also requires multiple inputs on your sound card.

- Four separate studio/monitor mixes—each getting its signal feeds from any audio channel, group channel, or FX return channel—are also available within the Cubase mixer. Each of the four independent studio sends offers level and pan controls. This is similar to using the sends and monitor sections on an analog board.

■ An integrated talkback function, which works along with an input on your sound card. Any microphone you plug into it is available in Cubase's control room.

■ A copy function to apply the main mix to any of the studio mixes with a single mouse click or key command. This is possible on some external digital consoles, but not on an analog board.

■ Since your click (metronome) is most likely coming from Cubase, the mixer includes a special click bus that is always patched in.

While the list of control room–like functions within Cubase 4 sounds very promising, you're still limited by the number of inputs and outputs on your sound card and by your computer's power. Even if your computer has the necessary power to remove latency while recording, you still may need an external mixer to submix other audio signals (such as the MIDI instruments in the previous example).

Bypassing the Sound Card When Recording a Band

Another way to simplify matters when recording bands is to use a digital console instead of an analog console (see Figure 7.23).

Digital consoles are usually a little more expensive than lower-end analog consoles, but they can save you a lot of patching by acting like a cross between a sound card, an analog mixer, and a patchbay. They also offer a user more hands-on control than working directly with the Cubase mixer.

Most digital consoles allow users to "build" the console to their specifications by adding special cards that offer specific input and output types as well as digital effects. Digital consoles give you the added advantage of access to Cubase's onboard digital effects, saving you the trouble of using external effects processors. You can usually run the outputs of the digital console straight to your computer through FireWire, cutting out the extra step of connecting to an external sound card.

Figure 7.23 The Mackie Digital X Bus Digital Recording Console.

One of the best features of using a digital console, or virtual console, is the ability to save your setups. By saving your setups, you can save loads of time in the studio, especially when you're recording the same type of band frequently. If you can afford a digital console, I highly recommend it to get the biggest bang for your buck.

Interfacing Your Cubase Studio with Another Pro Studio

If you've come to the conclusion that some things were just not meant for your Cubase studio and have decided to take a portion of your projects into a professional studio, you are not alone. One of the greatest things about Cubase is that it interfaces with just about any digital file format. This means that if you decide to spend time tracking in another studio, as long as you walk out of the studio with a hard drive or CD-ROM that contains the files in a Cubase-compatible format, you will be ready to edit, overdub, and/or mix at home.

Choosing the Right Pro Studio

Most professional studios are not using Cubase. They either have a Pro Tools system, Nuendo, some sort of digital hard disc or tape system (such as RADAR or ADAT), or an analog tape machine. If you can find a studio that uses Pro Tools or Nuendo, you will save yourself a lot of headaches and time. Anything not recorded on a DAW will most likely need to be transferred to a DAW before you will be able to work with the files in Cubase.

Note: Again, I'd like to reassure you that there will be little difference in quality going from a Pro Tools or Nuendo system. The main reason pro studios offer Pro Tools or Nuendo is they are more compatible with other systems and offer a few more features than Cubase. Keep in mind that Cubase project files will open in Nuendo, but Nuendo project files must be from the same software generation to open in Cubase. Cubase 4 can open Nuendo 4 files, for example, but not earlier Nuendo files. If Cubase and Nuendo share the same generation (version), they should even be able to share each other's files without a hitch.

If you have the means to transfer files from another digital recorder or from an analog tape machine, there's nothing wrong with recording to another format. The highest-quality format is usually DAW-based, though. Recording to analog tape is still popular, but 95 percent of the recordings made on analog tape are transferred to a DAW for editing and mixing. Bringing your computer and sound card along to the session is always an option if you're unsure of the setup. When the studio clock is ticking, it's often faster to use the recording format that the engineers are familiar with, so my advice is to reserve your computer as a last resort or as something to make transfers or backups to after the recording is finished. If you do bring your computer, you can also verify that the file format you have output will work in your system before you leave the studio.

Note: Recording using Broadcast WAV files is a great option when transferring audio files from one studio to another. It not only works easily when crossing platforms, but also contains a timestamp of the audio file that can be referenced in all DAWs.

Preparing for the Studio

There are several things you can do to save time and money, and ensure better results, *before* you take the band into a professional recording studio. A few tips:

- Practice, practice, practice. This may sound like a cliché, but if everyone in the band knows what they need to play before they get into the studio, you will have much better results.

- If you have prerecorded tracks you need to play with, bounce the tracks to a stereo mix that you can import into the studio's system for monitoring. Since you're using the tracks only to monitor, you will be able to go back to the original unbounced tracks later when you mix in your Cubase studio at home. For more on bouncing tracks, see Chapter 9.

- If you're using a lot of external or virtual synths, record the MIDI as audio files and then bounce the audio files so that you have one stereo mix of the synths to monitor with in the studio. This will save you from dragging all your synths to the studio and setting them up. You can always edit your MIDI and synths after the recording session in the comfort of your home Cubase studio.

- If you are used to using a particular sound for a click track, go ahead and record the click track as an audio track. The sound of the metronome is not universal. Sometimes an unfamiliar sound may throw off a performance. Also, you should know the exact tempo you would like to use for a song before entering the studio. If you have prerecorded tracks to import into the professional studio's DAW, then you will need to know that tempo in order to sync the tracks.

- Besides practice, all the musicians should be using instruments and equipment they are happy with. If they think the $75 guitar they brought is going to sound like a $4,000 guitar just because they're paying for a quality recording, they are going to be disappointed. Drummers should know how to tune their acoustic drums or find someone who does, both before the session and at the studio before recording. Bass players and guitar players should bring their tuners and have their guitars tuned with new strings at the start of the session.

- The band should be relaxed and comfortable and shouldn't go into the studio after playing a show the night before. Most likely your day in the studio will be long and somewhat tedious at times. Sometimes getting the right drum sounds can take hours, so the other musicians should bring something to keep themselves busy. Singers should not spend too much time rehearsing on the day of the recording. If a vocal take doesn't come out perfectly, it's one of the easiest things to fix in an overdub at home in your Cubase studio.

- For your protection, bring two external hard drives to save the files from the session. The last thing you need is a $200 hard drive to crash when it's the only hard drive that has your $2,000 recording session stored on it. If you can, make backups of your session on DVD-R. Usually a studio will also keep its files saved for a period of time, but don't trust *any* pro studio when it comes to saving your work. At the end of a session, you should have at least two backups of the files you need for your Cubase studio and two backups of the actual session in whatever file format.

- You can bring your computer and sound card. If you're using a desktop, it might be a pain, but when there is a drum kit or piano involved, packing up a computer should be the least of your worries. (Of course, you should be very careful when transporting any type of computer.) If the studio uses a Mac and you use Windows (or vice versa), having your computer there can be a good idea just to make sure your files are compatible.

- Bring a friend to run errands for you if possible. When a guitar player breaks a string and doesn't have a replacement, the band gets hungry, or somebody forgets something at home, that friend could become the most important person in the room. If you have a friend who is patient and actually likes the band, or is interested in learning more about recording, that's even better!

Those are just a few things that could help your studio experience run more smoothly. There are plenty of other things that can help you give you the best tracking experience ever. If you don't expect a studio to work miracles and you are prepared beforehand, you should be able to walk out of the studio with something you can use for years to come.

Important: Whether you decide to record to a click or not, always start recording a take with a two-measure count-in. This can be as simple as starting with a "1-2-3-4, 2-2-3-4," or maybe the drummer can click sticks for two measures. By recording a count-in, you'll make your life much simpler if you ever have to do any overdubs. The count-in can always be easily cut out in editing.

Wrapping Up After a Pro Recording Session

If the band is well-rehearsed and the recording engineer has been at the top of his or her game, by the end of the day, you should have at least one great take. Feel free to keep as many takes as you want—hard drive space is cheap compared with studio time. You never know when those extra tracks can come in handy. Remember that getting the best sound in the studio is half the battle, so make sure to allow plenty of time for the engineers to work their magic. In a perfect world, a band could record several songs in one day. In the real world, you should take as long as you need to get each track right before moving on. You don't want any regrets after you've left the studio.

You shouldn't try to mix a track the same day you recorded it. By the end of a tracking day, everyone will be too burnt out to make good mixing decisions. You should dedicate at least one full day to mixing each track you record.

If your band didn't record any overdubs in the studio, chances are that every track will be left uncut. All tracks should also have the same start and end times. Figure 7.24 shows how the end of a live session should look. See Figure 7.25 for how it should *not* look. The reason you want to leave all your tracks unedited and with the same start and ends times is to make the task of realigning the tracks easier when you import them into Cubase.

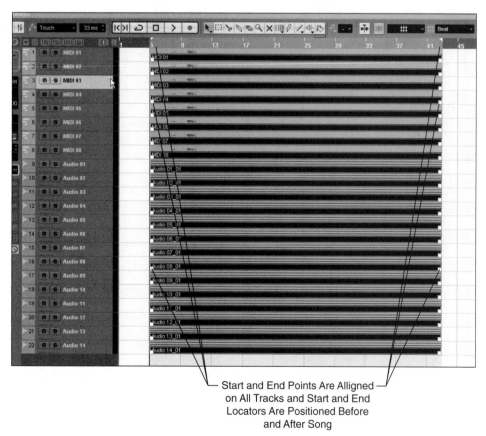

Start and End Points Are Alligned
on All Tracks and Start and End
Locators Are Positioned Before
and After Song

Figure 7.24 The way a live tracking session should appear before exporting (saving) the tracks.

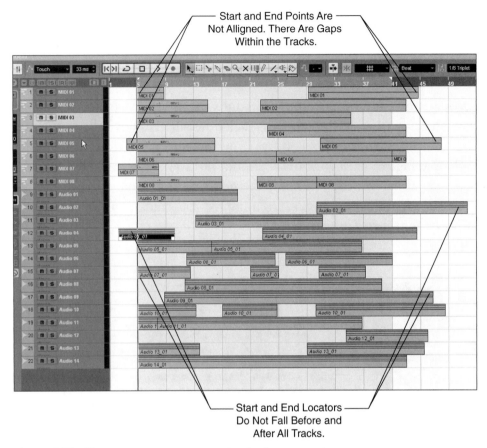

Figure 7.25 The wrong way to export tracks from a session.

The most important thing is that all tracks have the same start and end times during exporting. The track should start at least two measures before the song (including the count-in) and end two measures after the song ends (so you can make sure there aren't any sustained notes that get cut off). When you reimport the tracks into Cubase, they should look exactly like Figure 7.24.

If the engineer has used any effects plug-ins during the session, the effects should be rendered and saved as another track. This way you have the unaffected track as well as the affected track to work with. Most likely, you will not have the same software plug-ins that the pro studio has, so you should definitely make sure you capture the effect in its own audio track before leaving the studio. However the engineer finalizes the export, you should always get a copy of the entire project folder in the format (Pro Tools, Nuendo, etc.) the engineer used, just in case you decide to come back to the studio or use a similar studio.

Cubase, Pro Tools, Nuendo, and many other DAWs share the ability to import and export a type of file called an OMF file. This is a standardized file that can be used to save edit locations, start and end times, effect settings, pan settings, and more. You should always get an OMF file of the session you are working on. There is some confusion regarding OMF files. For instance, an OMF file *cannot* create an effect plug-in that you do not have on your system. It can capture effect settings, but if you do not own the plug-in, the settings will do you no good whatsoever. Even though an OMF file is a standardized file, a lot of problems can come up when you're transferring OMF files between incompatible systems.

To make things foolproof, you can have the engineer export each track separately as its own file. The export process usually goes fast, and most of the time you won't be recording more than 24 tracks. Make sure that the engineer has labeled each track upon export and has also labeled the tracks for the OMF file before exporting. Knowing that one track is the snare drum track, and another is the piano track will save you a lot of time down the road (especially if you're dealing with a lot of tracks)!

Make note of any special equipment used in the session. By keeping these notes with your recording, you'll always have a reference for how you got a certain sound. Also, keep the engineer's name and contact information handy in case you need to get in touch. Studio numbers are usually pretty easy to find, but engineers frequently move from place to place.

Last but not least, if you have your computer with you, try loading everything back into your computer before you leave the studio. You can try importing each track one at a time into Cubase by using the preexisting song—if you had prerecorded tracks—or creating a new song and selecting Import (from the File menu), then selecting Audio File and locating the saved file from your hard drive. The audio file will be imported to the cursor's location on the selected track. By adjusting your cursor and track selection, you should be able to rebuild your mix (apart from volume and pan settings). You can also try importing the OMF file from the same menu and loading the audio files from the appropriate directory. This process is usually more automated and faster, if it works.

Use this same process if you decide to take the edits and mix that you've done in your home Cubase studio to a pro studio for a professional mixdown. For more on editing and mixing, check out the next two chapters.

8 Basic Editing

If I had to choose the best reason to own a DAW such as Cubase, I would say for the power a DAW gives you when editing both MIDI and audio. Cubase has some of the best tools available for editing music in today's world. If you're wondering how bands sound so polished when you listen to a recording today, it's most likely because the producer knows how to edit audio and/or MIDI very well. Even the best performers in the world depend on these powerful editing tools to give them that extra edge in today's hypercompetitive music world.

Editing with a DAW such as Cubase can become very involved. The MIDI-editing features in Cubase are so extensive that I wrote an entire book called *MIDI Editing in Cubase*. I didn't even really touch on editing audio in that book, and editing audio can be even more complex than editing MIDI. In my world as a television music producer, editing MIDI and audio are equally important. But if I had to choose one over the other, I'd choose editing MIDI because it's what I've been doing since I started using Cubase in 1990. Because this book covers such a broad functionality of a Cubase studio, I've limited my explanations of MIDI and audio editing in Cubase to just a few simple methods.

While the subject of editing goes a lot deeper than what you can read in one chapter, I believe that once you learn the basics of the most important editing methods, you will be able to manipulate your recordings far beyond what you could do with another type of studio recorder (such as a tape-based machine or a hard-disk recorder).

This chapter has been simplified to cover copying and pasting parts, quantizing MIDI, pitch correction and manipulation, and timing correction and stretching. By using these editing methods, you can turn a mediocre performance into a good performance and a good performance into a great one.

Getting to Know the Toolbar Buttons

There are many tools you will use to edit MIDI and audio, but the tools you access from the Cubase toolbar buttons are the most universal and flexible available in Cubase. Cubase 4's tool buttons are grouped together on the tool bar. In Figures 8.1 and 8.2, I have provided a closeup of the tool buttons as well as the name of each button. Figure 8.1 shows how the tool buttons appear in the Key Editor, whereas Figure 8.2 shows how the tool buttons appear within the Project window.

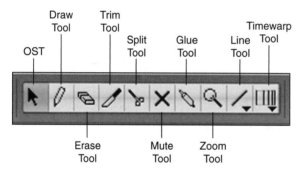

Figure 8.1 The 10 tool buttons located in the Key Editor.

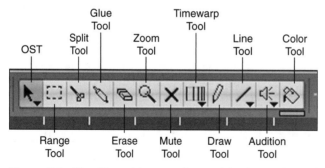

Figure 8.2 The 12 tool buttons located in the Project window.

Although there are 12 tool buttons in the Project window and 10 tool buttons in the Key Editor, I will go over only six of these tools here: the Object Selection tool, the Draw tool, the Erase tool, the Mute tool, the Split tool, and the Glue tool. These six buttons are common between both editors, and by using these buttons and a few other functions and edit windows, you can perform some of the most useful edits possible in Cubase.

The Object Selection Tool

Most likely, you are already familiar with the Object Selection tool. It used to be called the *cursor,* but Cubase has since changed to calling the mouse-controlled arrow icon (the pointer) the Object Selection tool and now reserves the term cursor for the line that scrolls through the song (formerly the *Song Position pointer*). Nonetheless, the Object Selection tool is definitely the most useful tool of the group. To keep things from getting too repetitive, I will be abbreviating the Object Selection tool to the acronym "OST" throughout the rest of the book.

Accessing the Tool Buttons Before I go into details about the OST, I'd like to point out something else that's very important about the tool buttons as a whole. If you move the OST anywhere within the note display and right-click your mouse, a pop-up menu appears (see Figure 8.3). If you examine the icons in the top half of the pop-up menu's left side, you may notice that they are the same as the icons above, within the tool-button grouping on the toolbar. This is another great way of accessing these useful tools without using the toolbar. These tools will remain in the pop-up menu whether they are displayed on the toolbar or not. I find it much easier to access these tools from the pop-up menu, but choose whichever way works best for you. One other way you can access these tools is by typing the corresponding numbers that appear next to each in the pop-up menu. Using any or all of these ways can help speed and ease the process of working in Cubase.

The most basic use of the OST is to select a note, part, or tool. From now on, I will refer to both notes and parts as *objects*. To select any object with the OST, position the arrow icon over the object and click your mouse.

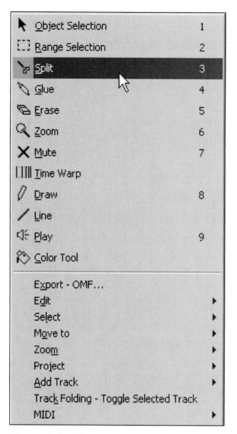

Figure 8.3 The pop-up menu's "toolbox."

To select multiple objects, simply hold down the Shift key on your keyboard while selecting each individual object with the OST.

Moving Objects with the OST

Another important feature of the OST is the ability to move objects within the note or part display. To move an object using the OST, click on the object and hold down the left mouse button. While holding the left mouse button, move the OST wherever you'd like to move the object, and then release the mouse button. After releasing the button, the object will remain in the new location. This process is called *click and drag*.

Note: Click and drag, or clicking and dragging, is the process of moving the mouse while holding down the left button. This comes up a lot throughout this book and when editing within Cubase.

One of the best features of the OST is that you aren't limited to working with one object at a time. When you click and drag anywhere within the note display over the objects you would like to move, the OST creates a box whose size you can adjust and use to select multiple objects.

To select multiple objects, place the OST somewhere in the note/part display, over the top and before the start of the objects in the measure. Click the left mouse button and drag the OST downward to the right, below the objects at the bottom. Notice how a box is created. This is the multiple object selection box (see Figure 8.4).

When you release the mouse button, notice that the objects within the selection box have all become shaded. This indicates that the objects have all been selected. Now you can move the entire group of parts using the same click-and-drag method you would to move one object at a time.

Selecting multiple objects with the OST may seem a little clumsy at first, but once you've done it enough times, it will become as easy as clicking the mouse.

Note: When selecting multiple objects, you should know that the box the OST creates does *not* have to completely surround an object to select it. Any object that has a section inside the box will be selected.

Changing Object Lengths Using the OST

The OST can also change the length of a selected object. To do that, select the object and position the OST on the right side of the object. A double-sided arrow should appear pointing left and right (see Figure 8.5).

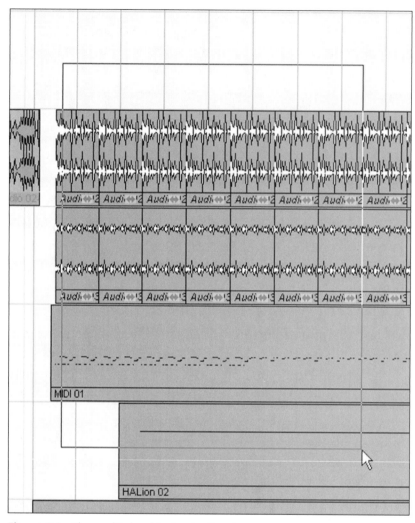

Figure 8.4 The multiple object selection box.

While the double arrow is present, click and drag the note to the right until it reaches the length you need, and then release the mouse button. The object should now be adjusted to the new length.

When using the OST to alter lengths in the Project window, you have three sizing options available from the button's drop-down menu: Normal Sizing, Sizing Moves Contents, and Sizing Applies Time Stretch.

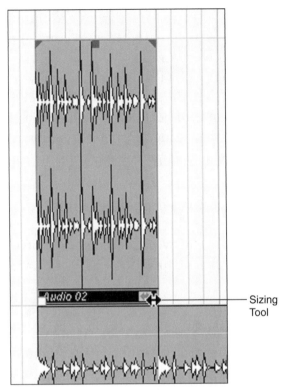

Figure 8.5   The OST displaying the Object Sizing tool, used to change length.

When the first option, Normal Sizing, is selected, the OST uses the same basic selection and sizing methods for parts as it does in the Key Editor when used with notes in the note display. Note that when you use the OST to change the size of the part, the part may get bigger or smaller, but the notes and events within the part do not move or change. This means that although the part itself is larger, nothing has been moved or changed within the part.

You may be curious as to how or why sizing a part using Normal Sizing could be effective while editing. There are times you may need to extend a part to the end of a measure(s) in order to make it fit into a predetermined space. For instance, let's say you have a verse in your song that is eight measures long. You have a string part that comes in at measure two and ends at measure five. Even though the part falls within the eight measures, you can extend the front of the part to come in at the start of the verse and extend the end of the part to the end of the verse without altering the actual part. Now when you copy and paste the part later, you won't have to worry about changing the timing or location of that individual track. It will always fall where it needs to within the verse. The extra length you added was merely for spacing. It adds nothing and does not affect the musical arrangement in any other way. Keep in mind that using Normal Sizing on an individual MIDI note in any editor will change the duration of the note.

The second sizing option on the OST button's drop-down list is Sizing Moves Contents. The difference between this and Normal Sizing is that when you resize the part with Sizing Moves Contents, the notes/audio files within the part actually change positions as you make adjustments.

The third option on the OST button's drop-down list is Sizing Applies Time Stretch. This option can be useful when you need to convert a groove that has been recorded at one tempo to fit into a new tempo.

Both Sizing Moves Contents and Sizing Applies Time Stretch can be very tricky to work with. Because of this, you can assume I'm talking about Normal Sizing in this chapter when I mention sizing parts. Later in the chapter, however, I will touch on Sizing Applies Time Stretch. For more information on Sizing Moves Contents and Sizing Applies Time Stretch, please refer to your Cubase manual.

Just as you can move multiple notes at once using the OST multiple object selection box, you can also *size* multiple objects at once. Simply select the range of objects you would like to size with the OST the same way you would to move multiple objects. Once you have selected the notes, move the OST to the left or right side of the selected objects, and the OST lengthening tool will appear. The tool will size everything between the selected parts.

The Draw Tool

Also located in the group of tool buttons is a button showing a small pencil. This is the Draw tool. Its main purpose is to *create* an object that doesn't already exist in your song.

After clicking on the Draw Tool button, you will notice that the button turns blue and what once was the OST has now changed into a small pencil icon pointer. To create a note or part, you use the pencil pointer to target a location on the note/part display and click the left mouse button.

Once you've created a new note, you can use the same pencil icon to lengthen it the same way you lengthened the note with the OST. With the pencil, however, you won't get a double-sided arrow because you can go in only one direction, which is to the right.

When using the Draw tool in the Key Editor, you can create music one note at a time instead of using a MIDI keyboard controller. This might seem a little tedious for a keyboard player, but the results of the Draw tool are the same as a MIDI keyboard's. This means that as long as you have an ear for music, you don't need the skills of a keyboard player to create music in Cubase.

Since this chapter concentrates on editing and the Draw tool's main purpose is to create, I will not go into details on the many ways you can use the Draw tool. It can, however, come in quite handy during the edit process, and it's important to understand its uses.

The Erase Tool

Another very useful tool is the Erase tool. Its icon resembles a small eraser. The Erase tool is used to get rid of objects you don't want in your project. Once you've selected the Erase tool from the toolbar, you'll notice that the pointer changes into a small eraser. To get rid of an object, all you need to do is click on it with the eraser.

You can also use the eraser to erase multiple objects at once using a method similar to selecting multiple objects with the OST. Once you have selected all the objects to erase, click on any of them and the entire range of objects will be deleted.

The Mute Tool

The Mute tool's button shows the letter X. It works similarly to the Erase tool, but instead of getting rid of unwanted objects, it silences them. Once you've muted a note/part, you can also unmute it when you want to hear it again. After selecting the Mute tool, you will notice that the pointer changes into the letter *X*. To mute an object, click on it. It will become shaded, and you will no longer be able to hear the object until you unmute it by clicking on it again.

You can also use the Mute tool to mute and unmute multiple objects by clicking and dragging to select the necessary objects, as you did with the OST. Even though this is a very useful tool, I will not use it in the editing techniques I will show you later in this chapter.

The Split Tool

The button with a pair of scissors on it is known in Cubase as the Split Tool button. When you click this button, you will notice that the pointer changes into a tiny pair of scissors. The Split tool is used to divide one object into two separate objects. When you use the tool to split a note, it actually creates a new start point for the new note on the right of the Split tool. This is similar to creating a new note next to an existing note. When you use the split tool to split a part, the part becomes two separate parts, which are divided by the point at which they have been split. This means that each part can now be handled as its own individual part.

Note: When splitting an audio part, you are not *cutting* the original audio track. You are creating a new end point for the left split side and a new start point for the right split side. The original audio file is safely stored separately on your hard drive. By resizing a part after it has been split, you can restore the audio file to its original state. This type of file handling is known as *non-destructive editing*.

To split a note or a part, position the Split tool pointer so that the tip is over the point where you would like to split the object. Left-click the mouse and notice that the object has been split, as indicated by a line through the original object.

If you are splitting a note into two separate notes, you can edit the pitch, velocity, length, and start and end times of each note separately.

If you are splitting parts, you can treat each side as a separate part. If you do not reposition the sides, however, there will be no audible effect from splitting the part.

You can also use the Split tool to split multiple parts/notes at once in a way similar to using the OST to select multiple parts. This can come in very handy when you need to separate sections of a song (verse, chorus, bridge, etc.)

The Glue Tool

The Glue tool goes hand in hand with the Split tool but works in the opposite way. This tool enables you to join two separate objects. When you select the Glue tool's button, the pointer becomes a small glue bottle. Position the glue bottle over the note or the part preceding the object you wish to join and click the mouse one time. The two objects will be "glued together" to form one longer part or note.

Note: Be careful of overclicking when using the Glue tool. Each click of the Glue tool will "glue" the object you're on to the *following* note. Too many clicks could lead to a messy, gooey blob, and nobody wants that.

The Glue tool can be used to glue multiple objects, as well, in a way similar to using the OST to select multiple objects. Even if there is a space between the object you're selecting and the object to the right, the Glue tool will fill the gap as it connects the two objects into one longer, seamless object. Be careful when glueing multiple notes together. Sometimes the move can result in notes getting stuck where they don't belong.

Quantizing MIDI

Before we get into some serious editing with the tools you've just learned about, I'd like to discuss one of the fundamentals of editing MIDI: quantizing.

Note: The *American Heritage Dictionary* has this definition for the word *quantize:* "to limit the possible values of (a magnitude or quantity) to a discrete set of values by quantum mechanical rules." In my words, it means defining the increment (in terms of beats) in which you would like your MIDI events to automatically be aligned to your magnetic musical grid. Keep in mind that in order to quantize, you must set your ruler to display time in bars and beats. Currently there is no other way to quantize in terms of time in Cubase.

Quantizing, simply put, is using Cubase to automatically reassign notes to what the program determines is the correct place in the bars and beats grid according to your preferred settings. This means that if your MIDI bass note falls slightly after beat 1, you can *quantize* the bass part so that the bass note falls exactly on beat one. Quantizing is a very useful tool for locking grooves together. The Quantize features in Cubase are extensive. It is helpful to know some rhythmic theory when working with quantization (for example, you need to know whether the bass player is playing 1/16 notes or 1/4 notes and whether they are played straight or played with a swing).

There are several ways to quantize a MIDI part in Cubase. The most common and easiest form of quantization is called *over quantize.* To over quantize a MIDI part in the Project window, use the OST to select the part you'd like to quantize, and then use your knowledge of rhythmic theory to determine the smallest increment of time used in the part (1/4 notes, 1/8 notes, 1/16 notes, etc.). Once you have determined the increment, select that increment's setting from the quantize display on the toolbar (see Figure 8.6).

Now with the correct setting, select Over Quantize from the MIDI menu at the top of the screen (see Figure 8.7). Your part will be automatically corrected so that the notes fall directly on the grid.

Once you have over quantized a part, you should play it back and listen to see if it sounds the way you intended. If it isn't right, you can revert to the original part by undoing your quantize. To undo it, select Undo Quantize from the Edit menu (see Figure 8.8).

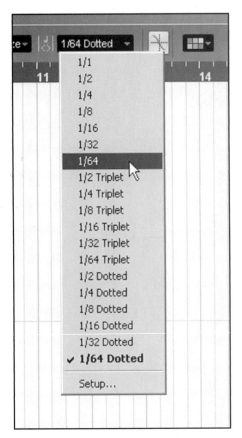

Figure 8.6 The quantize display.

You may want to experiment with another quantize setting. The quantize function can get very deep. Sometimes you may have parts that contain triplet feels and straight feels. Also, the parts may be played so poorly that quantizing puts the notes in the wrong place even if the settings are correct. Using the Quantize function is not always the best choice. Over quantizing can reduce the "human feel" of the track.

Some of the more complex types of quantizing involve using Cubase's iterative quantize or creating your own quantize groove. I will not dive into them in this book. If you would like to learn more about editing MIDI and quantization in Cubase, please refer to my book *MIDI Editing in Cubase*. It goes over MIDI editing in great depth.

Figure 8.7 The Over Quantize function in the MIDI menu.

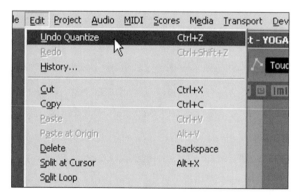

Figure 8.8 Undo your quantization to revert to the original, unquantized part.

It is possible to quantize an audio recording, but doing so can be very tricky. Cubase quantizes audio files in a way similar to how REX files work. The program analyzes the waveform and decides where the beat is based on the peaks and dips in the recording. This process is called creating *hitpoints*. Once the hitpoints have been generated, you can then quantize the hitpoints to fall within the grid at the defined setting (see Figure 8.9).

Hitpoints

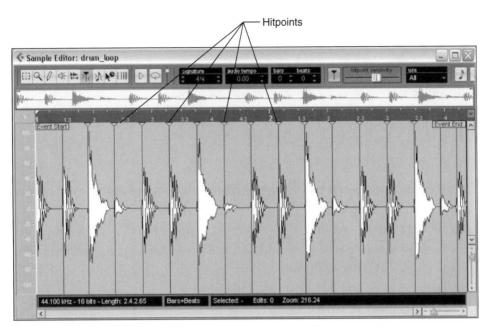

Figure 8.9 Hitpoints have been created for an audio file.

By using hitpoints, you can also create a groove from an audio file that you can use to quantize your MIDI tracks. This means that if you have a groovy live drummer who sounds great but is consistently ahead of or behind certain beats, you can quantize your MIDI bass so that it falls exactly where the drum groove falls. I go over this in *MIDI Editing in Cubase*, and you can also find more information on working with hitpoints in the Cubase manual.

The Snap Function

When working with MIDI and audio, the Snap function allows you to keep parts and notes organized as you move them around on the grid. It accomplishes this by "magnetizing" the grid so that the parts and notes can be moved only to certain places. This function is very important for performing quick and accurate edits.

The Snap Function Button

The button that looks roughly like this—>I<—is the Snap button (see Figure 8.10). With the Snap button activated, your notes and parts will

Figure 8.10 The Snap button pulls notes and parts into alignment in the grid like a magnet.

automatically move to the closest grid point (according to the setting you define in the quantize display) when you move a note. When a note or part falls outside of your grid settings and the Snap button is activated, the note/part is "pulled" to the grid like a fridge magnet to a fridge. If the Snap function is deactivated, the note or part will stick wherever you place it with the OST (which may not be perfectly aligned to the grid). Sometimes it's necessary to work with notes and parts outside the grid lines, so you have the power to turn the Snap function on or off.

The Snap Type Display

There are several ways you can control your Snap settings. One is by selecting the type of Snap editing that best suits your needs for a particular edit. The Snap button has a display just to its right called the Snap type display (see Figure 8.11). The graphic in the display changes according to the Snap type you choose. When you use the left mouse button to click on the display, a drop-down menu appears with eight different choices of Snap type.

Figure 8.11 The Snap type display and drop-down menu.

Snap to Grid

Snap to Grid is the most common Snap type, and the default. It's symbolized in the display by some lines crossing to form a grid. When using this type of snap, objects will move to the nearest line in the grid according to your settings in the quantize display. This is great for moving notes or parts to be directly on the beat or at the start of a measure.

Snap to Grid Relative

Sometimes you may *like* the fact that an object falls a little before or after a beat, but you need to move it to the next measure for editing purposes. Snap to Grid Relative moves an object that doesn't fall on a beat but without affecting the natural placement of the note. It does this by calculating how far your object is from the grid, and when you move the note, it uses that same calculation to place the note accordingly next to the grid. This is an invaluable way of keeping a performance while moving objects around in the note/part display.

Snap to Events

In some cases you may not want the object (or event) to be moved according to the grid at all. You may want your objects to snap to other objects. In this case your objects become "magnetized" to each other and stick to each other when moved. This could get really messy if you aren't careful, so to help prevent a MIDI pileup, Cubase still snaps to the grid at measures. An example of snapping to another object would be if you wanted an object to start as soon as another object ended. If the previous note or part length doesn't end on a beat, this is one way you could easily get the next object to fall directly after it.

Note: A MIDI event is a fancy way of describing anything recorded with MIDI. In most cases a MIDI event will be a note, but when we use the word *event*, it could mean *anything* recorded with MIDI—not just a note.

Shuffle Snap

This unique snap setting works a little differently from the rest. Let's say you have two objects that are side by side in the display and you don't like the order they're in. You would rather have the second object come before the first. In this case, you can use Shuffle Snap to make the objects swap places. With the Snap function activated, just drag the first object past the second object, and they will reverse their order. This snap is one you probably won't use very often, but you'll be glad you have it when you need it.

Magnetic Cursor

Let's say you want to place a bunch of different notes to all start or stop at the same place and that place doesn't fall on a beat. You may want to try the Magnetic Cursor setting. When you use this setting, everything you move toward the cursor will jump to its exact location on the timeline. This can be very handy when you're trying to create an offbeat punch with several parts or notes playing at once. I will demonstrate this in the following exercise.

The Crazy Snap Combos

If your need for snap goes beyond what we've gone over so far, then you're *snap crazy*! The good news is that Cubase can accommodate your needs to a certain degree by offering combination Snap types. It has three combinations, which include the Grid and Cursor combo, the Event and Cursor combo, and the Event, Grid, and Cursor combo. Of course, these variations just twist two or three different types together, and if you're really snap crazy, I'm sure you'll figure them out on your own!

Prepare to Snap

Before you edit any part in Cubase, it's always a good idea to set and activate your Snap function. To do so, you first have to decide what increment you would like to work in. In the Project window, you have three choices (see Figure 8.12): Bar, Beat, or Use Quantize. In the Key Editor or Drum Editor, you simply use the quantize display to make your snap setting. Remember that if you need to work in smaller increments than the snap setting will allow, you can always

Figure 8.12   Choosing the snap setting in the Project window.

deactivate the Snap function. A simple way to activate/deactivate the Snap function is by using the J key on your computer's keyboard.

Because editing is usually done on a much larger scale in the Project window, snapping to either a bar or beat can come in quite handy. When the Snap function is set to a bar or beat and you use, for example, the Split tool to split a part, the split will occur only on a bar or beat. When you move a part, it can be positioned only on a bar or beat. If you need to move a part or note in finer increments, you can always select Use Quantize and then select a setting from the quantize display.

If you are unhappy with any edit or move that you make while you are snapping, remember that you can undo any move or edit by selecting Undo from the Edit menu.

Copying and Pasting Parts

Now that you've learned about some of the basic editing tools in Cubase, it's time to learn how to use them to edit your recordings. One of the most common edits to make is the simple copy and paste. The reason pop music sounds so polished theses days, some people say, is that a musician only has to play *well* for two bars, and the rest is copy and paste. Because of this, producers are able to take only the best parts of a recording and use them over and over again throughout the song. If one chorus sounds better than another, why use the worse-sounding chorus?

When you're cutting and pasting in Cubase, this means you can use the best-sounding drum, bass, guitar, vocal, and keyboard parts over and over again without having to settle for a somewhat sloppy performance.

Producers can concentrate on getting each section of the song perfected and spend less time trying to perfect the whole song. Maybe this principle sounds ridiculous to you because you're used to playing a song from start to finish, but if you think about it, you will find that 9 times out of 10, an instrument or vocal will repeat within a song. This means that when you record an entire song, the musician is actually providing several takes of the same part. In theory, cutting and pasting is really just a time-saving feature. Another great thing about cutting and pasting is you can reproduce a sloppy performance over and over and it will sound like it was meant to sound sloppy because it's exactly the same throughout the song!

There are several ways to copy and paste MIDI and audio parts in Cubase. I will demonstrate the easiest and fastest way. This method involves using the tool buttons and a couple of keys on your computer keyboard. First, audition the parts you have recorded by playing back the track. Locate and identify the repeating sections of each part. Usually a part repeats for one bar or several bars. Set your Snap function to the increment you need to edit your part. (If the part repeats in one-bar or four-bar phrases, set your Snap function to Bar. If the repeating part is only two beats long, set your snap to Beat.) Most likely, the Bar setting on your Snap will be sufficient for making some general section edits. Once you have set your Snap to the appropriate setting and activated the snap function on the toolbar, you're ready to make your first cut with the Split tool. The goal is to cut each part into a section according to the repetition in that section. You may be cutting the part into sections of the song (such as verse, chorus, intro, ending, and bridge), or you may be cutting the parts into one- or two-bar phrases that are repeated throughout a section of the song (such as a drum part that repeats the same beat every two measures). Figure 8.13 shows a drum part that has been split into various sections to identify the part that's being played.

By splitting your original part into equal, repeating parts, you have created new sections that you can rename if necessary. If there are sections you know are not up to your quality standard, activate the Erase tool and click on the sections to get rid of them.

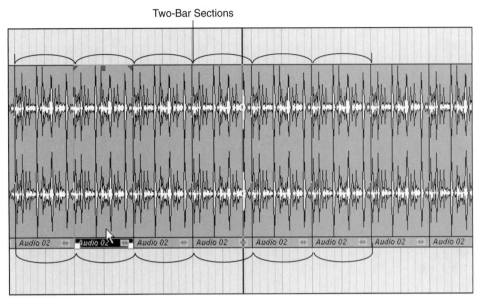

Figure 8.13 An audio recording of a drum groove that has been split into two-bar sections.

Note: Remember that deleting an audio part does not remove the audio recording from your hard drive and it's always possible to undo any mistake you make while you're editing. If you're concerned with losing some of your hard work, you can always periodically resave the entire project as a new project (e.g., Project name + date, or project name + 1 (2, 3, 4, 5, etc.) Also, if you will be editing a MIDI track, it's sometimes a good idea to try quantizing the part before you start to cut. If you try quantizing the whole part and don't like the way it sounds, try quantizing just some of the notes that are close to the bar line by using the Key Editor and selecting those particular notes. This should help keep you from cutting the wrong notes from parts.

Once you have removed the bad parts, you should be able to get a better look at the good parts that are left and see the holes where sections need to be replaced (see Figure 8.14).

Now it's time to select the OST and take one of the good sections to fill in where one of the bad sections used to be. Hold the Alt key on your

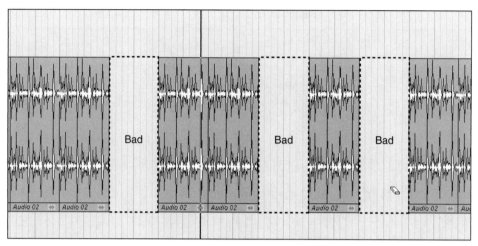

Figure 8.14 The bad parts have been removed from the drum track and are ready to be replaced.

keyboard while clicking and dragging the good section to fit into the gap left from the deleted part. Once you have the good section in the right place, release the mouse button and then the Alt key. Your good part has now been duplicated in your old part's hole.

You can repeat this process to fill the remaining holes on your track with copies of the good parts. Make sure you put the appropriate parts where they belong. You may want to play back your track to confirm you are copying and pasting the correct parts. When you are finished copying and pasting, the track should look similar to the way it did at the start of the edit (with the split points in place, as in Figure 8.13).

At this point, if you have been editing a MIDI track, the MIDI track is functioning the same as if it were never edited. The track will play from the start to end as it would had it not been edited. However, if you've edited an audio track, Cubase will be working a little harder for you. Even though the copied part *appears* to be the actual intact track, it's actually just representing your copy-and-pasted parts. Instead of playing the audio track from start to finish, it's actually replaying the section of the original recording you copied over and over again as it is repeated. Figure 8.15 should help you understand how Cubase works with edited audio tracks.

Figure 8.15 The way Cubase handles an edited audio track.

Though this non-destructive copying and pasting trick can be deceiving, as you've probably heard by now, it works well. Once you are happy with the sound of your track, it's good practice to construct a new audio file so that Cubase does not have to work so hard. If you are editing a MIDI track, use the Glue tool to paste the parts back together into one part (as shown in Figure 8.16).

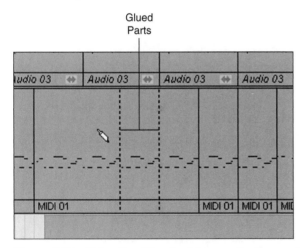

Figure 8.16 Using the Glue tool to reunite the parts of the track into one solid part.

Crossfading a Bad Audio Edit

If you're working with an audio track, it's possible that your edits may not sound as seamless as you want them to sound. This might be due to slight imperfections with the timing (since the audio is not quantized and not as calculated) or because of other variations. If this is the case, try rearranging some of the copies after identifying the problem. Once you have the parts in what seems to be the best order, you may still have some audible noises or glitches at the edit points. Crossfading your audio parts can eliminate those problems.

Here's a quick example of how and when to use a crossfade. I recorded a bass track, and then I later chopped it up with the Split tool and copied the parts I liked. Unfortunately, the point at which I split the bass part had a sustained note, and whenever the track plays, I can hear a click at the split point. See Figure 8.17 for a look at my bass part and the split point.

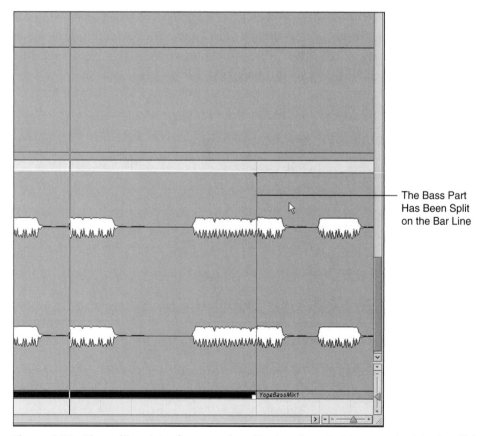

The Bass Part Has Been Split on the Bar Line

Figure 8.17 The split point of my newly edited and copied bass part with the click problem.

While I'm in the Project window, I'm going to set my Snap to Beat and activate the Snap, and then take one side of the split point (in this example I'll use the left side) and use the OST to extend the part with Normal Sizing selected so that it overlaps the previous part for one beat (see Figure 8.18).

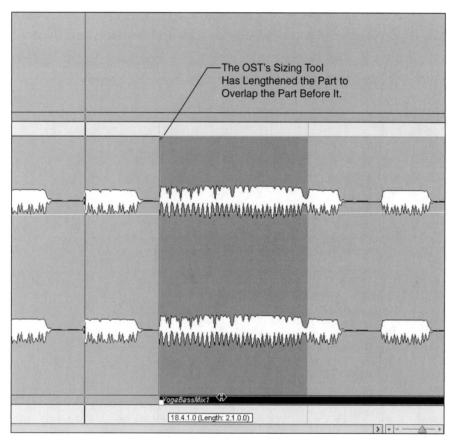

Figure 8.18 I've resized the second part of my bass section so that it overlaps the end of the first by one beat.

Note: Notice how a little more of the original audio part has been revealed from the resized part. The audio has not been stretched or moved within the audio track. This has simply moved the start time of the part to a new position so that it starts one beat earlier. This should demonstrate the power of non-destructive editing.

Even though you can't see the original part under the newly resized one, it's still there and hasn't been moved. Because of this, both tracks are technically *overlapping* for one beat. Now that the two parts are overlapping, you can create a crossfade between the two parts so that they fade in and out of each other for a nice smooth transition.

To create a crossfade between the two parts, first select both parts with the OST by creating the multiple object selection box around the two parts, as shown in Figure 8.19.

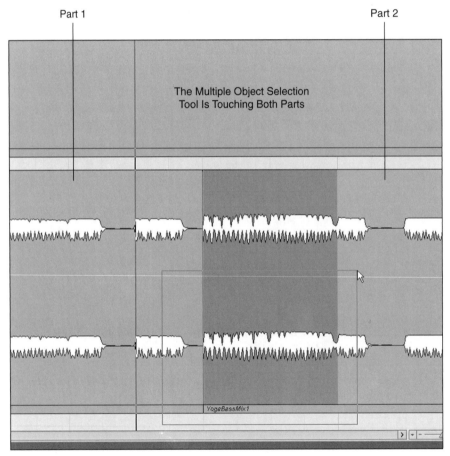

Figure 8.19 Selecting the two parts for a crossfade with the OST's multiple object selection box.

Once the two parts have been selected, press the X key on your computer keyboard. A crossfade for one beat should appear in the overlap that you have created, as it does in Figure 8.20.

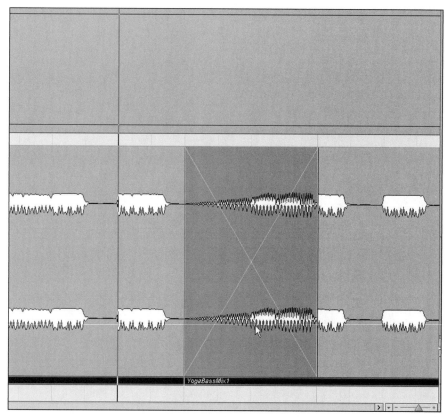

Figure 8.20 A crossfade for one beat has been created.

Most likely you won't need the crossfade to be a full beat long. What's great is you can now use the OST to modify the length and position of the crossfade. In Figure 8.21, I have disabled the Snap so that I can work in very fine increments, then I resized the crossfade with the OST so that it was much shorter. Lastly, I moved the crossfade to a position that worked best for a smooth transition.

If you take a closer look at Figure 8.21, you'll notice that I actually moved the end of the crossfade to the right just past the original start point of the part I originally extended to the left. This allows for a smooth fade between the original and the copied part without any audible noise.

Once you have finished crossfading all your audio edits to get rid of audible noise at the edit points, you can get back to our original plan, which was reuniting these audio tracks so we can work with one audio

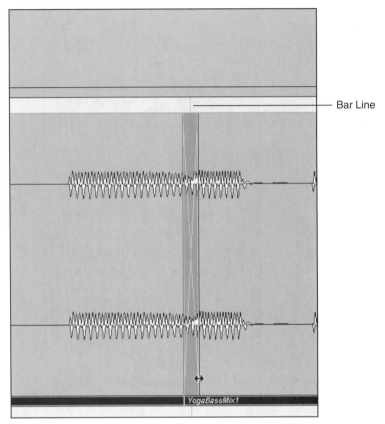

Bar Line

Figure 8.21 The crossfade has been resized and repositioned with the OST to make a smooth transition.

track again. You can glue these tracks together again (as you did with the MIDI track earlier), but sometimes the crossfade gets lost in this process. What I prefer to do is create an entirely *new* audio part from the edited audio parts.

To create a new audio part, use the OST's multiple object selection functionality to select the entire track of edited parts. Once all the parts have been selected, open the Audio menu at the top of the screen. From the audio menu, choose Bounce Selection. A message box will show that a new file is being written. After the file is written, another message box will appear asking if you would like to replace the events. Since our goal is to simplify matters, choose Replace Events. A part will be displayed, and all your edits will show as one solid file once again (see Figure 8.22).

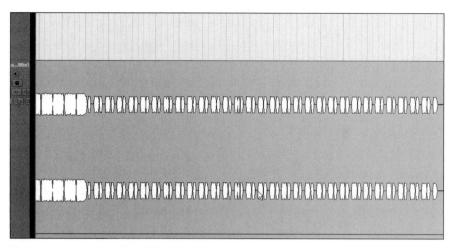

Figure 8.22 The audio edits have been bounced to create a new audio file.

Keep in mind that your old track still exists if you need it. You can find it and reimport it into Cubase from the audio pool (see the Cubase manual for details). Before moving on, take a moment to listen to the newly bounced file and check for errors.

Note: When using any sort of processing (such as *bouncing* in the previous example), audio glitches are a real possibility. Always check (and double-check) to make sure everything sounds good before moving on. You can always undo these steps to get back to where you were, but if you take several steps after the fact, you may have to sacrifice some of that hard work to get back to your safe point. Also, once you save and close your song, the undo history is lost, and it will not be easy to get back to the previous stage unless you saved your work under another name before.

Pitch Correction

There are third-party VST plug-ins available for auto pitch correction. These can come in handy for quick fixes, but Cubase comes with tools you can use for correcting pitch without having to use a plug-in.

Notes recorded with MIDI can easily be adjusted using the OST from within the Key Editor. You can also use the Transpose tool to transpose MIDI pitches up or down or even to match a scale template. When it comes to correcting MIDI pitch, there are no limitations within Cubase.

For this section on editing, I would like to focus more on audio pitch correction mainly because you're bound to run into more problems with a singer or a guitar player who is out of tune than a keyboard player. MIDI pitch correction is mostly aimed at fixing wrong notes, whereas audio pitch correction can not only change the note's pitch but can also affect the fine-tuning of a note.

I'm not going to lie. Pitch correction can be a very tedious task and requires that you have a good ear. As a producer, you have to be able to determine whether the note is slightly flat or sharp in pitch. This is not an automated process, and the more you understand and can hear pitch, the better off your pitch-correction experience is going to be. Cubase comes with a great pitch-correction/altering software processor simply referred to as Pitch Shift. To open and view this processor, you need to have the audio part you wish to alter selected, and open the Audio menu, select Process, and select Pitch Shift. The Pitch Shift window will open (see Figure 8.23).

Before we start shifting pitches, you need to know the easy way to get the proper results. Similar to the way we isolated the bad parts with the Split tool when copying and pasting parts in the previous example, you need to find the bad *pitches* and isolate them with Split tool. If you have a lot of bad pitches, it's probably better to record another take of the instrument or vocal or find the good notes in the existing take and copy them to replace the bad notes, just as we copied and pasted the drum loop in the previous example.

For this example, I'm taking a vocal track and isolating a word that was sung slightly flat (see Figure 8.24). Notice that I've both isolated the note and identified that it was flat before attempting to change the pitch.

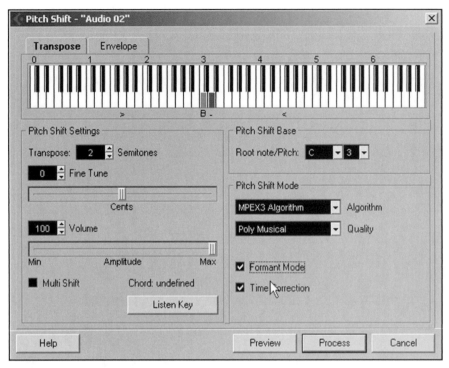

Figure 8.23   The Pitch Shift window in Cubase.

Note: Sometimes it's hard to identify whether a note's pitch is sharp or flat. If the vocal sounds better once it's processed, you made the right choice, and if it sounds worse, you can always undo the process and try again.

Now that the word is isolated and selected with the OST, I open the Pitch Shift processor from the Audio menu. Since I am making slight tuning adjustments, I will be working in cents as opposed to semitones.

Note: *Cents* are an increment of pitch between semitones. A semitone is also known as a half step. Cubase uses a Cent slider to determine the increments between the current pitch and a semitone. With the Cent slider set in the middle, it has no effect on the pitch.

When the Cent slider is positioned all the way to the left, the pitch is one semitone lower. When the Cent slider is positioned all the way to the right, the pitch is one semitone higher.

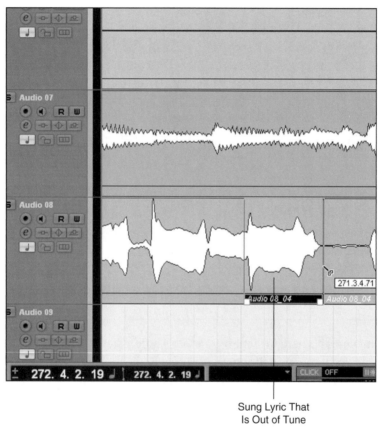

**Sung Lyric That
Is Out of Tune**

Figure 8.24 The word that was sung slightly flat has been isolated.

Even though the Pitch Shift processor in Cubase allows you to set a pitch-shift base, there is no need to determine the note that you are going to be shifting. We are simply going to be tuning the current pitch slightly higher so that the note is not flat. There are features such as a Listen key and a keyboard that are there to assist you, but if you know what you're trying to accomplish before you even open the Pitch Shift processor, you will find that you will not need these tools.

Since I'll be making only a slight tuning adjustment to this word, I will set the Transpose setting to 0 (zero) semitones. The note that was sung is slightly flat, so I will adjust the Cent slider somewhere toward the right, between the center and the right side, as shown in Figure 8.25.

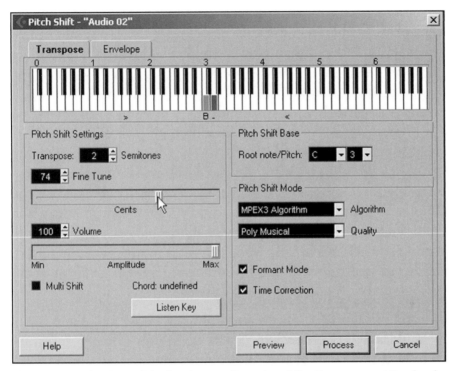

Figure 8.25   The Cent slider has been adjusted and the Transpose setting has been set to 0 (zero).

The amplitude should always be set to Max unless you need to lower the volume level of the pitch. I find that this is another tool that is not really necessary and something you can change after the processing just as you would any part during the mix session. (For more on mixing, see Chapter 9, "Mixing It Down.")

There is a section in the Pitch Shift processor called Pitch Shift Mode. The algorithm that comes with Cubase is the MPEX3. This is the actual processor involved in processing the signal, and it's made by another company called Prosoniq that Steinberg licenses for use with Cubase. If you're like me and most of the world, even though the MPEX3 offers seven quality settings, there's really only one setting you need and that's the *best* setting. The only price you pay for using the highest-quality setting is in having to *wait* longer during processing. This setting should be set to Poly Complex or Poly Musical for all pitch shifting you do (unless for some reason you're aiming for low quality).

The way audio pitch shifting works is it slows down or speeds up the frequency of the given pitch. Back in the early days, they used to record vocals at a low speed and then play the tape machine back at a higher speed to alter their pitch. This is the same trick that Alvin and the Chipmunks used to get the chipmunk sound. Since most of us don't want our vocal performance to sound like chipmunks, an advanced formant processor has been created to eliminate the tonal character-istics normally associated with pitch that has been sped up. For the most part, you'll always want to have this box checked, unless you are going for a more synthetic sound. Another problem with the old-school way of adjusting pitch was that when you changed the speed, you had to adjust the speed of the entire mix or else the tracks would not play back in sync. By using time correction, you can be sure that your processed part will still be in time with the rest of the track.

So, to sum things up, for the most part you should always have your quality setting on Poly Complex, and Formant Mode and Time Corr-ection should always be checked. Since we're only slightly adjusting the pitch of the note, the only real adjustment we should have to make is to the Cent slider.

Note: Cubase includes a Preview button to hear what the sound will sound like after it is processed. Personally, I find that this is a waste of time. Only after the sound is created will you be able to hear the isolated sound itself. You'll be much better off processing the signal and then listening to the track to hear the processed note along with the original track so you can hear how the two parts sound together.

Once my setting has been made, I click Process. Since I'm only proc-essing one word, the process time should be pretty quick. I can then play back my track and listen to the change I've made. Remember, if you don't like the way it sounds once it's been processed, you can always undo it and try again. If you don't like the change, make sure you undo the changes and go back to the original recording before attempting to apply more pitch shift. Each time you process the signal, you will lose quality from the original recording, and this will become more noticeable the more times you process the signal.

Note: For the best quality, you should always process from the original source recording, as opposed to a recording that has already been processed multiple times.

Of course the Pitch Shift processor is not just limited to tuning. It also works well when you need to shift to a completely different pitch. The higher or lower you go with pitch, the less natural the sound becomes. At this time, there is no such thing as a perfect pitch shifter when making drastic changes. Feel free to experiment with it, though, as it works better for some instruments than others.

If you want to have a little fun with your recording, you can try using the envelope-based Pitch Shift processor by clicking the Envelope tab just over the keyboard in the Pitch Shift window (see Figure 8.26).

This processor allows you to create pitch bends from low to high or high to low. This can do so much as add a little tremolo to a vocal or create an octave slide up or down to the correct pitch. This works very similarly to the transpose features except that this time you select a pitch bend range as opposed to a simple pitch adjustment. The pitch bend range setting determines how high or low in pitch you can go. The higher the range, the more dramatic the result. Once the range has been set, you then use your mouse to define points where the pitch will rise and fall within the audio clip (see Figure 8.27). You can also adjust the type of pitch curve that best suits your needs by adjusting the curve kind.

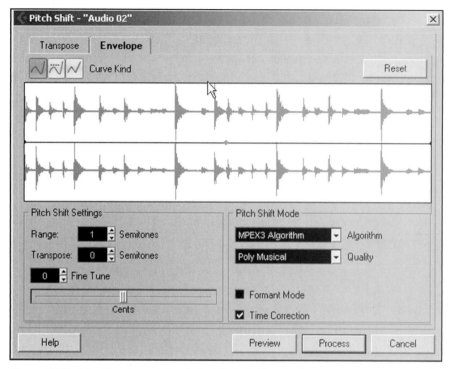

Figure 8.26 The Envelope tab of the Pitch Shift window.

The preview is usually a waste of time, and it's hard to get a good sense of the sound until it has been processed. So once you make a setting, it's best to just process it and listen. If you aren't happy with the result, undo your process and try again.

Time Stretching and Timing Corrections

Audio timing corrections, such as a bass note that falls slightly ahead or behind the beat, can be handled similarly to copying and pasting parts and pitch correction. This first step again is locating the notes or beats that are out of time.

Note: Working with details, such as locating a note or word that needs to be isolated, can be much easier if you know how to use your *zoom controls*. Cubase has many different ways you can change your view. If you haven't familiarized yourself with these methods by this point, I highly recommend that you get more information on using the zoom controls in Cubase. Using these tools will greatly increase the speed and flow of your work.

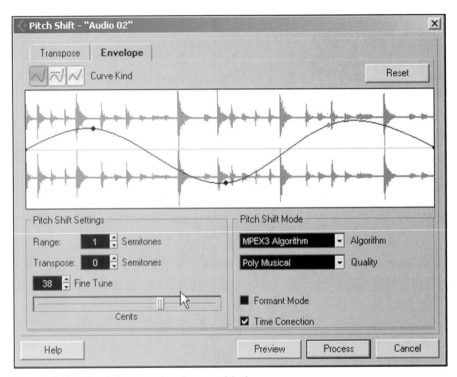

Figure 8.27 A pitch curve has been added.

Finding a word or a beat that needs isolation can be a little tricky at first. You need to learn how to identify the beat by the way a waveform looks, and by studying the waveform as you are listening. The waveform should be zoomed so that you can see the peaks of the wave as the track scrolls by. You can also use the ruler to help you identify where the problem is. As you listen to the track, first try to identify where the problem occurs without even looking at the waveform. Does it happen in measure 12 between beats 2 and 3? Does it fall slightly *ahead* of beat 2, and should it fall *directly on* beat 2 instead? Making these mental notes will make finding the error much easier, and finding the mistake is more than half the battle.

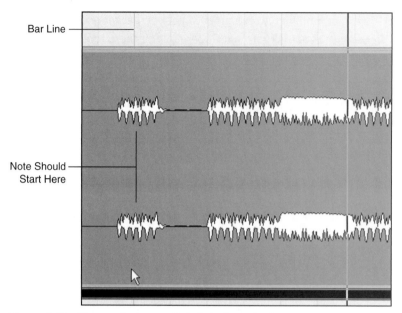

Bar Line

Note Should
Start Here

Figure 8.28 The peak occurs slightly before the beat, meaning the note hits too early.

Once you have determined where the timing issue is and your zoom is set appropriately, you can use the ruler to compare where the peak of the audio file is with where it should be (see Figure 8.28 for my example).

Note: When it comes to fine-tuning things such as timing and pitch, you first need to become a perceptive judge of what sounds off. Sometimes the more you look at a recording, the more you may notice that there are a lot of things that are off. A lot of times there's nothing wrong with some pitches or beats that are slightly off. Usually it's the slightly off pitches and beats that really make a performance shine. If you want perfect performances, you should get robots to record the music. In editing only you can decide what the word *off* really means.

Now that I've identified and found the problem, it's time to isolate it. Like an audio surgeon, you can use the Split tool to cut the audio file slightly before and after the problem note. You will most likely need to deactivate the Snap to make this sort of precision cut (see Figure 8.29).

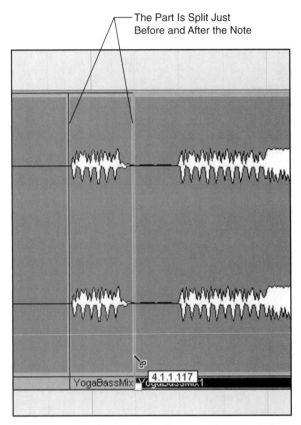

Figure 8.29 Isolating the off note with the Split tool.

Once the note has been isolated, you can use the OST to physically move the note so that it starts right on beat 1 of the measure. Most likely this will cause a slight gap before the edit and an overlap after the edit (see Figure 8.30).

At this point, you should listen to the track again to see if it sounds the way you intended it to sound. What you should be listening for is the placement of the note. Most likely there will be an audio glitch due to the gap and overlap you created when moving the note.

If the note is still not falling in the correct place, try using the OST to move the note slightly forward or backward on the timeline and listen again. Continue this process until you have found what you believe to be the best position for the edited note. Once your note is in position, you may need to fill the gap and crossfade the overlap using the

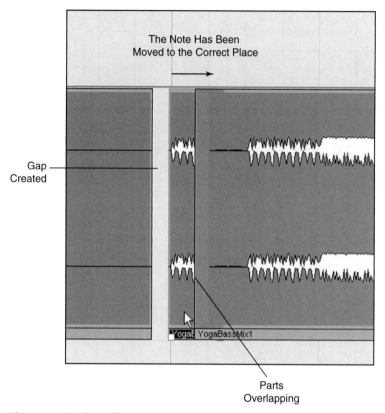

The Note Has Been
Moved to the Correct Place

Gap
Created

YogaBassMix1

Parts
Overlapping

Figure 8.30 The off note has been moved to fall on the correct beat according to the ruler.

methods demonstrated earlier in this chapter. In this case, because the note was moved slightly to the right on the timeline, I may need to lengthen the left side of the edit so that it merges with the original edit point, and I might need to crossfade the right side of the edit so that there is a smooth transition back into the original track. I may even need to split the edited note one more time so I can crossfade just the end of the note back into the original track (see Figure 8.31).

The ultimate goal is make a smooth transaction with the note now in the correct place. Once the edit and all other edits have been completed for the entire track, you can bounce the audio track (as we did after crossfading in the previous example) and your track will appear as a new solid track with the timing corrections permanently in place (see Figure 8.32).

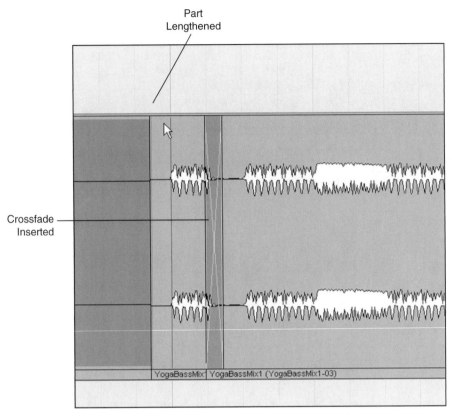

Figure 8.31 Adjusting the length of the edit and crossfading it back into the original track.

More and more, editing audio is becoming one of the most creative tools for music producers to use. One of the most common editing techniques is to use pre-existing samples and drum loops within a production. The big problem with using audio samples, however, is that they have all been recorded at specific tempos, and if your song is at another tempo, the sample will not work without adjustments of either the song's or the sample's tempo. This next brief example will demonstrate how to edit *any* sample to fit into a predetermined tempo.

The secret to altering samples is a process known as *time stretching*. With time stretching you can change the tempo of a sample without altering the pitch characteristics of the sample. This technology has been available for years, but it keeps getting better and better. There are a couple ways to time stretch audio in Cubase, but one of the newest

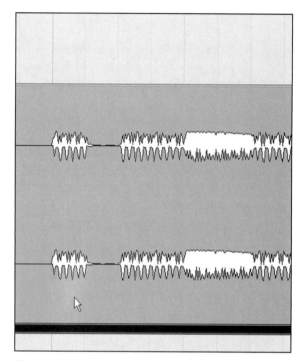

Figure 8.32 The newly bounced audio track with timing corrections.

and easiest ways is the Sizing Applies Time Stretch feature on the drop-down menu of the OST. With it you can make a sample fit into your tempo without even knowing the tempo of the original sample!

The first step is to determine how long your sample is in bars and beats (e.g., two measures, one measure, two beats, etc.). The next step is to import the sample into Cubase on its own newly created audio track. To do this, from the File menu, select Import and then Audio File, then locate the audio sample from your hard drive. Alternatively, you can import a track from an audio CD using a similar method.

Note: Ultimately, it's best to import a pre-edited sample. A program such as WaveLab can be used to edit an audio sample so that it has a clean in point (such as on beat 1), and possibly a clean out point. However, if you don't have a WAV or sample editor, it's still possible to work with samples in Cubase.

Once you've imported the sample, place it on beat 1 of any measure in the project. At this point, it's likely that the sample will not musically fit with your project's predetermined tempo (see Figure 8.33).

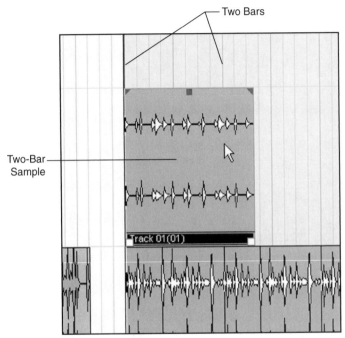

Figure 8.33 The original two-bar sample has been imported into the current project.

By examining this two-bar sample within this project, we can determine that the sample is longer than two bars. This indicates that the original sample was *slower* in tempo than the current project. All we really need to do to convert this sample back into a two-measure groove is apply the proper time stretching, and the tempos will automatically match.

By activating the Snap and changing the Snap setting to Bar and the OST sizing option to Sizing Applies Time Stretch, we can return the length of the sample to its original two bars. The time stretch will automatically adjust the sample to the correct project tempo (see Figure 8.34).

Now, when the sample plays back in the project, the tempos will be locked in perfect time.

This same time-stretching technique can be applied to any sample, whether it's a full arrangement, a drum loop, or a guitar riff. Any sample

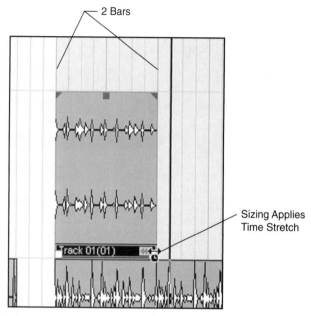

Figure 8.34 The sample has been resized to two bars with the OST's Sizing Applies Time Stretch option.

containing a pitched instrument, of course, will need to be adjusted to fit the key center of the current project. Using the Pitch Shift processor to transpose an audio sample to match the key of the current project can also be a powerful tool in making the sample work flawlessly within the project. Of course, only a good ear and some knowledge of musical harmony can define the key center and pitch adjustments that need to be made in order to create a great-sounding project.

When it comes to correcting timing issues with MIDI, most of what you need to fix can be accomplished with quantizing and the OST in the Key Editor. Even though time stretching can be applied to a MIDI track, the time-stretch effect physically moves the notes *off* the grid. The beauty of working with MIDI is that MIDI tracks always play at the tempo of the track, so there really is never a need to time stretch a MIDI track.

Again, what we've gone over in this chapter merely scratches the surface of the powerful editing capabilities of Cubase. I believe that using just the tools you learned about in this chapter, you could accomplish some amazing-sounding recordings, but if you'd like to learn more, explore Cubase on your own and with the Cubase manual.

9 Mixing It Down

After you've recorded and edited your tracks, you're ready for the final mixdown stage in Cubase. Like everything else, mixing down can be as easy as you want it to be. The more advanced and particular you get with mixing, the more complicated the mix will be to create.

There are several key elements of mixing down that I would like to cover in this chapter. Just as I offered the basics on editing in Cubase, I will narrow the mixing topics here to what I believe are the most important, essential topics to cover during the mixdown session. If you skipped over the last chapter on editing, you might take a little time to familiarize yourself with the tool buttons before you continue. I will once again refer to them throughout the chapter.

The key elements I will touch on include the following:

- Mixing audio levels

- Exporting MIDI tracks as audio tracks

- Automation

- Using real-time virtual effects processors and EQ

- Exporting a final stereo mix

Each of these is very important in the mixdown stage in Cubase.

Mixing Audio Levels
Usually when people think of mixing, they think of a recording engineer sitting behind a million-dollar console with flying faders concentrating on the sound coming out of the incredible-sounding control

room while some rock stars lounge around the studio patting each other on the back at how great they all sound. Indeed, that's the ideal situation for most of us, but mixing has nothing to do with a million-dollar studio. The art of mixing is simply the art of blending the audio signals of multiple sources in a way that works best for the collective arrangement. To achieve the best mix possible, I most often start by concentrating on the big picture (listening to all the tracks) and deciding what is the most important part of that picture. Once I decide which part that is, I concentrate on making that part sound as good as it can possibly sound, and then I decide what is next important (and so on), until all the tracks have been blended. Inevitably, as each part is added to a mix, something else is taken away from that original part. As each part is added, I concentrate on blending the new part to the big picture so that it doesn't take away too much from the original part.

While mixing is the final stage in a recording studio, most professional producers are really mixing audio tracks *before* the Record button is even pressed in a studio. You may wonder how it's possible to mix without having an audio track recorded. The mix starts with the musical arrangement itself. A lot of bands can play a song for years without hearing a valuable outside perspective as to what is working and what isn't in an arrangement. A good producer knows that some musical parts can get in the way and even take away from the great sound of another music instrument. Therefore, mixing technically starts with listening to a live band perform, analyzing how to integrate the music's components in the most flattering way possible, and then altering the way the music is performed—all before a Record button is even pressed.

The great thing about editing is that you don't have to have an entirely clear picture up front of what is working and what isn't. You can always use your critical ear to help you decide later on, and then use your editing tools to cut parts of the arrangement that are interfering with the most important piece of the puzzle. (Often this is the vocal track or track that contains the song's melody and/or lyrics.)

If you've done your work along the way, by the time you get to the mixing stage, getting a great mix will involve blending audio levels of different tracks, using EQ and effects to enhance the sound quality of the overall mix, and then exporting the audio into a standard stereo audio file you can put on CD or whatever media you choose.

Today, with the mixing tools that Cubase has to offer, you simply do not need a million-dollar mixing console to create a mixdown. You don't even need a *virtual* mixer to create the perfect mixdown. Cubase, as well as other DAWs, has completely redesigned the way we look at creating a mix. In the old days, before automation, you either needed to bounce audio while mixing to create complex mixes, or you had to have a team of engineers operating audio faders as the mix was playing. And if you didn't get it right, you had to try it again. If you had to do a remix for some reason, you had to rebuild the entire mix from scratch using cryptic notes. Those days are long gone, and now you can program a very detailed and accurate mix (with one engineer) and *save* it so that you can always recall it later.

Cubase has a virtual mixer, but I hardly use it because it's so much easier and more efficient to mix tracks in the Project window. Some people like to use a mixing control surface for a more hands-on approach, but I just don't believe that control surfaces are necessary. Great mixing in Cubase requires using your ears and your eyes much more than your fingers. Control surfaces are really necessary only when you're working on the fly and demand speed and efficiency. If you're taking your time and programming a mix in Cubase, a mouse and your computer keyboard are the only tools you will ever need.

Note: You may be familiar with the phrase "less is more." This makes some sense when mixing and recording. You have a virtually unlimited number of recording tracks in Cubase, but the more tracks you try to mix together, the more you risk losing your most important elements in a mix.

Building a Mix in Cubase

The first step in mixing is isolating the most important part of the mix and making it sound as good as possible. The best way to accomplish this is by first listening to all of the tracks and then deciding which is the most important. Once you know that (the element might be on multiple tracks), you then mute the remaining tracks and concentrate on that part.

To mute the other tracks in Cubase, click the Mute button for each individual track (see Figure 9.1) using the OST (Object Selection tool).

Figure 9.1   A track's Mute button.

Once the other parts are muted, focus on your most important part. Make sure that there are no audible editing glitches. Listen to the part from start to finish. Is the level consistent throughout the track or tracks? Consider this part the foundation of your entire mix. Without it, the rest of your mix will fall apart as you build it. At this point you will want to make level adjustments and add any effects to this part until you're sure you will be satisfied come the final stage of mixing (more on making level adjustments and adding effects later in this chapter).

Once you are completely satisfied with your foundation track(s), add the next most important part of the mix by selecting and unmuting the appropriate tracks in Cubase. Take the time to listen to how adding this new part has changed the sound of your first part. Now it's time to compromise between the foundation and the newly added track. This could consist of lowering the volume or changing the EQ of the new track, the foundation track, or both. Does the newly added track sound as good as it can sound? Could the track stand alone? It also may be necessary to *solo* the newly added track to hear how well the new addition to the mix stands by itself. To solo a part, click the Solo button for that particular track (see Figure 9.2). When soloing, you can make adjustments to the level or EQ to listen to how it affects the part. When you are finished making adjustments, deactivate the solo and once again listen to the foundation track and the newly added track together. Continue this process, with adjustments, until you are completely satisfied with the way these two parts work together.

Figure 9.2   The Solo button on a track.

This process of adding parts to a mix is known as *building a mix*. You should continue to add tracks, making larger adjustments to the newly added part and minor adjustments to the foundation parts. Once all the tracks have been added and all adjustments have been made, you should be ready to either export the mix or start getting more creative with it (more on both of these later).

As you're building your mix, you might find that things start to fall apart, start sounding much less defined than they originally did, or that, overall, the mix just doesn't cut it. It may be necessary to either start over with a new mix or retreat from your last several steps. One of the best ways to take a few steps back in Cubase is by using the *Edit History* (accessible from the Edit menu). The Edit History acts as a list of every action you made when working in Cubase since the project was opened (see Figure 9.3). The last action taken is at the top of the list, and the first action is at the bottom of the list. By clicking on a prior action, you will restore the project to that state, and this will allow you to create new actions from that point. You can also use the Undo feature in the Edit menu, but sometimes it takes several steps to get back to a place where you can restart.

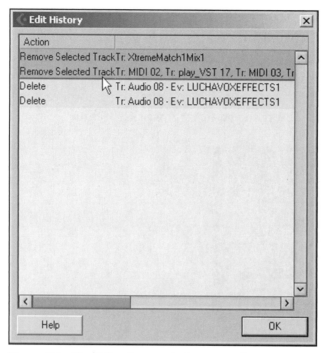

Figure 9.3 The Edit History window is useful for backtracking as you build your mix.

Making Volume Adjustments in the Project Window

You don't need to open Cubase's virtual mixer to make adjustments to the levels of your tracks. There are several easy ways to make volume adjustments within the Project window.

The easiest way is by adjusting the volume within each part using the OST. You can do this like you changed the size of a part with the OST in Chapter 8, "Basic Editing."

First select the audio part you wish to adjust with the OST. Then position the OST over the small blue box in the center of the part (see Figure 9.4). Once over the blue box, the OST will turn into an up-and-down arrow pointer volume control (see Figure 9.5). By clicking and dragging upward or downward, you will be able to adjust the level of the selected part. As you adjust the volume, the waveform is also redrawn to reflect the level changes (see Figures 9.6 and Figure 9.7).

Using this simple method, you can make quick and accurate volume changes for each part. What's great about adjusting the levels by part

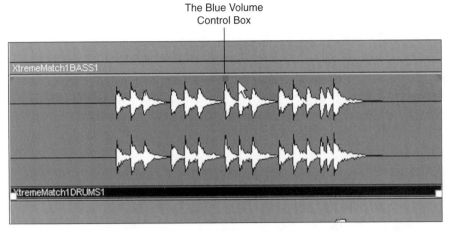

Figure 9.4 Adjusting levels using an audio part's blue volume control box.

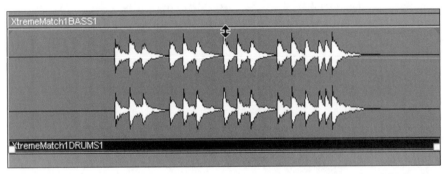

Figure 9.5 When placed over the blue volume control box, the OST becomes the volume control.

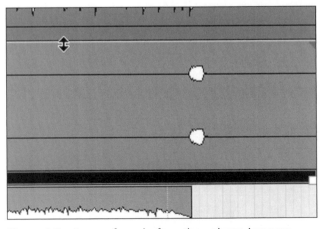

Figure 9.6 A waveform before the volume increase.

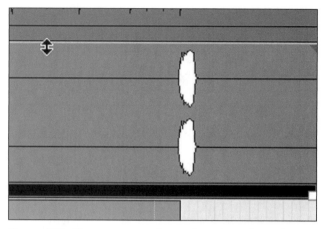

Figure 9.7 The same waveform after the volume increase.

(as opposed to the entire track) is that you have the ability to isolate small sections and make finely tuned volume adjustments. This can be achieved by first cutting the section of a part that may be slightly too low in volume and then adjusting that section using the OST's volume control (see Figures 9.8 and 9.9).

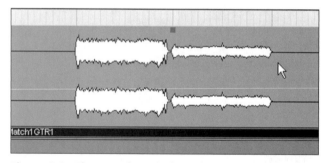

Figure 9.8 The waveform before the quick volume fix.

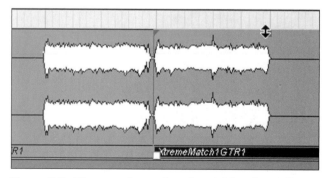

Figure 9.9 The waveform after the quick volume fix.

By using this method, you can quickly isolate a note or word that is slightly lower or higher in volume and needs to be adjusted.

You can also fade levels in or out using the OST to select either the left (fade in) or right (fade out) blue box in the upper corners of the selected part. This works in a way similar to selecting the part volume, except this time you drag the OST to the left or right to change the length of the fade in or fade out (see Figure 9.10).

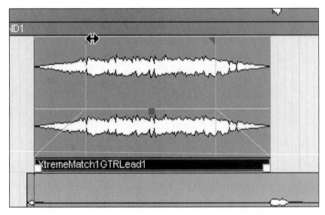

Figure 9.10   Fading a part in or out with the OST.

If controlling the overall volume of a part, or fading a part in and out, is still not enough, you can use the Draw tool to create points within the audio part and then use the same tool to draw an envelope volume increase or decrease on the actual waveform (see Figures 9.11 and 9.12). This is very similar to the method we used in creating a pitch envelope in Chapter 8.

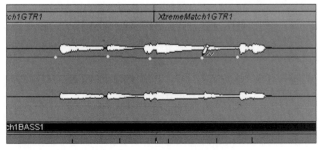

Figure 9.11   Creating envelope wave points with the Draw tool.

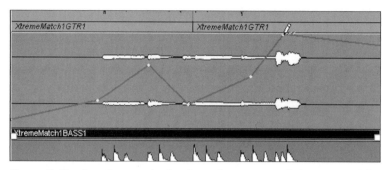

Figure 9.12 Creating gradual volume increases and decreases within a part using the Draw tool.

Once you're finished making your volume adjustments, you can bounce your part sections into one solid audio part as I demonstrated in the last chapter. This is not always necessary but could come in handy, especially if you will be taking your mix to another studio.

For those familiar with the old-school way of mixing (with a mixer), this method may seem a little strange at first. This is the most recently added method of mixing in Cubase, and with it, I find that I rarely need to use the other methods. I feel that mixing will become more and more advanced based on this particular method.

Instead of showing you every possible way to adjust volumes in Cubase, I've limited this discussion to this one particular method so I can address other important areas of mixing. If you want to learn more about automation subtracks and the mixer, the Cubase manual contains a lot of useful information on both of these subjects. I will demonstrate using an automation subtrack a little later in this chapter.

Exporting MIDI as an Audio Track

I've skipped over MIDI tracks in this chapter so far because MIDI tracks cannot be mixed the same way an audio track can. Even though MIDI is a powerful tool, I favor working only with audio tracks for the final mix. Since the ultimate goal is a stereo or surround-sound audio mix, there isn't much benefit to keeping your MIDI tracks in the MIDI format during the final mixing stage. Usually, creating audio files from your MIDI tracks will free up some of your system's resources.

The method used to convert MIDI tracks to audio tracks depends on which synth you are using with your MIDI tracks. If it's an external synth, you will need to patch the external synth to two (stereo) physical inputs on your sound card and record the audio from the synth to its own stereo audio track. Once the audio has been recorded, you can mute your MIDI track and continue using your synth's new audio track in place of the MIDI track.

If you are using a virtual synth, you can export the audio from the MIDI track into its own audio track. Using the export feature is fast and creates a new audio track within your project automatically.

First, solo the MIDI track that you need to convert into an audio track and make sure the left locator is at the starting position (or earlier for the synth part) and the right locator is at the ending position (or later). Now, from the File menu at the top of the window, select Export and then Audio Mixdown (see Figure 9.13). The Export Audio Mixdown

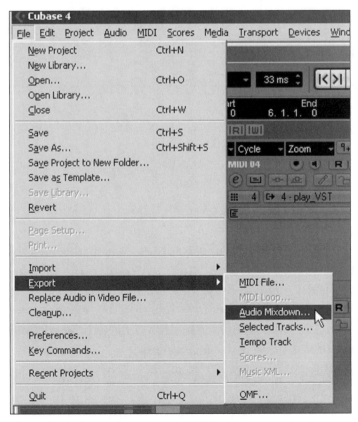

Figure 9.13 Preparing to export MIDI as an audio track.

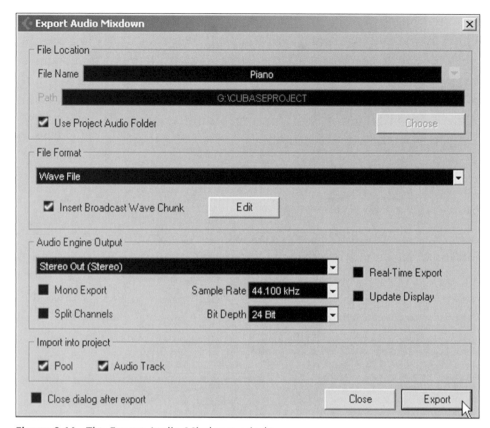

Figure 9.14 The Export Audio Mixdown window.

window opens (see Figure 9.14). This is the same window you will use to export your final mix of the entire project.

When exporting a MIDI track as an audio track, you first need to name the track (perhaps based on the synth sound), and then select the folder (file path) you wish to export your audio track to (which most likely should be the same folder as the project you're working on). For simplicity's sake, you can check the Use Project Audio Folder check box or use your computer's browser to select the location by clicking the Choose button. The file format should usually either say Wave File for Windows systems or AIFF File for Mac systems.

The Audio Engine Output can read Stereo Out or the output of the virtual synth you are exporting. (If you choose to export directly from the virtual instrument's output, you will bypass any effects you may be using from Cubase.) Mono Export should be checked if you wish to create a mono track instead of a stereo track. The sample-rate and bit-depth settings should match the project's settings. Real-time export is not necessary unless you hear a glitch or poor sound quality from the audio mixdown of your MIDI file. If the audio quality is substandard, a real-time export will record the audio from the virtual instrument as the project plays from start to end in a very similar way to recording an audio track from an external synth. Both the Pool and Audio Track check boxes should be checked in the Import into Project category.

Once you have chosen your settings, click on the Export button, and the track will be converted from a MIDI track to an audio track while displaying a progress bar. Once this is complete, a new audio track of the soloed MIDI track should appear within the project as the bottom track within the track display. You can then mute the original MIDI tracks and check the audio file by playing it from start to finish to make sure there are no glitches from the processing. Once everything checks out, you can mute the MIDI track, deactivate the virtual instrument, and continue converting the rest of your MIDI tracks using the same method.

Everything I have covered in this section is very similar to the method used to create a file for a final mixdown. I will discuss this in more detail at the end of this chapter.

Automation

By using the method I demonstrated for making volume adjustments in the Project window, you are automating your audio levels. There's no need to see flying faders or do any other sort of programming to create the proper balance of audio levels.

On the other hand, Cubase is designed to automate a lot more than volume levels. In fact, almost everything in Cubase can be automated, including the virtual instruments and effects. One such feature is what Cubase refers to as an *automation subtrack*. Each track in your Project window contains a virtually unlimited number of automation sub-tracks. To access an automation subtrack, position the OST so that

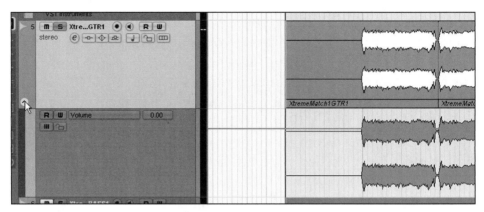

Figure 9.15 The automation subtrack lane display.

it is in the bottom of the shaded area displaying the track number on the left side of the track display (as shown in Figure 9.15). A small arrow indicator will appear, allowing you to display an automation subtrack. When you click on this arrow, a track appears (usually a volume automation subtrack). By using the OST to select the Automation Type field (usually where it says Volume by default), you can open a drop-down menu displaying every type of automation subtrack possible (see Figure 9.16). If you aren't satisfied with the list, you can also choose More for innumerable other options.

In case you need more than one type of automation simultaneously on any given track, you can open multiple automation subtracks using the OST to select a hidden + (plus sign) at the bottom-left side of the automation subtrack (see Figure 9.17). Using this +, you can continue to add as many automation subtracks as necessary (see Figure 9.18). Alternatively, you can hide these subtracks by clicking the − (minus sign) above the +. Hiding the automation subtrack does *not* remove the automation. It hides only the view. To get rid of the automation, you need to delete the subtrack by right-clicking on it and selecting Remove Selected Tracks or by selecting the same option from the Project menu.

Once you have selected the type of automation you need, you can use the Draw tool to create events within the automation subtrack, like a left-to-right pan (see Figure 9.19). The green R button (read automation) on the subtrack also needs to be activated when using the pencil (if it isn't already activated).

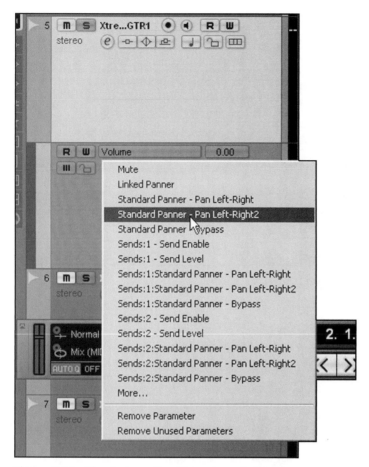

Figure 9.16 The Automation Type drop-down menu.

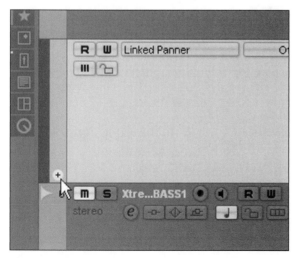

Figure 9.17 The Add Automation Subtrack (plus sign) button.

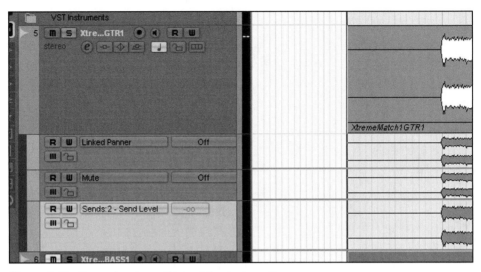

Figure 9.18 Several automation subtracks in action.

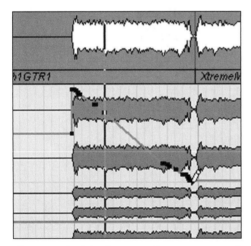

Figure 9.19 The Draw tool creates a pan from left to right on the automation subtrack of an audio track.

If you'd like to hear the track without the automation but don't want to actually delete the setup, you can disable the automation temporarily with the Mute Automation button, indicated by three vertical lines (see Figure 9.20).

I will cover other great automation features in more detail in the next section.

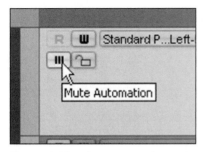

Figure 9.20   The automation subtrack's Mute Automation button.

Real-Time Virtual Effects Processors

One of the more creative elements of mixing is adding special effects to audio tracks. Adding the right reverb to a vocal can really bring out its warmth and special characteristics. Adding a little delay to a guitar solo can make it sound larger than life. Adding some chorus to a bass can give it a much richer and fuller sound. Adding processing is where a mix can really start getting more experimental, and there is no right or wrong effect to add to a particular type of track. If you can imagine it, you can make it happen with the virtual effects processor plug-ins that come with Cubase.

Depending on the version of Cubase you're using, you have up to 50 effects processors at your disposal—without even considering that you can use multiple instances of each effect. There are also up to 16 MIDI effects plug-ins available. Could you imagine trying to fit all of this processing power into a studio rack if each processor were its own hardware unit? Purists might use some higher-end external processors during mixdown, but more and more people are switching to using only plug-in effects processors such as those that come with Cubase.

Here's just a sampling of the plug-in virtual effects processors available in Cubase 4.1.

- 4 delays: Mod Machine, Mono Delay, Ping Pong Delay, and Stereo Delay

- 3 distortions: Amp Simulator, Distortion, and Soft Clipper

- 11 types of compressors and limiters

- 2 types of EQ, plus 4-band EQ on every audio channel

- 17 filter and mod plug-ins such as a flanger, chorus, tremolo, tone booster, and ring modulator

You may find that you don't really like the sound of a certain processor. If so, you can always buy additional plug-ins from third-party developers to add to your already massive collection.

The EQ Section

While Cubase comes with a ton of plug-ins, the most basic and important processing tool in Cubase is the EQ. Using the right EQ setting can really help isolate the instruments in a mix. EQ helps parts stand out in the mix and keeps parts from stepping outside their necessary space. The art of using proper equalization can take years to perfect. This art entails being able to identify a frequency that you like or dislike and then cutting or boosting the level of that specific frequency on that track to fine-tune the mix.

The easiest way to access the EQ section for any track is by clicking the *e* button on the track display (see Figure 9.21). When you do, a window displaying the track's EQ, as well as the insert and send effects, appears (see Figure 9.22).

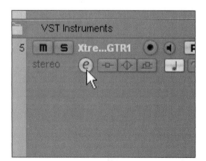

Figure 9.21 The e button on an audio track.

Cubase's EQ section can have up to four active parametric bands of EQ, each with a range from 20 Hz to 20 kHz. Each EQ can be boosted or cut up to 24 dB. And each EQ band offers a choice of two parametric types. The Q (or bandwidth) of the EQ can be adjusted by using the green slider at the bottom of the EQ setting or by changing the numeric value in the same field (see Figure 9.23). The high-band (eq4)

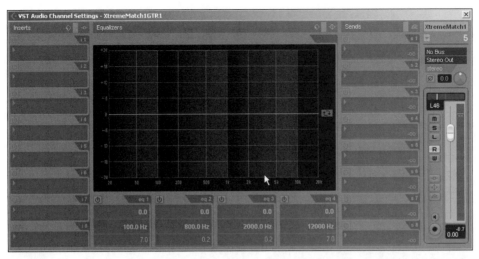

Figure 9.22 The track's effects and EQ settings in the VST Audio Channel Settings window.

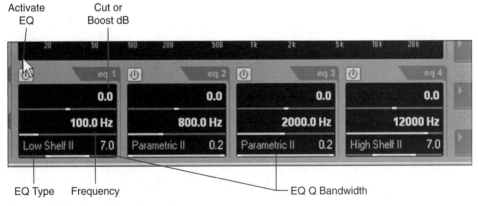

Figure 9.23 The EQ settings close up.

can also be set to be either four separate types of high-shelf EQs or two separate low-pass EQs by changing the setting within the EQ Type field. The low-band EQ (eq1) can also be set to either four low-shelving EQs or two separate high-pass EQs using the same method.

The easiest way to set an EQ is by clicking in the EQ field at the frequency you would like to adjust and at the cut or boost level you would like to adjust it to. By clicking in four different places, you will activate each band of EQ. You can then reposition each point until you have the EQ setting you are happy with. After you set your EQ, it may look something like Figure 9.24. If you want, you can also use the presets we touched on in Chapter 5, "Recording Vocals."

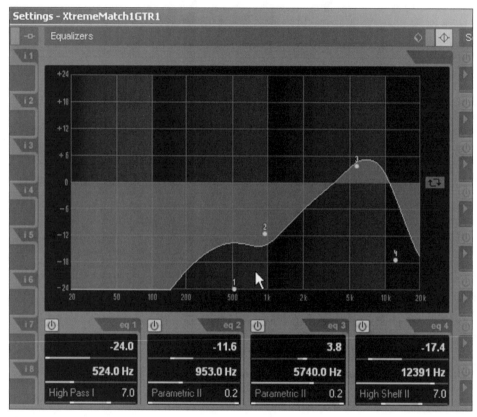

Figure 9.24 Four active bands of EQ.

Note: Be very careful about boosting frequencies. 24 dB is quite a boost and most likely will cause a clip (a distorted digital signal) in the final mix. Clips are very difficult to remove from a mix after it is finalized, and they should be avoided as much as possible before the final export. You can tell if your signal is clipping by a red signal indicator on the transport's output level meter.

The basic idea behind proper EQing is to give each part its own EQ range. Certain instruments sound better in some ranges than other instruments, and most instruments share a range with several instruments. By narrowing each instrument's bandwidth and cutting unnecessary frequencies, you can go far beyond simple volume-level adjustments in your mix.

Using Real-Time Effects

Unfortunately I can't go into detail on each effects plug-in that comes with Cubase. I will, however, demonstrate how to use at least one effect so you can apply the same process to all the other plug-ins available.

There are two ways to use a plug-in effect: as an *insert effect* and as a *send effect*. Insert effects are used on individual tracks, whereas send effects are used on multiple tracks at once. If you have one vocal track that requires its own reverb, an insert effect would be the proper type to use. If you have several drum tracks that want to share the same reverb, a send effect should be your choice.

To create a send effect, open the VST Connections window from the Devices menu and select the Group/FX tab. Next, click on Add FX. An Add Fx Channel Track window will appear (see Figure 9.25). Use the drop-down menu on the Effect Type field to select the effect for

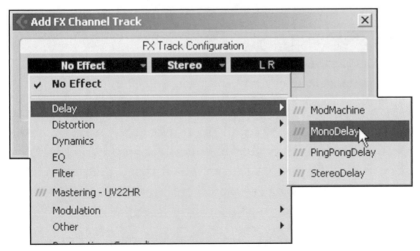

Figure 9.25 The Add Fx Channel Track window within the VST Connections window.

which you would like to create a send. Once the effect has been selected, you can close VST Connections window and select the *e* button on the track you would like to send to that particular effects channel. Once the VST Audio Channel Settings window has appeared, click in the first send's name field. The effect you have selected in the VST Connections window should appear within this field (see Figure 9.26). Choose the effect and make the setting adjustments necessary for the effect you are using. Alternatively, you can create the same send effect by selecting Add FX Track from the Project menu.

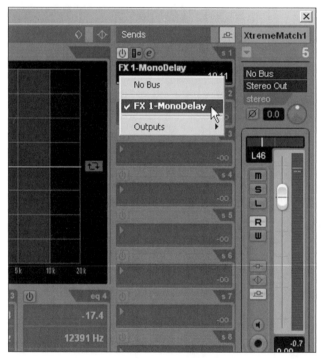

Figure 9.26 Sending the audio channel to the existing send effect.

When you have finished with this track, select the same send for the other necessary audio tracks. Since all the tracks are sharing the same effect, one setting on the effects plug-in will affect all the tracks. Using a send effect can save processing power, but if that's the only reason you're using it, you should know that there are other ways to save processing power.(I will touch on this a little later.)

An insert effect is much easier to select. First click the *e* button on the track you wish to process, and when the VST Audio Channel Settings

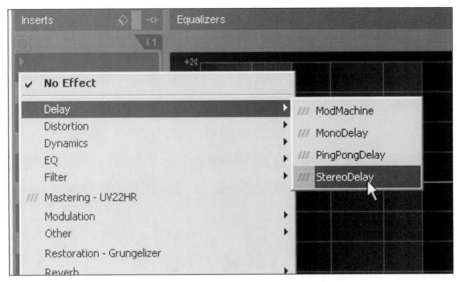

Figure 9.27 Setting up an insert effect.

window opens, select the effect you need by clicking in the name field under the insert effects, located on the left side (see Figure 9.27).

Whether you decide to use an insert effect or a send effect, once the effect has been loaded into the VST Audio Channel Settings window, you can access and modify the effect by clicking the *e* button located by the Effect Type field.

Automating Real-Time Effects

One of the greatest things about mixing in Cubase is that everything can be automated. Real-time effects processing is no exception.

To automate an effect for any audio track, first load the appropriate effect, as I showed you in the previous example. Create an automation subtrack for the track you would like to automate (see the "Automation" section earlier in this chapter). Try to locate the effect you wish to automate for the audio track within the Automation Type drop-down menu. If the effect is not listed, select More. If the effect is listed, select the parameter of the effect you would like to automate and skip to the next paragraph. After you select More, an Explorer window called Add Parameter will appear (see Figure 9.28). Browse to the appropriate folder (Ins or Sends) and find the effect that you would

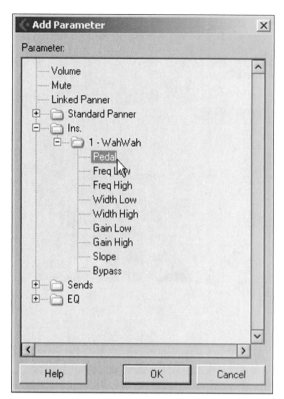

Figure 9.28 Locating the proper effects parameter for automating from the Add Parameter window.

like to automate. After you select the effect, select the parameter of the effect you would like to automate.

Now that you have your automation subtrack for your effect set up, you can activate the Write Automation button (W) located at the top of the effect (see Figure 9.29). Once this button is activated, you should notice that the button is also activated on your automation subtrack. Now you are ready to program the automation. Click Play, listen to the track, and use the mouse to maneuver the virtual knob or slider for the particular parameter you are automating. When you are finished, you should notice that the automation subtrack now contains several events to represent the moves you made. By deactivating the Write Automation button and activating the Read Automation button (R), you can now hear and see the automation you have just created (see Figure 9.30). You can also edit the events using the Draw tool in the automation subtrack if necessary.

Write Automation
Button Activated

Knob Controlled
During Playback

Figure 9.29 The Write Automation button on the effect's virtual control surface.

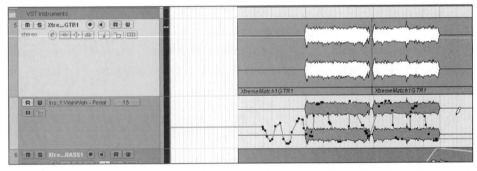

Figure 9.30 The Read Automation button on the automation subtrack and the newly created automation events.

While you are recording (or programming) your automation with the Write Automation button enabled, you can actually control several parameters at once. If you would like to see the parameters, you need to open the appropriate automation subtrack for each parameter (refer to the "Automation" section earlier in this chapter for details about using multiple automation subtracks).

Saving System Resources When Using Real-Time Effects

One of the only drags about using real-time effects is that they eat up a lot of your computer's processing power. This means that the more effects you use, the more likely your system is to encounter errors and/or crash during a mixdown session.

Because of this, Cubase has incorporated a feature called *freezing*. Freezing a track that is processed is sort of like taking a snapshot of the track with the effect and then using the snapshot instead of the effect. When you freeze your track, it sounds identical to the track being processed in real time, except that it's *not* being processed in real time. Freezing a track allows you to keep it both in its unprocessed state and processed state. If you decide to change the effect later on, you simply deactivate the freeze feature, adjust your effect, and refreeze your track.

I've been exposed to Steinberg's freezing technology since the release of Cubase SX, and to be honest, I found it to be just another way of bouncing tracks with effects (something I have been doing for years to save processing power). For me the whole idea of freezing a track is a waste of time in the studio. Bouncing tracks with effects is just as simple and I believe sounds just as good and works faster than freezing an effect. The other great thing about bouncing tracks with effects is that it's a universal solution to the age-old processing problem, not just something you can do using only certain versions of Cubase. Bouncing audio tracks with effects will works with any DAW and any version of Cubase.

Since I feel that knowing how to bounce audio tracks with effects is more important, I'm not going to demonstrate the freeze feature. Instead, I will demonstrate how to bounce audio tracks with effects.

The process for bouncing audio tracks with effects is similar to the method I demonstrated for exporting MIDI as an audio track earlier in this chapter. The first step is to solo the track you would like to bounce with effects, and then export the audio track just as you did the MIDI track in the earlier walkthrough. Once the track has been reimported as a new track into Cubase, mute the old track and listen to the bounced track to make sure it still sounds as good as the original. If it doesn't, you may want to try the Freeze feature or try changing your export settings to a higher bit depth. If the track sounds identical, continue using the new track as a substitute for the old track. If the old track is not playing, it will not take any processing power. However, by deactivating the effects on the old track, you will be saving a little juice for your system (see Figure 9.31). If you need to go back and

Figure 9.31 Deactivating the original effect after bouncing tracks saves processing power.

change your effect, you can mute the bounced track, unmute the original track, and reactivate the insert effect or send effect on the original track and make the appropriate adjustments. When finished, you can rebounce and create a new bounced track.

Bouncing audio tracks with effects is a non-destructive technique that's been used for years. Although I'm very impressed with the sonic quality of a frozen track, I think you will find that bouncing audio tracks is a very efficient and great way to get the most out of your system and project. Always keep an open mind to any new ways or ideas that you come across, but also keep a strong hold on any tried-and-true methods you learn while working in Cubase, and you will remain at the top of your game.

Getting Creative with a Mix

There is no one secret to achieving the perfect mix. Ultimately, you should be able to hear everything in the musical arrangement clearly and distinctly. Going beyond that is entirely up to the person controlling the mix. Obviously, there are a lot of records that sound amazing, and even though the sound often cannot be reproduced live, there is definitely something to be said for a recording that takes a band or song to new levels.

Often the person responsible for such sonic advances is a band's creative producer: someone who can hear the power of a song but somehow manage to multiply that power by 10 using his or her own imagination in the studio.

The tools I have shown you for both editing and mixing can be very powerful if used by someone who has the creative gift in the studio. I want to point out a few powerful tools you should not ignore when working in Cubase. These are tools that can come in very handy but are not used by everyone. Unfortunately, I can't get into details, but you can dig into the Cubase manual and other resources to learn more about them.

- Other audio processing (not real time), such as reverse, phase reverse, and resample

- Other editors, such as the Key Editor, Drum Editor, Logical Editor, and List Editor

- The tempo track, Time Warp tools, and Musical mode

- The Audio Editor, hitpoints, and slices

- ReWire and virtual instruments

Using the tools and methods I have shown you, the tools listed here, and your imagination and trained ear, you should be able to create a mix as good as any you hear on the radio today.

Exporting a Final Stereo Mix

When your mix is sounding as good as it possibly can, you're ready for the final export.

Exporting a mix is no different from exporting a MIDI track to an audio file, or bouncing an audio track with effects. There are only a few changes in the Export window that you should consider when making the final export.

- You don't need to export your mix to the project folder, but keeping your mixes in the project folder may make them easier to find later on.

- There are several file formats to choose from when exporting. Using WAV64 files may be something you should seriously consider if you plan on having your mix professionally mastered as they are becoming more and more of a standardized format. If this is the case, you should speak to the person in charge of mastering your CD and ask about preferred formats.

- Even though CDs play at 44.1 kHz and use 16-bit technology, using higher sample rates and bit depths during recording has been proven to increase sound quality. Even if your project was recorded at a lower bit depth and sample rate, upgrading those for your final mix will make a big difference in the sound. If your intention is to create a CD afterward, you can use a process called *dithering* to convert your mix to match a CD's specs.

- Using real-time export will be slower but will most likely provide better results than not using it because sometimes certain plug-ins and instruments react with glitches or errors during the speedy export process. Slower processing almost always means more accurate processing.

- Unless you're exporting your final mix at the same bit depth and sample rate as your project, you should most likely leave the import options (Pool and Audio Track) unchecked. If these are checked, you will be forced to change the bit depth and sample rate of the imported file.

- Another reason to use real-time export is you can watch your output meter and make sure that there aren't any peaks in the red while the song is playing from start to finish. Any peak during the export will result in audio clipping and will create digital distortion in the final mix. Even if the digital distortion is inaudible, it can create problems for you down the road.

Exporting a mix is easy. Once your mix is created, you should be able to play it back on any device or program that plays the file format you selected during the export procedure. Always save your project after you have finished a mix. It's a good idea to include the date of the mix in the name of the project so you know exactly which version you're pulling up. You may find yourself coming back to a mix for remixing later.

Again, I believe that the way I've shown you to mix in Cubase is becoming more and more of a universal standard and using a virtual mixer or an external control surface in some ways is like taking a step backward. If, however, you are used to using a mixer and this new way seems inferior to you, please take the time to explore using Cubase's mixer as it should provide more of an old-school approach to mixing. You can find many more details on Cubase's mixer within the Cubase manual.

Epilogue: After the Mix

I've given you a lot of information about Cubase and how you can use it in a home recording environment. Now it's up to you to take it to the next level. Always keep your eyes and ears open for changes in technology, and check the Steinberg Web site (http://www.steinberg.net) once a month to keep up with the latest program updates and releases.

In this book, we've gone over everything from setting up a Cubase studio on your computer to mixing a project down to two tracks. You may be wondering, where do I go from here?

The first and easy answer is to use mastering software such as Wave-Lab to put the final touches on your mix and create a CD that includes other tracks you may have mixed (see Figure E.1). Mastering is a whole new art and can take years to perfect. If you want the best results for a finalized CD, you're probably best off seeking the assistance of a professional mastering engineer. Once you have a mastered CD, creating MP3s and uploading your songs to iTunes or other sources is a breeze.

My goal was to point you in the right direction so that you know what's out there. As you can see, Cubase is a massive program. We barely scratched the surface of the editors, and we didn't even touch more than half of the program's functions. If you are serious about creating music with Cubase, I highly recommend you check out my other book, *MIDI Editing in Cubase*. MIDI is one of the most powerful tools you can use for music creation. Whatever your needs, it's important that you take this knowledge and put it to good use again and again. Practice makes perfect. The more you use the program, the faster and the better you'll become at it.

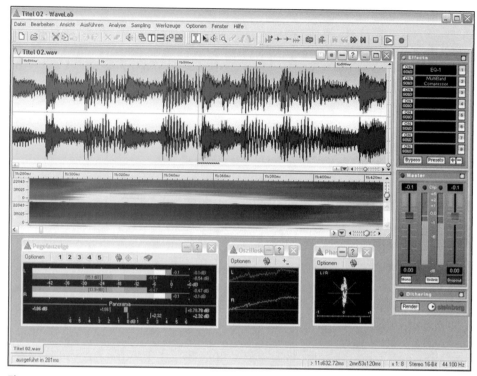

Figure E.1 Steinberg's WaveLab mastering software, the next step in your audio adventure.

Customizing Cubase

There are many ways you can customize Cubase to make your working experience more pleasant. Taking the time to establish a workspace, create project templates, and set up your preferences will allow you to dive right into creating music rather than wasting a lot of time trying to get the technical side of Cubase up and running.

Workspace in Cubase refers to the visual layout. Setting up a workspace allows you to determine which windows should be active, what size each window should be, and where each window should be located. As you've probably already figured out, you can have a lot of windows open in Cubase at one time: the editors, mixer, effects, VST instruments, project browser, transport, and so on. A lot of times you'll want your windows all to appear a certain way for a certain task. For instance, during mix-down you may want to see your mixer, your VST instruments, the Project window, and some audio plug-ins. When working on drums, you may want to see the Drum Editor, a VST instrument panel, the Project window, the transport, and the VST performance meter. Making a workspace is like setting up your desk the way you like to work.

Creating a project template is similar to setting up a workspace except that it sets up everything the way you like it from the start of each *project*. This can be very handy if you are an artist who creates a lot of music using the same tools regularly. Using a project template, you can save all your track names; automatically load and set up both your VST instruments and plug-in effects; determine what types of tracks you would like to display, as well as how many of each type; and set your windows exactly the way you like them. Just imagine how much time this could save you.

Setting up your preferences can also save you loads of time and make Cubase work the way you want it to work. Selecting Preferences from the File menu (Cubase menu on a Mac) brings up a dialog box for default settings. From here you can establish the way things look in Cubase (Appearance), the way the editors work (Editors), the way different types of events are displayed (Event Display), and many other general setups. I highly recommend that you take the time to browse all the preferences to get an idea of what you can change to better suit your needs.

One of the newest additions to Cubase 4 is the Media Bay. The Media Bay is a powerful file-handling system you can use to browse, filter, and organize all the media files on your computer system. Those of us who have been doing this a while are very familiar with the problem of file management when you have thousands of samples and file types to sort through. This alone can make finding the right sound a very difficult task. The Media Bay has been designed to make this task easier, and I highly recommend taking the time to explore the feature and read up on it in the Cubase manual.

Going Beyond Cubase

Even though Cubase has everything you need to create music, you will find that once you learn it all, you'll want even more. Fortunately, there are plenty of third-party developers out there to keep you satisfied for a long time.

The first step you'll probably want to take is exploring other manufacturers of VST instruments. Steinberg offers many Cubase-compatible VST instruments that aren't included with the program. You can find these plug-ins listed on the Steinberg Web site. Because Cubase is such a popular program, most manufacturers have designed their VST instruments to work with Cubase. For VST instruments, check out companies such as Native Instruments, East West (www.soundsonline .com), and Big Fish Audio, or just do a Web search for "VST instruments" or "virtual instrument" and see what pops up.

Besides VST instruments, you can also explore audio-processing plug-ins. Even though Cubase 4 comes equipped with some excellent audio plug-ins, you may find that you need others. The more you use your plug-ins, the more you'll become aware of what you need, and if you look hard enough, you'll find it. I have found third-party developers that have created better-sounding reverb and compression plug-ins than you'll find packaged with Cubase. Sometimes the plug-ins cost more than Cubase itself! The best way to look at it is as money you're saving on hardware.

After obtaining more VST instruments and audio plug-ins, you may find that you need other programs to work with. For instance, Reason might offer you more flexibility and inspiration than Cubase for the type of music you're writing. Steinberg is very aware that Cubase can't do it all, which is why it has ReWire. ReWire allows you to work with several programs simultaneously by sharing the audio engine of Cubase. If the other program you're using doesn't work with ReWire, you can always export your file in a format that Cubase understands, such as a Standard MIDI File.

Index